The Gift
A Runner's Story

Paul Maurer

ISBN: 1-4116-6925-8

ISBN-13: 978-1-4116-6925-3

Printed in the United States of America

www.pcmaurer.com

Dedicated to Sue. My own "Marie".

Thank you to my family for their encouragement and support. Special thanks to Jon K., Kevin J., Scott D., Chris L., Weldon, Danny K., Tom, Vicki, Eddie S., Amy, Jim S., Peter B., Dan H., Jeff R., Jonathon and Angela H. for their technical help, thoughts and insights.

"To give anything less than your best is to sacrifice the Gift"

- Steve Prefontaine

Chapter One

The top step sagged under his weight as he watched the landlord brush aside the cobwebs and open the apartment door. The creak of the hinges did little to forewarn him of the rank odor about to escape from the small room and assault his senses.

"Jesus, this place stinks," said the runner as he walked across the doorstep.

"What do you expect?" asked the old landlord chewing on the moistened stub of an unlit cigar. "Lifestyles of the rich and famous for four hundred bucks a month?"

There was no reason to dispute the point as he looked over the studio apartment. After a quick survey of the cracked paint, stained carpeting, and yellowed linoleum, he grudgingly admitted the humble dwelling was an undeniable fit for his meager belongings.

"It's perfect. Reminds me of Hef's mansion."

The landlord looked at him quizzically before responding. "And don't forget Mr. Brett Rodgers," he said as he looked at the application, "rent is due the first of the month…and oh yeah, no parties either."

"Not even for me and one and a half of my closest friends?"

He knew he wouldn't be living there long…eight, nine months tops he had estimated. With sixteen credits left before getting his masters degree in exercise physiology, he was set to graduate from the University of Milwaukee by the fall. He had come to view his latest re-location as another regretful passage in his life that he would weather just as he had so many times before. But deep down there wasn't a whisper of a doubt in his mind that he was destined to leave this town as inconspicuously as he had arrived. When he heard the winter swells howling outside the window, he wondered where those very same winds of fate would blow him in the future.

He climbed down the back stairwell and felt the cold blast of a January snowfall hit him squarely in the face. The Wisconsin winter was in full force and he found it hard to take a full breath. He laughed out loud as he walked toward his car in the back lot. "I look like the damn Beverly Hillbillies moving into town," he said looking at the snow-covered mattress attached firmly to the roof of his rusted Civic. He remembered the shaky ride he had taken from Ohio and was ultimately grateful the car had at least gotten him to Milwaukee in one piece. After a pensive look at the band-aids he had stuck on the balding tires in a moment of whimsy, it suddenly dawned on him; the car was a parallel of himself – a little beat up but still running.

With his frozen breath hanging in the air he started to unpack his humble personal treasures from the old vehicle. Even working alone he knew the three suitcases of clothes and boxes of books and magazines wouldn't take him long. He struggled with the cardboard boxes one by one and felt the familiar burn in his legs as he climbed the steps. He gladly welcomed the sensation and he was more than ready to let even the simplest of workouts begin.

The front door squeaked to a close behind him and soon his cold hands rifled through the largest box. He carefully pulled out a cardboard tube and slowly slid out the contents as if it was a family heirloom. It was the one thing he wanted to see at this moment and he needed to know it had survived the daylong trip. He unrolled the old dog-eared poster and spread it out on the bare floor before looking intently at the picture of the runner in flight and its underlying caption.

"To give anything less than your best is to sacrifice the Gift," he read aloud. The legendary distance runner Steve Prefontaine had spoken the sentence over thirty years ago, but to the runner, the statement was still as meaningful as the day it had been recorded. He smoothed out the poster and carefully tacked it on the wall. "It's just you and me, my man, you and me."

In his mind, Prefontaine had always been the gold standard for United States distance runners because of both his record setting times and unyielding desire to win. But as painful as it was to admit his own shortcomings, he knew that so far he had barely scratched the surface in truly utilizing his own gifts. The unrelenting burning in his gut told him the stay in Milwaukee was his last chance at fulfilling the promise he had so far squandered recklessly. After admiring the lone wall decoration, he took a deep breath and picked up a permanent magic marker from the box. Under the poster he wrote directly on the wall the day's date.

"Happy freakin' New Year," he said. He moved to the far end of the peeling wall and continued writing in bold letters, "Olympic Trials – August 10: Baton Rouge". He felt his hand clench the pen harder when he inked in "5,000 meters – 13 minutes 25 seconds". He had been taught long ago that a goal was just pissing in the wind until it was written down. After he stepped back slowly from the wall he admired his artwork. "There's a lot of space between now and then. Let's see what we can fill it with." He considered the answer to his own question as he dragged the wet mattress into the corner of the room. While looking at all of his worldly belongings piled up haphazardly in a heap the thoughts drifted through his head... a running gypsy... long distance white trash...a bum on the run...

"Snap!" the rubber band around his wrist echoed in the room. The tingling skin was the runner's reminder to himself not to let the errors of the past have a hold on the future, and like one of Pavlov's dogs, he had decided to reward any negativity with a jolt of self-inflicted pain. He had vowed the race he was now entering was a new one, and from this day forth would be only laden with positive thoughts.

He stretched out on the well-traveled mattress and thought of his checkered past. He drifted back to the glory days of high school in Connecticut where he had recorded a record time of four minutes and four seconds in the mile run. He remembered the feverish recruiting battle fought between the elite running programs of Stanford, Arkansas and Colorado as they lobbied for his talents. Yet, it was the nearby campus of the University of Connecticut that seemed a natural fit, and after signing a letter of intent he was immediately hailed as the savior of a struggling track program. The "golden boy" he was lovingly called by the university press as they fawned over the new recruit. The seniors even took to calling him "Midas" to never let him forget the high expectations that he was destined to carry on his lean shoulders. When his first year concluded with third place in the conference championships and the "freshman of the year" award, everything was right on schedule.

He could still hear the ring of the phone call that would forever change the smooth course he was on. He automatically closed his eyes as if to snuff out the memory, but still could not avoid re-living the searing pain he experienced when his mother told him his father had suffered a heart attack. *He didn't make it,* her quivering voice stated painfully. His father had been both his high school coach and the one person who helped him make any sense of disorder in his life. And now he was gone. His disorientation to her words and the immediate sensation of confusion multiplied exponentially when his mother's sobs echoed over the phone lines.

He thought of the funeral and the sense of estrangement and coldness he felt towards his mother. The emotional isolation he had developed toward her for the last five years only intensified when she arrived at the wake in a decidedly inebriated state. Just as he had done countless times before, he justified her behavior to the throng of well-wishers who had come to pay their last respects. He had long ago come to terms with his parents divorce when they separated over her drinking, but since then had only maintained minimal contact with his mother. As painful as it had been, he had come to the hard-edged conclusion that it was best to let her live alone in a seemingly perpetual alcohol induced haze.

He remembered how the color of the campus had taken on a decidedly different hue when he returned to take summer courses and continue his training. The months drifted along uneventfully, but he felt a gradual loosening of the emotional connection towards the campus he had spent the prior nine months acquiring. The daily run through the parks and trails was still a constant in his life, but the zeal for training had already begun to fragment imperceptibly. The carefree nature of the collegiate nightlife was soon a given on his daily agenda, and the beckoning of the lights from the pub windows seemed to call to him just as powerfully as the nectar did to the butterflies that flittered through the fields during his midday runs.

He once again ran cross country in the fall with the supposed intention of building strength for spring track, but as the months passed there was a slow erosion of the necessary self discipline. The parties, girls, and good times drew him in deeper and he knew anything was his for the taking. In those mornings that he woke up in his own bed he would still squeeze in the obligatory miles, but it wasn't long before both his running and studies began to suffer. He could still recall the pounding of his head in the morning where his runs would wait for a few hours…if they came at all. He was just out having fun he justified. Not a drunk like his mother.

He performed adequately in the winter indoor track season, but without the proper base of miles, he began to get injured. Throbbing shins, inflamed achilles, sore knees…just like a car in need of maintenance he began to have breakdowns at the most inopportune of times. His coaches assumed it was just the normal wear and tear that distance runners undergo, but deep down the collegian knew better. When spring brought the outdoor season he continued to experience various injuries and the coaches began to hear whispers of his barroom exploits. He remembered one morning, deep in the throes of a hungover state, being called into the coach's office where he successfully fought to reassure them of the exaggeration of the tales.

He rested his heels on the wall of the apartment and absently kneaded the egg-sized knot of scar tissue in the back of his left hamstring. The memory was still fresh in his mind of seeing himself standing on the bar stool to "load the cannon" with a shot of Jack Daniels. The exhortations of the surrounding crowd still rang in his ears as they urged him to down the rust-colored liquid. He remembered throwing his head back to swallow the contents of the shot glass and the resulting unexpected fall through the air as the stool buckled under his weight. Upon awaking in the local hospital, he was confronted by a gray haired physician that informed him of his battered condition. A "severe concussion" the doctor had called it but he knew that was the least of his worries. The fall had caused a major tear in his left hamstring and would eliminate any running for the next few months.

He could still feel the crutch digging in his armpit as he hobbled to the coach's office. "A lush…a damn lush," his coach had called him. "A waste of talent. A waste of a scholarship." He wasn't stripped of the scholarship, but when his grades continued to plummet, the decision was soon made for him.

He started to feel like a nomad and wandered from college to college accumulating credits, but never finding a permanent home. In his mind's eye he still emotionally linked each school to the fastest performance he had attained during his short lived attendance. After Connecticut he transferred to nearby Boston College where he ran a 4:02 mile until in the "best interests of all parties" he switched schools again. He resurfaced at tiny Southeastern University where he teased his newest starry eyed coaches with a personal best of four minutes flat. But after violating team rules and multiple missed practices, he left the campus by so called "mutual agreement". His latest move ended at the grounds of Kent State University where on a whim he began to test the difficulties of the 5000 meter event. He could still remember the day the track gods aligned the stars and allowed him to beat the Olympic qualifying standard by a scant two seconds. His ensuing celebration resulted in a drunk and disorderly charge that again stripped him of the opportunity to compete on university soil.

Interspersed among the increasingly rare solid performances, he recalled the agony of a series of crash and burn races. "Consistency breeds success" his father used to say, and he knew he was a poster boy for the flip side. Even with all of his undisciplined ways the sporadic solid performances of the talented runner still landed him notice in the monthly periodical the *Track and Field News*. The magazine was the runner's own bible and the mere listing of his name spurred him on to increased training. But the unavoidable lure of the neon bar lights and the resulting lack of consistent training assured him of only intermittent success.

He remembered trying to make sense of his Kent State predicament and the acknowledgement that once again a move was imminent. When the phone rang that day he recalled the pain of another slurring phone call from his alcoholic mother and her incoherent rambling. After hanging up on her once again, he bolted out the door and by sheer habit walked toward the local running store to sift aimlessly through the discount shoe bin. As he waded through the bargain shoes, he looked up toward the old poster as if it was calling to him from the wall. Although he knew it to be irrational, the three decade old quote from the famed runner seemed to be speaking directly to him and the directionless path he was on. The desperation in his voice convinced the salesperson the poster was better off with a new owner.

He had since been sober for three months and slowly felt the old power returning to his twenty-six year old legs. So here I am, he thought... living an uncertain future in an unknown town.

"I think I need a run," he said aloud.

Chapter 2

He had always looked forward to running in the falling snow secure in the knowledge that he would have the roads to himself. After methodically digging through the battered suitcases in search of his cold weather running gear, he layered up quickly and was soon ready to explore his new surroundings. An intended quick check of his features in the bathroom mirror turned into minutes when he studied the pair of bloodshot eyes that stared back at him. He scratched at the puny five o'clock shadow that dotted his drawn face and was surprised by the unexpected mottled appearance of his hollowed cheeks. Pretty as a picture, he thought as he turned and retreated from the fatigued image the daylong journey had created.

He made his way out the front door and stood on the wooden porch as he tucked his dark curls securely under his wool hat. With the cold air filling his lungs, he quickly bound down the front steps like a child at play even in the absence of a singular running route. He decided to head towards nearby Lake Michigan knowing it was the only specific landmark that he couldn't miss. As he had learned from his other relocations, it would only be a matter of time before he knew the tangled maze of the city better than a homeless man.

He began his run and felt the familiar rush of freedom encompass him as he stomped through the newly fallen snow. His shortened stride ensured safe landing, and he licked at the melting flakes as they fluttered onto his warm face. He felt drawn toward the lakefront and after studying the horizon he caught a glimpse of the icy blue of the lake. He studied the white boulders that protected the land from the steady onslaught of the water as it pounded in at an unrelenting pace. *"Here by the sea and sand...nothing ever goes as planned,"* he thought to himself as he recalled the lyrics from his father's favorite rock album of years gone by. He shook his head to clear his mind from the past and focused on the scenery that surrounded the long hill of the parkway. In the distance he noticed three runners approaching quickly from the opposite direction and he welcomed his first contact with the locals. He could hear their noisy chattering even through his thick hat, and the natural kinship he felt toward other runners emboldened him to interrupt their run with a half-wave from a gloved hand.

"Hey guys," he asked as he carefully slowed to a stop, "how far does this road go? I just moved in and I don't feel like getting lost."

They stopped their run before answering and he guessed them to be collegiate runners only slightly younger than himself. "Three miles downhill and at least ten our way," said the smallest runner with a knowing look on his face. "But if you want to, you're welcome to tag along with us. We'll take it slow for you and show you around."

He looked at the pint-sized runner and could feel the energy flowing from his boyish face. It struck him as funny the runner thought he would have to slow the pace for him until the realization hit that he had put on his oldest and rattiest gear. "Schleppers" he used to call the faded and saggy sweats back east. He wore them for comfort, but knew instantly he would never be mistaken for anything but a jogger when compared to other runners and their customarily sleek outfits.

"That would be great," he replied without protest. He didn't feel the need to haul out his running resume just yet.

"We'll show you the campus," said the animated runner as they trotted away together. "There are some nice routes around here. By the way my name is Chris Logan, but everyone on the team just calls me 'Logan' almost like I don't even have a first name."

9

The tallest of the runners laughed before he offered his own commentary. "He has a lot of nicknames. Every week it seems he gets a new one. Tell him about 'Dangle'," he urged with a gleeful look on his face.

"It's a long story, a very long story," said Logan.

"Christ," groaned the third runner quietly as he rolled his dark eyes. "Not again."

"Ever since I can remember I've been cursed," he started to explain with an exaggerated look of pained resignation. "What my jealous friend has a problem with is I'm special in a manly sort of way. A regular freak of nature."

"Or just a freak. Anyways, I'm Ron but you'll probably hear them call me 'Hollywood' more often than not. I'm still not really sure why, though," said the tall runner as he held out his hand.

"He hopes it's because he's such a studly blond thing," said Logan. "But it's really because we think he's destined to become a fruity hairdresser on the west coast."

"You're so full of shit," said the now irritated runner with a shake of his head. Brett knew they had played this game many times before and waited patiently for it to run its course. After a moment of muffled laughter the last of the runners offered his own introduction.

"And I'm Jon," said the quietest runner as he too offered a firm handshake.

"Jon?" Logan replied. "No one calls you that pussy name ever since we caught you flexing in the mirror. You're stuck with the name 'Rip' until we say otherwise."

Brett waited until the chuckling died down before he began his own introduction. "Well… Logan, Rip, and Hollywood, it's nice to meet you even if you gave me more information than I needed. And for the time being I just go by Brett, even though I feel sort of out of place without a nickname."

"Hang with us awhile and we'll think of something stupid," said Hollywood as he wiped the salty combination of sweat and melted snow from his eyes.

"I get the feeling that will be easy for you guys."

"Check out the new guy," said Logan with an amused grin on his face. "He's trashing us already. I think we could use another smart ass running degenerate in our little group."

He smiled and felt an instant bond with the threesome when they automatically continued on their trek through the snow. They formed a single line that followed the pathway of other adventurous runners that had already made an appearance on the route. Brett felt pleasure in running with the trio, and some of the feelings of isolation that had set in started to fade when they continued on their journey. After noticing the school issued wind jacket outfitting Rip he spoke up once again. "Are you guys on the team here?"

"Yup," replied Logan from the front. "We all run track and cross-country. However, just like now I'm always a step ahead of these posers."

It didn't take Hollywood long to respond when a well placed shove on Logan's shoulder sent him tumbling face-first into a waist high snow drift. "European tactics," he shrugged, "get tough or die."

"You bastard!" shouted Logan in muffled tones as he attempted to extricate himself from the powder.

The still moving runners chuckled to themselves as they clearly were not threatened by the menacing tone of the now trailing runner. "As Logan was saying before he left us, we all run for the school," said Hollywood. "I prefer track as opposed to running through the cow fields getting all covered with crap. Cross country always makes me feel like I'm in a herd of sheep just playing follow the leader."

"Maybe you ought to run from the front once in a while then," challenged Rip to his cohort. "Show some balls for a change. Anyways Brett, we are all juniors and as you can probably tell we are the best of friends."

"Do you all live together?"

"Hell, no," said Logan as he re-joined the group from the rear. "We tried that last year and almost killed each other. Being together a few hours a day is enough."

The foursome continued on with their run through the elements and the dialog took a natural pause. Brett could scarcely believe the beauty of the snow covered landscape and re-thought his stereotypical notions of the aging Midwestern city. As they slowly climbed up the steep hill that led toward the campus, he took one last look back at the lake. Even through the beachfront land was covered with snow; it garnered up the memory of the many youthful barefooted runs he had taken along the Atlantic Ocean. His eyes continued to trace the unfamiliar horizon until he saw an animated collection of people congregated on a distant shore.

"What's going on down there?" he asked pointing to the people milling around on the frozen beach.

"Polar bears," said Rip. "Bunch of yahoos jump in the lake every New Year's Day. We stopped and watched them for awhile."

"Yeah," said Hollywood, "this one fat ass came out from the lake and his folds were frozen together."

"And there was this old dude shaking so much I thought he was having a seizure," offered Logan. "Those guys are whacked."

Rip shook his head as he looked out at the crowd in the distance. "And people say runners are nuts."

They jogged as a group into the concourse of the sleepy campus and the academic buildings buffeted them from the winds howling off the lake. The architecture stood mutely as the runners trotted gingerly across the cobblestone flooring of the grounds. A small collection of lights shone dimly from the windows where the most dedicated of academia engrossed themselves in the pursuit of a higher education. The three locals took turns answering the newcomer's rapid fire questions and they enjoyed pointing out the many sites located at the heart of the campus. Brett tried to absorb the information as best he could before forming his most important question.

"Is there a track around here?"

"The pit of despair? I've left pieces of my soul in that place," said Hollywood.

"And parts of your lunches," added Logan.

"It's around the corner," said Rip as he squinted his brown eyes and a sudden seriousness washed over his face. "Follow me."

He guided them to the fence surrounding the track, but even with the snowfall Brett could still make out the shape of the familiar oval. He had no control over the sudden pounding of his pulse as his well trained neurons braced for yet another potential competition. Fully imagining the roar of the crowd, he felt the familiar knotting of his gut when a sudden rush of adrenaline seeped into his bloodstream. He scarcely remembered his tour guides until his daydreaming was interrupted by Rip's calm voice. "We won't be out there until spring."

"So we better enjoy runs like these now because when Coach Wickers gets his meaty paws on us it's all over," moaned Hollywood.

"With his twisted workouts we'd hurt less if he would just pull our toenails out with a pair of pliers and get it over with," suggested Logan.

"He is tough," said Rip speaking for the group. "But fair. It's Rex you have to worry about."

A quizzical look crossed Brett's face as he processed the unfamiliar name. "Rex?"

"Sexy Rexy, Wickers' assistant coach," offered Logan. "He was a hotshot runner a few years ago and still holds the school record in the mile at four minutes and three seconds. His name is on the record board, which he'll remind you of more than once."

The sheer mention of the assistant coach seemed to raise the intensity of the conversation and Brett watched Hollywood's snow-soaked gloves clench at the mesh fence surrounding the outskirts of the track. "He's an arrogant jerk. A pretty boy without a hair out of place."

"Jealous?" asked Logan.

"Watch it," warned Hollywood. "I ain't afraid to get dirty."

Brett noticed the flash in the runner's eyes as if a raw nerve had been touched. He suspected there was a story behind the anger that might one day come to light. He intuitively felt the other two runners retreat from the potential conflict that had unexpectedly edged into the dialog. The silence was broken when

Rip spoke up again. "We all just stay out of Rex's way. It's the safest route to take. By the way, Brett…do you race?"

"I have in the past," he answered without specifics. "But not lately."

They seemed to accept the vagueness of his answer and started up the run again as they eased past the campus workout center. The outline of the massive structure stood out in stark contrast to the cluster of small and weathered buildings that surrounded it on all sides. When the runners trotted into the shadow it cast, they suddenly stopped as if they had been commanded from above. Their breath hung frozen in the air as they all looked in longingly through the oversized windows. The glass was frosted at the edges, but the effects of winter did little to impede the runners' view of at least a dozen sweating coeds spinning on the stationary bikes. The foursome was in rapt attention and squinted steadfastly through the snowflakes to focus on the attraction inside. The eye pleasing sight caused a collective silence until it was broken with a sigh from Logan. "Ahh, to be one of those bicycle seats for only a day. Don't you guys go anywhere. I'll be right back."

Without further explanation he sprinted toward the entrance of the center. They turned back to the window and noticed the spinning class beginning to empty. With amusement they watched as Logan began to creep in from the back of the room and make his way towards the vacated bike of a particularly shapely coed. As a satisfied smile crossed his face they watched him sniff the seat deeply and absorb the pungent memory of its previous occupant. The three howled from outside the window when he feigned a look of ecstasy and dramatically fainted to the floor. They were still laughing when he rejoined the group a moment later.

"Smelled like fish," he said answering the obvious question.

Unable to resist his own contribution to the comment Brett added a clarification to the description. "Like tuna if I remember correctly."

"You're as sick as he is," said Hollywood with an expression that registered a mixture of both disgust and delight.

By the tone of his new friend's response he knew he had just solidified his entry into the band of runners. Heaven help me, he thought to himself.

Chapter 3

He awoke with the corner of his wool hat lodged over one eye and gloves on his hands in what had been a futile attempt to ward off the nighttime chill. He had anticipated a long, cold night but never anticipated the paper thin walls would fail so miserably in the battle to keep out the Wisconsin winter. After a series of blinks, he focused on the beaten interior of his new location, and had to think hard to recollect his latest home base. He arose with the blanket still wrapped around his shoulders and peered through a small circular opening in the window left uncovered by the overnight accumulation of snow. While watching the wind whip the drifting snow, he felt an unmistakable cold breeze on his cheeks as the cold air wafted through the porous window pane.

"God-forsaken tundra," he complained as he pulled the blanket even tighter around his lean frame.

He shivered uncontrollably as his body tried to shrug off the cold the best it knew how. Sleep had come slowly the previous evening despite the cumulative fatigue of his long drive through the Midwest. He absently studied the blowing snow and re-lived the midnight awakening that had once again disturbed his rest. The dream was always the same. Once again it began as a simple run with the flowing motion he had become so accustomed to. He felt the warmth of the noonday sun on his face…and heard the squawk of seagulls flying over the Connecticut hillside. The sound of his own rhythmic breathing echoed in his ears as he covered the ground with an unusually effortless stride. Ahead in the distance he spied a lone bicyclist pedaling over a well worn dirt path that bordered the panoramic cliffs of the Atlantic Ocean.

The steady cadence was maintained and the gap between the biker narrowed as they approached from opposite directions. He fought to catch a glimpse of the rider until a broad smile lit his face when he happily recognized the familiar features. *Dad!* he shouted with a wave of his hand. His father's proud face returned the greeting silently and he rose up a single hand to acknowledge the wave. As the runner's heart pounded he watched when a look of alarm crossed his father's face and the bike unexpectedly started to careen out of control. The runner looked on helplessly at the terror in his father's eyes when the spinning wheels struck the refuse scattered from a cliffside party held the night before. He rushed toward the unstable rider in a full sprint and reached out to steady the vehicle as it wobbled drunkenly on the trails. But before he was able to reach his father, the runner suddenly labored as if knee deep in wet sand, and he groped wildly in an attempt to reach him before disaster struck. His father's pleading eyes drilled at him while the bicycle veered toward the jagged cliff overlooking the ocean. The sound of the waves echoed and he watched in horror as the suddenly abandoned bicycle soared over the edge and crashed toward the unforgiving rocks below. He awoke to the sound of his own uncontrolled breathing and after bolting upright in bed he felt the sweat-soaked blanket clinging to his body as it had so many times before. When the shaking died down he slumped back into his mattress knowing that a fitful sleep was sure to follow.

Still looking out the window he tried in vain to forget the insistent dream until his attention was diverted by a hardy jogger negotiating his footing over the slick sidewalks. The jogger jarred his thoughts back to the previous day's events and the local runners he had met up with on the lakefront run. In their closing conversation Rip had told him of the local running store where he worked a few hours a week, and Brett remembered the invitation to stop by. The option to leave his current surroundings was immediately more appealing when he took stock of his latest residence and the accompanying bleakness of the ramshackle apartment. Even the filtered morning sunlight did little to accentuate the rusted radiator and scratched floorboards that bracketed the room. The monotonous drip of the leaky kitchen faucet only succeeded in further darkening his already dampened mood. He reluctantly dropped the one remaining blanket from his shoulders and made his way stoically toward the bathroom.

A quick lukewarm shower did little to shake him from his doldrums. What else could he expect living in a dump like this, he thought. "Snap," went the rubber band. "What pleasant ambiance… perhaps some potpourri would freshen the place," he said aloud in an attempt to reverse the negativity.

He soon made his way out to his car and was both surprised and pleased when it started on the first turn. With the pistons chugging in the engines own fight for warmth, he scraped the windshield clean from its overnight accumulation of snow. After climbing back into the cold interior he affectionately patted the steering wheel, and hoped the slick tires could guide him safely to his desired destination. He drove the vehicle carefully over the heavily salted roads and blasted his challenged defroster to its maximum in a hapless attempt to clear the foggy windows. Even through the frozen air he could still smell the hanging scent of the yeast fermenting in the nearby breweries as yet another vat of beer was prepared for mass consumption.

"Milwaukee," he said with more than a trace of disgust. "I'm gonna be marooned in this cow town with a buncha beer-swilling cheese eaters."

He looked out at the dirtied slush and narrowly avoided the rush of an oversized snowplow as it hurled the remnants of the storm toward the curb. He returned the somnolent glare of the sleep-deprived truck driver and took a deep breath while he death-gripped the steering wheel in concentration. With the tension building in his shoulders he fought to guide his car over the slippery terrain until he happily found the running store without any difficulty at all. Given the impeccable directions Rip had provided he was fast getting the feeling his new friend's nickname was appropriate, and he judged him to be someone you could always count on. After securing a parking spot he slid out the door before making his way up the neatly shoveled front walk. The glass door's entry bells performed their customary jingle when Brett focused in on a familiar face.

"Morning, Rip," he said in an amiable greeting.

The runner smiled in return and looked up from the front counter. "Glad you found the place, Brett. Come on in. You're the first person to brave the weather so far and make it here."

He stomped his shoes on the salt-ringed welcome mat and returned the smile before he responded. "It does suck out there. I'm lucky I didn't end up in a snowbank."

"It'll clear up soon," he reassured the transplanted runner. "Anyways, because it's so quiet it'll give me a chance to show you the place."

He watched as Rip diligently straightened up the front counter. "So how long have you worked here?" he asked.

"The last two years or so. Coach Wickers knows the owner of the store from way back when and I think a lot of the university runners have worked here over the years. Tony has run this place since the seventies, but he doesn't like to work the floor anymore."

"There's a lot of nice gear in here," said Brett as he viewed the assortment of sports watches nestled behind the glass case. "Too bad I can't afford any of it."

"I know what you mean. But at least I get a nice discount."

"Are you from Milwaukee originally?" asked Brett casually as Rip stepped out from behind the check-out counter to peer out the front window.

He shook his head from side to side before responding slowly. "Nope. I'm from a small town about two hours north of here. I picked the school because they have a good education program and I hope to teach someday. But I ran in high school and figured I'd give it a shot here. I never even broke ten minutes for the two-mile until my senior year, but I seem to keep improving year by year. Wickers is pretty cool to run for and he got me p.r.'s in every event last season. He even gave me a partial scholarship this year and I'll be damned if I'll let him down this year in track."

Brett appreciated the runner's candor and commitment to the program and continued on with his probing. "What's the story on Hollywood?"

"Our international man of mystery? He doesn't talk much about high school but I know he took third in state at Illinois. The eight hundred meters I think. Logan says he has some serious issues with his family back home and because of it he keeps his personal life pretty close to the vest. We think he comes from money, but like I said he won't talk about it much."

"And Logan?"

"Do you have an hour?" said Rip as he moved toward the entrance and wiped the condensation off of the glass door. "As he may one day tell you even though he didn't run at state his senior year he was still the 'true' champion in the mile. But too bad for him he was suspended from the state meet because he was caught in the girl's locker room after the sectional meet. Apparently he hyperventilated and passed out after catching a view of the girls' soccer team in the shower. He fell *out* of the locker he was hiding in and hit his head on the bench. Of course, the girls' parents went nuts and he had to serve a one meet suspension. He's over it by now and claims the vivid memories of the event ultimately made it all worthwhile. He'll even show you the scar on his forehead to prove that it's the truth."

Brett smiled and nodded as if his questions had been answered. "He seemed a little feisty yesterday so I kind of guessed he had a sordid background. But I get the distinct feeling it'll be fun to run with you guys."

"That remains to be seen," Rip said in a doubtful tone as he walked toward the racks of colorful gear. "Anyways, I've got some time so how about I show you around."

He followed his guide as they walked through the aisles of the modest store where a series of neatly stocked racks of shorts and singlets were prominently displayed. The necessary winter gear covered the center of the store and circular racks bulged with the protective clothing. As they both examined the high tech goods priced beyond their meager reach Brett couldn't resist a comment.

"Gore-tex, fiber-tech, chafe-proof, odor-proof, wind-proof and water-proof," he read reciting the tags on the gear. He shook his head in disgust at the latest of the never-ending fashion parade and was proud to think of himself as old school. "Just give me some semi-clean socks and a pair of shorts that won't ride up and I'm good to go." He backed away from the expensive garments and stopped abruptly when he felt a barrier from behind. He turned to face a small table filled to capacity with a wide assortment of discounted running paraphernalia. *50% Off!* screamed the orange sign on the sale table. The runner immediately flashed back and automatically examined the walls as if expecting a replay of his last running store experience.

Rip noticed his consternation and spoke up in a questioning tone. "Are you all right?"

He quickly recovered his temporarily misplaced focus and responded: "I'm fine. I was just daydreaming for a bit. I was hoping you might be able to squeeze me into your employee discount for all of these shoes on the wall." Brett studied the pegboard wall that displayed the latest wares created by the multitude of corporate giants. Even a brief glance at each shoes distinct logo was enough to cause him to recite the names of each company. Asics…New Balance… Mizuno… Adidas… Brooks… and impossible to ignore was the ubiquitous Nike brand. The colors nearly jumped off of the fabrics as the yellows, silvers, blues, and reds decorated the nylon outers that nearly spoke to the runner as he memorized the styles. "Beast", "Free", "Wave", "Supernova", shouted the tags that dangled from the shoes. He admired the graceful lines and designs and was almost like a patron at an art museum. But as he looked beyond the visual appeal, he sensed both the promises they held, and the disappointments they may bring. He reflected on the graveyard of old running shoes in his trunk each of which could tell a different story.

"C'mon," said Rip interrupting his musing, "I'll introduce you to Tony."

They walked toward the stock room and Brett studied the multiple columns of neatly stacked shoe boxes. He wished for an unlimited expense account to quench his insatiable appetite for new shoes, but settled on living vicariously through the well organized stock. He nearly spoke up his desires to Rip, but held back when he saw the owner of the store slamming down the phone. "Damn it!" he shouted as they strode toward his invoice covered desk. He stood up as the two runners approached him and Brett noted the still lean appearance of the gray haired man.

The lines on his face were drawn tight and the hollows of his cheeks were accentuated by the hawk-like nose and alert eyes that seemed to measure them as they neared his disheveled work area.

"Tony, this is Brett. He just moved into town for school yesterday and I invited him by. Hollywood, Logan and I met him on a run and showed him around campus."

"DangleWood on your first day?" he said blending their nicknames. "Things can only get better for you. Those two puds are so joined at the hips their only chance to get laid is meeting up with a horny set of Siamese twins. Nice to meet you," he said extending his hand and offering a no-nonsense greeting.

"Likewise," said Brett trying to ignore his distinct imagery of being a bug examined under a microscope.

"So where you from?"

"Out east. I'm just finishing up my studies in exercise physiology. Rip was nice enough to invite me by."

Tony pursed his lips while he sat back in his office chair. Brett wondered what he had said to offend the man until he spoke up in an edgy voice. "Exercise psychiatry," he hissed.

"Physiology," he corrected the old man tentatively.

"Whatever," he replied in a nearly inaudible grunt. The stare returned as the owner stared intently into his eyes and measured the need for further discussion of the topic. Seemingly bored with the usefulness of pursuing any more explanation of the runner's education he continued with his oratory.

"It would do my heart good if all you bucks would spend less time studying about running and more time doin' it. I get tired of reading about 'Isashabo Keloid' from Ethiopia. Why some hard-headed Polack from Milwaukee can't kick butt is beyond me."

Brett was quiet as he let the red coloration of the store owner's forehead return to a more normal skin tone. With Rip standing silently at his side he waited until the time was right before responding. "I promise I don't study that much. And I can't say that I totally disagree with you about running more. And lastly I'm *half* Polish if that's any consolation."

Tony considered his remarks as the conversation ran its course. The older man suddenly sighed when he remembered his irritation of the phone call from a few moments earlier. Turning his attention to his employee, he spoke in a voice that approached a growl. "Rip, I just got off the phone with Peter and he called in sick again. I'm gonna let the little pissant go, but I'll need you to cover a few extra shifts until I find someone new."

Rip paused before answering and Brett watched his eyes dart around the stockroom nervously. "I can't Tony. Track and school are starting up again and I can't spare time."

"Shit!" complained Tony. "I'd rather see my proctologist again than be out there for eight hours looking at runner's feet. Damned ugliest things on earth in my opinion."

The room quieted and Brett noticed Rip's discomfort in his inability to help out his boss. Breaking the silence, he boldly spoke up to offer his own assistance. "Maybe I can help."

"You have any experience?" asked Tony while he stroked at the gray stubble that shadowed his chin.

"Supinator or pronator? High or low mileage? Recreational or elite? I think those shorts look nice on you Martha. They cover nearly all of your cellulite," Brett answered in a mock sales pitch.

Tony's expression changed into what seemingly passed for a smile. "Humor and knowledge. A potent mix. I'll give you a shot but only if you swear to never try on the jog bras."

"Logan," said Rip shaking his head.

"I promise," said Brett solemnly as he flashed the Boy Scout oath.

"Stop by tomorrow and Rip can show you the ropes. Just don't screw up or you'll find a pair of size eleven Pegasus stuck up your ass."

"Fair enough," said Brett.

The conversation ended abruptly when Tony sat down at his desk and impatiently flipped open a ledger. Even without a goodbye it was obvious their first meeting was at an end. As they walked back to the sales area Rip attempted to explain the owner's demeanor.

"It might seem otherwise but Tony's a pretty good guy to work for. He was supposedly a heck of a runner but developed a bad wheel. You can't get him to talk about it, but I heard he ran the marathon in the '68 Olympic trials. The old timers say he was pretty talented in his day."

Brett nodded and gazed at the high shelves lining the four walls that had been filled to capacity with aging plaques and trophies. Golden memories of the glorious days of youth he thought. And as he studied the tarnished hardware he wondered if it was the old man's daily reminder of his own unfulfilled gift.

Chapter 4

The freshly transplanted runner had shared a few casual runs with his three new friends and had become increasingly comfortable with the lay of the land. In the short time they had been able to spend together on the roads, he had been able to glean more than the initial thumbnail sketch of each of the runners' ability. Logan and Hollywood both admitted to eclipsing a mile in four minutes and ten seconds when they finished in a hotly debated dead heat last season. Brett suspected that even with all of the good natured give and take bantering they delivered, it was clear they each possessed superior competitive instincts. Rip was more vague about his specific exploits, but admitted to running in the "low fourteens" for 5000 meters and once grinding through a 2:29 marathon. Brett recognized this as mid-major collegiate times but had realized long ago that more than one distance running champion had blossomed from such humble beginnings.

With the winter break nearly over, the veteran runner knew the three runners would soon be joining up to train exclusively with the track team again. He intuitively recognized that it would be next to impossible for him to gain the fitness he needed by running solo, and Rip had suggested that he talk to their coach and see if somehow he would be allowed to work out with the university athletes. He found asking the coach more than a bit humbling, but knew it was necessary to achieve his ultimate goal.

As he slowly walked through the athletic complex in search of the administrative offices, he felt an unmistakable lump in his gut. His wet shoes squeaked on the freshly waxed floors and he meandered the halls feeling as lost as a mouse in a maze. He knew he was distinctly out of place as a non-scholarship athlete, and he had an overpowering urge to remain as inconspicuous as possible in the unfamiliar setting. But realizing the pressing need of completing his task, he took a deep breath when he stood outside the office marked "Coach Wickers". With the door slightly ajar he felt the invitation to enter was implied and he cautiously eased the door open to its fullest width. He was immediately confronted with the icy gaze of a heavyset man at his desk with the brim of his baseball hat pulled down to nearly completely cover his forehead. When the runner studied the weathered face and unflinching eyes, he decided that Logan's advice to "throw the old man some bull" would earn him expulsion from the facilities at a record pace.

"Excuse me, Coach," he began. "My name is Brett Rodgers and I'm a grad student starting up this semester. I've been training with a few of your runners over the break and I was wondering if you might let me work out with your team during the season. I…"

"Who you been running with?" the coach interrupted in a gravely voice.

Brett paused before answering as he struggled to remember his new friends' names. "Chris, Ron and Jon."

"I believe they're generally known by other names, but I know who you're talking about. Rip's a good kid but the other two have been a wild hair up my ass since the day they stepped on campus."

"Yes sir," he said respectfully. He waited silently for the conversation to continue and his eyes were drawn to the framed picture hanging behind the coach. Brett estimated the young discus thrower captured in a faded black and white photo to be no more than twenty.

"Quite a physical specimen," commented Wickers as he read the thoughts of the lean runner. "That was probably a hundred years ago and almost that many pounds. I'm guessing you're a distance runner like the others."

He knew he was being measured up and the nervous runner self-consciously brushed the straggles of curls off of his forehead while a trickle of sweat in his armpits only added to the

26

discomfort of the meeting. "5000 meters primarily. I ran in college out east but now I'm out of eligibility. I still compete some on my own."

"Rodgers. I know that name. You ain't the Rodgers that ran for Connecticut a while back are you?"

"Yes, that's me," he admitted aloud and watched as the coach squinted hard in concentration.

"I was out there at a meeting years ago and I met some coaches that said you were slicker 'en goose turds. One had such a woody for you I was ready to call childhood protection. I saw you in the meet results for awhile, but then I heard you had crawled into a bottle and were drinkin' yourself to the bottom."

Damn the grapevine, thought Brett. An unexpected gauntlet had been set out in front of him and he took a deep breath to help steady himself. He considered his words carefully before he answered. "I screwed up more than once, but that part of my life is over. I haven't had a drop in a long time and all I'm looking for is a place to train. Between you and me, I've qualified for the Olympic trials in the 5000 back at a time I still had some focus. I have eight months to play catch-up and all I'm asking for is a little help."

"You said you're all done drinking?" the coach asked as he placed his hands behind his head and leaned back in his leather chair.

"Yes," he answered as bluntly as he could, "I'm looking for a fresh start and I hope it's here."

Coach Wickers paused and studied the honesty in his face. "I tell you what, Mr. Rodgers. I believe in second chances and if you're half as slick as they said you were, I'll show up at the trials wearing a pair of ice skates. As far as your three new buddies are concerned Hollywood and Logan are my problem but Rip's got a real chance. If I see you messin' him up, the deals off."

"You won't regret it sir," he replied extending a hand that was soon engulfed by the coach's sausage-sized fingers. When the grip was released their eyes met again and the runner felt the fear of god hammered deep into his psyche. At that moment the mutual promise made between the two accelerated to the cusp of a vow...a vow the runner hoped would remain unbroken.

"The team is meeting in ten minutes at the gym for a talk. I expect all my runners to be there. That includes you," he said directly as he returned his attention to the oversized computer on his desk. Brett turned and walked out silently. His shoulders dropped as he exhaled loudly and reflected on a paper cut being a better experience than the last ten minutes. He walked mindlessly through the halls until he located the gym and sifted through the crowd of animated athletes.

"Brett," shouted Rip from the outskirts of the gathering. "What did he say?"

"I'm in," he replied. "As long as I don't get in your way or use up all the hot water."

"He's a real sweetie-pie isn't he?" asked Logan as he climbed to an open area in the gym bleachers. The others followed him as they squeezed into the cramped quarters that was rapidly filling up with a legion of athletes.

Brett opened his eyes wide and nodded in agreement. "He's a regular teddy bear. But at least he seems like a straight shooter."

"Yeah," offered Hollywood, "as long as you run through a wall for him he won't shoot you."

"Isn't that what a good coach does?" wondered Rip. "Anyways I'm glad you can run with us. I get tired of listening to these two whiners all the time."

Logan feigned indignation as he puffed out his chest at his decidedly non-threatened friend. "We'll see what the year brings hard ass. If I remember last season, you were sniffing my shorts in every race."

Rip stood up as if to face the challenge head on. "If I were you, I'd enjoy that memory as long as you can. Because it's going to smell a bit different this year."

Brett smiled as he listened to the trash talk of the runners. He had seen the pissing matches a thousand times before, and knew ultimately the track would end the debates unequivocally. "Time will tell," he said in a succinct fashion. "No pun intended."

When Coach Wickers strolled into the gym the small talk vanished and the cavernous gym quieted immediately. "Welcome, gentlemen," he said in a commanding voice as he anchored himself in front of the aluminum stands. "I trust you are all well rested from your break?" He waited until the expected murmur from the team died down before beginning again. "We have a new season upon us and I believe the makings of a championship caliber team. And in building such I look forward to the challenges ahead." Brett mistakenly thought the burn of Wickers' eyes was meant for him until he noticed Logan smiling back at the old coach.

"I'll fill you in later," the little runner whispered to him with a nudge in the ribs.

Wickers continued in his deep baritone. "Most of you know my assistant coach Rex Lindsay. He'll help me in many avenues and fill in for me when I am unavailable." Brett watched the assistant step forward in his black on black ensemble and nod confidently toward the athletes. He wondered if he was becoming paranoid as he now sensed direct eye contact from Wickers' right hand man. While he fidgeted in his bleacher seat the old coach began again. "Lastly, we have my oldest friend in the world. His given name is Myron but if you call him that, he will chew your arm off like a rabid pit bull. 'Dog' as he is affectionately known is our trainer and can treat anything from hiccups to hangnails. He long ago earned my trust and in doing so will have yours. Use his services and heed his advice."

Brett looked at the old trainer and immediately had a vision of "Santiago" from Hemingway's *Old Man and the Sea*. His sunken cheeks and white stubble belied the energy emanating from his vibrant blue eyes. He smiled cordially to the group without saying a word, but the calm he projected was somehow comforting. Brett suspected he had guided decades of athletes in their individual quests and relished his job as a lay healer of the runners' physical and emotional sins. When he stepped back Wickers continued on with his introductory greetings.

"Some of you do not know me well at the moment. But soon you will discover I am not a nice man. My grandchildren might beg to differ, but unless you can prove to me that you are a byproduct of my loins do not expect a bedtime story. I recruited each of you because I believed you demonstrated the minimum level of proficiency for my program. And now my job and responsibility is to pull you from your Momma's bosom and teach you how to compete like a champion. Some of you may not survive my methods, but to the ones that do I will make you one simple promise. And that is when you look in the mirror four years from now, that you will be proud of what you see. You will observe that as a member of my team you will have grown from a boy to a man. And that will not be by chance…but by plan."

He quieted as he let the words sink in to the desired depth and Brett sensed the emotional connection the coach's well chosen words had made with the athletes. The confidence he exuded was palpable and he watched earnestly as Wickers proceeded to introduce the newest members of the team one by one. After the long line of introductions was made he thought that he had been able to stay under the other runners' competitive radars when the coach unexpectedly asked him to stand. "And we have one other new runner in our group," he said. "His name is Brett Rodgers and although he is ineligible to compete in our program, I will be allowing him to train with us. If the internet is accurate, he has run a mile in four minutes flat among other accomplishments." He looked at Brett evenly before he spoke in a steady voice. "I trust you will all break him in slowly."

His face reddened immediately as he felt the team measuring up the magnitude of his past achievements. He had hoped to be able to run in anonymity, but that idea had gone swiftly by the wind. When he sat down and attempted to meld into the bleacher seats he saw the star gazing of the underclassmen and heard Logan's unmistakable voice resonate from behind. "Coach, did we hear you say four flat?" When Wickers nodded his head he continued. "In that case I think I just shit my pants. Do you mind if I go clean up my mess?"

After shaking his head in resignation Coach Wickers responded. "Mr. Rodgers, you just might want to reconsider which one of us is truly in need of help. You or me."

Brett smiled before he spoke. "I have my own cross to bear. Yours just happens to weigh one-hundred and thirty pounds."

Chapter 5

After stretching lazily in the corner Brett reflected on how easily he had blended in with the university team. He even looked forward to the daily afternoon practices and the perfect antidote they provided to the sedentary nature of his class work. With the team scattered around the antiquated gym, he kept a sharp eye on the clock after Coach Wickers had made it clear he expected all of his athletes to be dressed and ready for the 3:30 start. "Discipline is the key to success" he often stated, and when the clock ticked to the designated time he strode confidently to the front of the group.

"Gentlemen," he called. "Park it and listen up."

Brett had quickly learned to enjoy the coach's pre-workout lectures. Like the rapture of a traveling revival show, he wrapped a spell around his runners using his homespun wisdom to drive a point home with an absence of manufactured bluster. When they settled down he furrowed his brow in concentration and tugged at his well traveled baseball cap. He studied the group before narrowing his eyes as if sharpening his thoughts for the attentive audience.

"Boys, there are three things I demand a University of Milwaukee athlete to remember as he competes on my team. The first is that the moment he slips on his black and gold singlet that he will carry himself with class and dignity. And anyone who breaks that rule will find himself outside of this gym for the duration. Please remember that as we travel and compete in the spring. The second requirement is that all of my athletes will maintain excellence in the classroom. Without a sharp mind no matter how fit the body becomes in the end you will fail. On the track and in life. And I will not allow that to happen while I'm on watch. Understood?"

The crowd of athletes murmured in agreement. Wickers then surveyed the group as he reached into his windbreaker pocket and lifted an object in the air. "Can anyone tell me what this is?" he asked as he lifted an enormous jockstrap above his head.

"A gigantic slingshot?" suggested Logan.

"Possibly, but not the answer I'm looking for. Anyone else?" he asked the athletes again. Before they truly had a chance to answer he continued. "I'll tell you what it is. This is the garment that I expect all of you to fill when you are on the track competing on my team. I demand that each of my athletes will have the biggest rocks of anybody in their respective events. Each and every one of you will look your opponents in the eye and at the necessary time demonstrate that you are the meanest son of a bitch in the valley. I expect you to crawl on your hands and knees if that is what it takes to achieve victory. I will not tolerate anything less than your best effort when you wear the colors of our university. You will all compete with courage and when needed summon the required strength from the very depth of your being. The effort I expect of you is non-negotiable. Is this understood?"

The athletes again mumbled their answer.

"I said is this understood?" he roared as his voice boomed through the gym.

The sudden shout of the team startled those students milling around the periphery of the team meeting. Brett wished for a race at that very instant, but logged the speech into his memory banks for future reference. With admiration on his face he watched the coach charge to the blackboard to chalk in the afternoon's menu. The distance runners began their warm-up jog to prepare for the effort in front of them. Brett led the way as he had already seemingly inherited the mantle of leader even without the ability to compete for the team. His past achievements and age separated him from the underclassmen's inexperience and they seemed eager to follow his lead. He had learned to accept the burden as repayment for the chance to utilize the facilities and benefit from Wickers' experience.

"Ladders today boys," said the coach. "Starting at one-half mile we will build up to one mile at quarter mile increments and then descend back to a half mile. At 4:40 pace with a two-twenty jog in between. No stopping. Completed as a group or there will be an extra four quarters as my present to you. Line up and let's get going."

"C'mon kids," taunted Rex from the back of the group. He was strategically out of earshot of Wickers which undoubtedly emboldened his remarks. "Lead the way, Brent."

"It's Brett," he corrected. "With two t's. Write it down if you need to." The team sniggered when the newest runner verbally pushed back in a determined bid to be nobody's whipping boy.

"We told you he's a loser," whispered Logan. "I knew it was a matter of time before he'd get to you."

"We think of Rex as an 'equal opportunity asshole'," chimed in Hollywood. "He'll shit on anyone."

"Forget about him, guys," suggested Rip. "Let's just get ready for the workout."

Brett knew Rip was right, but he still seethed at the unnecessary arrogance of the assistant coach. Apparently ignorant of the tension Coach Wickers blew his whistle to signal the start of the first interval and the group slowly accelerated into motion. The coach watched with interest as Brett tempered his natural tendency to push the pace and instead accepted his coach's demand to stay as a group. But when the stress of the workout increased, Brett was frustrated to find it more and more difficult to keep the pack together. Notwithstanding his exhortations the collection of freshmen and walk-ons struggled to maintain contact with the hardened upperclassmen. As the repeats accumulated, the runners' breathing elevated even faster than the unwanted lactic acid did in their bloodstream. Brett briefly reconsidered his decision to train with the team when he barely sensed the anticipated burn he had experienced in countless past anaerobic workouts. He was not surprised that even with the dulled intensity he still felt his competitive juices slowly boiling over to the next level. When he looked over the cast of distance runners in varying degrees of distress, he tried to control his innate desire to go for the jugular and press the pace of the workout to unprecedented heights. But remembering the coach's pre-workout speech, the veteran runner knew the day's effort was a team building exercise and he reluctantly accepted Wickers' firmly stated wishes.

"Come on you guys," Brett encouraged the fast fading runners. "This is the last one of the day. Focus and it'll soon be over."

He noticed the coach eyeing him as they hit the starting line for the final time. He wanted nothing more than to blast the last half mile repeat, but he honored the goal of the workout and willed the pack to stay together. When the group of wheezing runners finally struggled past the finish line they felt the weary satisfaction in the completion of another hard effort. The older runner looked to Wickers as the other team members began the slow trot of their cooldown laps.

The veteran coach read his mind and waved him over. "Rodgers. Four more quarters at sixty-two seconds per. On my whistle."

He walked to the white line in silence while the other runners watched from the calm of their easy jog. Freed from the bonds of the team he exploded into action and ran the solo laps at the prescribed intensity. Wickers paid close attention to him and nodded in acknowledgement when he completed them as expected. The runner felt the fatigue he had always found strangely comforting and soon joined his teammates in the few remaining laps of the day.

"Thanks, coach," he said as he jogged toward Wickers. "I needed the extra work."

"Is that right? I could never have figured that out on my own."

He smiled back when he recognized the grizzled old coach had been one step ahead of him all along. But there was still one question he felt the need to ask. "Coach, this may seem weird, but I was wondering where you got the idea for your speech today?"

"I was just trying to get your attention. And I decided to hit you horny bastards where you live," he said with a satisfied smile.

And for what was starting to become a common occurrence Brett once again looked at the coach with an ever deepening feeling of respect.

Chapter 6

He followed behind the team bus and admired the undulating midwestern scenery while imagining the view from inside the Greyhound windows. Unable to travel with the team due to university regulations, the unattached runner had to be content with trailing closely behind in his trusty Civic. While choking on the spewed fumes of the bus he imagined the noisy horseplay taking place as the team traveled down the interstate. Almost as if on cue Logan splattered his lips against the rear window in his perpetual attempt at cheap humor. He found himself laughing out loud at the low-brow antics, but upon the fade of his smile he recognized his yearning to be on the massive vehicle with his friends.

"Madison, ten miles," he said aloud as he read the road sign. The Milwaukee runners were competing against the mighty University of Wisconsin Badgers in an infrequent intrasquad meet. The Badger runners were the pick of the litter with an annual stock of high school All-Americans assembled from across the nation. Brett himself had chosen Connecticut over the collegiate powerhouse in a recruiting war soon after completing his stellar prep career. But whenever the opportunity arose Coach Wickers chose to compete against the intrastate rivals in spite of the Big Tens squad's impressive array of talent. In a never ending battle to challenge his athletes, he knew the Wisconsin runners drew a formidable line in the sand for his own crew, and he took great interest in which of his David-like athletes weren't afraid to sling it against the Goliath squad from Madison. When the bus finally reached its destination and pulled into the campus parking lot, Brett slipped his vehicle in close behind. After the team exited he re-united with the group and walked toward the imposing domed structure that housed the indoor track.

"I've been here before," he stated offhandedly to Rip. "Back in my youth at U-Conn I think we were here for an invite."

"How did it go?"

"I think I did okay but it seems a million years ago." He didn't explain further and chose to spare his friend from learning about his trail of collegiate misfirings. What he could recall much more vividly than the past race itself was his trek through the infamous State Street bars. His final stop of that evening ended on a bar stool at "Bucks Tavern" and a resulting foggy morning wake up with an un-recognizable coed. He recalled silently slipping on his clothes and sneaking away minus a sock in a frantic rush to escape undetected. After he had scrambled back to the team hotel for the early morning red-eye, he remembered how his ragged appearance elicited a sharp look of displeasure from the coaches already waiting at the check-out counter.

"This place looks awesome," stated Rip as he brought Brett instantly back to the present. "What I wouldn't do to train here."

"All the glitter can blind you. Personally, I think you're a better match for Wickers and his 'dirt under the nails' philosophy. I get the feeling he likes guys he's got to clean up a little."

"So you think I'm like some trailer trash?"

"He probably needed a firehose to get the cow dung off your boots," Brett replied. "But maybe, just maybe, you're better off because of it."

"I guess." They hitched their travel bags onto their shoulders and traversed over the red brick walkway that led them to the entrance. They couldn't help but notice the hundreds of bricks with donors' names etched in the stone to recognize past monetary contributions.

"Look at all these names," Brett commented. "Probably all rich alumni."

"It would be nice if we had a little more money," Rip replied. "Last week I saw Coach Wickers folding towels for god-sake. By the way he told us you're going to run the mile with us. How was he able to get you in the meet?"

"By promising their coach I might be able to push the pace in the 'A' race. Apparently he doesn't hold our team in the highest regard and Wickers told him I would 'hang in there' as long as I could."

Rip's countenance took on a decidedly irritated nature as he considered the nature of the comment: "Smug bastards."

But even as the statement hung in the air his confident demeanor seemed to waver when his senses were assaulted by the spotless facility. As they stepped through the doors of the venerable fieldhouse, the red pigment nearly exploded from the surface of the indoor track. The silver aluminum stands that lined the oval already contained a smattering of track aficionado's, but even their small numbers hinted at the expected crowd that would gather for the upcoming event. The bronze plaques that lined the walls bore the names of the legendary Badger greats and testified to the greatness of the long-standing program. "Herold, Bremser, Lacy, Branta, Hacker, and Favor," recited Brett as he read the names of a few of the celebrated parade of past All-Americans. When he looked beyond the awards a forty foot Bucky Badger loomed on the far wall and sneered at him in bold letters that he was the fresh meat entering a "Badger Crossing". The mass of Wisconsin runners circling the track in their cardinal red warm-ups only heightened the intimidation that seemed to well up in the visitors. Wickers was not oblivious to the effects on his athletes and called them to attention.

"Follow me, gentlemen," he shouted pointing to an open area. He was followed closely by Rex who obviously reveled in his status as assistant coach. Brett quickly had the unsightly visual of the fair haired gofer as a parasite on Wickers' butt in need of a quick excision. But with more important things to worry about than a personal grudge, he willed his energy to focus on a more positive and productive element. The team walked behind Wickers as he boldly crossed the lanes of the track and interrupted the long stream of Badger runners already deep into their warm-up. After they stowed their gear, the team sat at attention still seemingly spellbound by the pack of Wisconsin athletes circling the track.

"I feel like a virgin ready to be sacrificed," Logan whispered to Brett.

He knew his friend to be only joking, but it still surprised him because he had never before seen even a hint of wavering in his bravado. Without saying a word he turned his attention to the burnt red surface of the artificial track and visually traced the parallel lane markers that ringed the oval. He had never been able to explain the contrasting feeling of excitement and calm that overtook his emotions the moment his toes hit the track. He knew the track would never truly be home, but as the dual feelings continued to flow, he understood that for the moment it provided a modicum of comfort. And just as he had so many times before, he accepted the contradictory sensations and mentally prepared himself for the impending battle.

"Eyes up," Coach Wickers interrupted from the edge of the track while he waited patiently for their full attention. "It appears to me that some of you may believe that we have arrived on a new universe as a result of a ninety mile drive down I-94. I used to feel the same way when I learned that the Wisconsin coach has master's degrees in both psychology and kinetics while I myself have trouble spelling those words. However, because of an unforgettable incident occurring during my last visit here I have ceased to fear a return to this facility.

"A few years ago a highly regarded Wisconsin miler was apparently suffering from an intestinal malady prior to competition. Although I give him credit for his courageous attempt, he was ultimately unable to manage his distress and developed a rather obvious case of the 'runs' during his event which left a greenish trail down the back of his legs."

"Sick!" shouted Logan among the groans of the team.

"Of course I agree with you," continued the coach. "But the moral of the story is that I learned in glorious technicolor that Badger a-holes quiver under pressure just as much as anyone else's. To help you remember this fact when you run by this 'Badger Crossing' sign behind me I suggest you read it as 'Badger's Squatting'. This will undoubtedly remind you that

Wisconsin boys stain their shorts just as badly as anyone else."
He listened to the muffled laughter and knew his point had been
made. "Men of Milwaukee, I suggest we now prepare ourselves
for the performances we are capable of."

The shouts of his athletes startled the runners in red as they
continued their warm-ups on the track. The speech achieved the
desired effect of breaking down the wall between the two squads
and all previous bets were off. Wickers looked at Brett stoically
but was unable to hide the satisfied twinkle in his eye.

With Hollywood nursing an achilles injury the other distance
runners began their prepatory routine. They stayed together as a
group and jogged through a methodical two mile warm-up. After
its completion, Brett noted the runners' sweaty sheen that he had
always somehow considered a strange form of emotional
cleansing. The flow of sweat soon hit a full boil when the milers
completed a series of striders at an ever increasing level of
intensity. He tried to collect himself with a deep sigh and felt the
usual pre-race jitters mounting, but still called Logan and Rip
over for a final consultation. "On a small track we need to work
together. There are eight laps to the mile here and an opening is
all one of us may need. If you see it, make your move"

"Gimme an inch and I'll take the mile," said Logan as Rip
nodded in agreement.

"I'll remember that. Now let's get this done." He was
pleased to see the old attitude return to his friends and they began
the long, slow walk toward the starting line. They were met there
by four red-clad opponents who toed the turf as if readying it for
the upcoming race. To the runner this instant was the worst of
times and he stood impatiently while exhaling the deadened air
through his dry lips. The aged starter recited the cursory
instructions and Brett longed for the race to begin. The words
were more blurred than usual, and he sensed the distinct
arrogance of the Wisconsin runners and the casual approach they
were taking toward their opponents. Brett stood alertly in his old
white singlet between his two black clad teammates and was
unable to avoid overhearing a mop-topped runner snigger about
the "Oreo cookies from Milwaukee". The snide remark was all he

needed to stoke his internal fury to the desired level needed for the day's competition.

When the seven runners lined up on the track their collective breathes seemed to be held in anticipation of the starter's gun. The echoing blast sent them exploding out of their crouch and accelerating down the track where Brett immediately felt the jostling of red singlets as he fought for position. Two angular shoulders sandwiched him and the resulting battle sent him crashing face-first toward the rough artificial surface. He instinctively performed a graceless "tuck and roll" that landed him stumbling on his feet but body lengths behind the pack. He fought against his natural rage but denied himself the gut-level reaction of sprinting and regaining quick contact with his competitors. After performing a quick internal body check he noted only a burning in his shoulder that he knew would do little to impede his ability to forge on. So that's the way it's going to be, he thought as he focused on the string of runners ahead.

The competitors covered the first lane by grouping themselves in two's and stormed the small track to an appreciative crowd. The duo of black shirted Milwaukee runners tailed behind and Brett worked the next three laps hard in order to recapture the lost ground. He zeroed in on the trailing jerseys and step by step willed himself to regain connection with the leading pack of runners.

" 'Bout time," Logan grunted as he looked out the corner of his eye.

Brett nodded silently as he analyzed the situation. If he attempted to pass, it would likely mean being forced out a minimum of two lanes by the well coached Wisconsin runners, and he calculated that team tactics were the only way he could recover from his early fall. He wordlessly tapped Rip on the elbow from behind and motioned towards the two closest opponents. His friend intuitively responded by pressing closer to his nearest competitors causing them to close up a slight gap in their ranks. In a veteran recognition of the move both Logan and Brett strode by strongly on the backstretch when the unexpected acceleration caught the competing runners off guard. The hard effort winded them briefly, but also bolstered their spirits because of the now free sailing they had toward the two leaders. Brett charged ahead of his tiring friend knowing there were only two laps remaining for him to salvage the race.

"Hang on," he pleaded to Logan through his gritted teeth.

"Find…the inch," he rasped back.

He continued his fight toward the frontrunners and Brett knew they were again battling the same concern. To run wide meant likely defeat as he doubted he could manage the extra yards it would demand. The sound of the bell signaling the final lap seemed to awaken Logan because he boldly pounded wide and challenged the outside Badger runner. The reaction was swift when the opponent angled towards lane two in an automatic response to cut off the intruder. Brett suddenly understood his friend's remark and bolted through the tiny crease created between the duo of Wisconsin runners when the race entered the final backstretch. With the small crowd growing increasingly animated he matched strides with his floppy haired nemesis while the mural of Bucky Badger looked on. His anger at the Wisconsin runner's "cookie" starting line remark demanded a well-timed response.

"Dunk…this…squatter boy," he growled at the now struggling runner and returned a hard shoulder before flying by him in the race to the finish line. He felt his chest break the tape and he sucked in the dry air while he waited for his friends to hang on for a well deserved fourth and fifth place finish.

A red-faced Wickers bounded up to greet his weary runners while a host of befuddled Wisconsin athletes looked on. The sweat dripped off the tip of his nose and Brett watched the Badger coach study him blankly before a hint of recognition seemed to cross his face. But he knew whatever runner the skilled coach remembered from years gone by was at best a cheap imitation of this year's model.

Chapter 7

The dog days of running had set in for the group when the gray dreariness of February overtook the landscape. The matted grass and barren trees only added to the sluggishness the runners felt as they battled through the winter blues. Their lives had become increasingly robotic with the daily grind of the early morning run, followed by class, and capped off with the afternoon workout.

On another bleak morning Brett grudgingly awoke in order to put in the required miles of easy running. As he lay in bed he took turns telling himself he was either "flushing the system" or "paying the price" required to gain the physical and emotional strength needed for success. But he still fought the daily nagging thought that the only true motivator of the early run was to avoid the guilt he would invariably experience on those infrequent days he slept in. Entangled further in his thoughts was the constant tug of war he fought between reason and fitness -- or its mirror image of obsession and burnout. Still struggling with the jumble of emotions he heard a pounding on his front door that signaled the arrival of a rare morning entourage.

"I'm coming," he shouted sliding out of bed clothed in his baggy sweats. He performed a quick brush of his teeth and slapped a handful of water on his face before exiting the bathroom. After grabbing an old sweatshirt and a pair of his training shoes from the pile on the floor he met his friends on the porch.

"Ain't you pretty in the morning," said Hollywood. "You look like my dirty wash basket."

Brett shook his head as if cautioning the other runners. "Not today, Hollywood. I'm tired and my hamstring is acting up."

"Tendinitis?"

"I guess," he answered with a shrug.

"Tendinitis…and bursitis," commiserated Logan in a subdued rap rhythm.

"Heels are bruisin'…blisters oozin'," joined in Hollywood as the battle began.

"Dehydration…inflammation."

"Snapping tendons…shin splints bendin'," countered Hollywood.

"Calves are twitchin'…rashes itchin'."

"Runner's knee…and bloody pee."

"Penile frostbite…quads are too tight," rapped Logan.

A look of concern crossed Hollywood's face when he struggled for an appropriate response. "Ahh! You win…again," he finally admitted in disgust. "I thought I had you this time."

The running rap did little to awaken Brett as he plodded mechanically into the start of the miles. On days like this when his motivation waned, he longed for a normal morning that included indulging in the bacon and eggs he could smell wafting from the small windows of the bungalows. He admitted running didn't always lead itself to the simple pleasures of life, but without it knew that other unexpected moments would have passed him by.

"Penile frostbite?" he asked aloud to his friend. "How did you ever think of that one?"

A proud smile overtook the smallest runner's smooth face. "I'm an art-tist. The bro's call me 'D-Mile'."

"As in you suck in de' mile?" asked Hollywood as he sniggered under his breath.

The comment hung in the air when the runners suddenly caught a view of the thick blanket of mist drifting over the lake. The lakefront landscape was an awe inspiring sight that made even the most difficult of runs seem manageable. Brett had hoped that this morning would be no different, but so far both the scenery and the verbal give and take had done little to shake him from his doldrums. The other runners recognized this and quietly looped through the campus as they completed the requisite miles. When each hit the necessary mileage they were eventually dropped off at their homes one by one.

Brett soloed to his apartment and reluctantly re-lived the previous evening. He reflected on the unexpected surfacing of an overwhelming urge that overtook him when he battled the frustration of a particularly hard assignment. The desire for a drink hit him in waves as the night had progressed, and it was all he could do to subdue the unwanted calling. A long muffled voice reappeared from his subconscious and rationalized the usefulness of a single drink to calm his anxieties. It was only after a study of the poster and the hard earned mileage on the wall that he cinched up his running shoes and bolted out the door for a quick getaway. When the steps accumulated and turned into miles the destructive need slowly faded until he deemed it safe to return to the flat. He recognized the symbolism of literally running away from his problem, but accepted it was better than the beer-soaked alternative. But he still wondered uneasily if the addictive qualities he had shown in the past could continue to be controlled by the twice daily injection of endorphins he administered to himself.

With only a few blocks remaining in the morning run he watched the activity of the campus streets multiply. The combination of groggy students and hardened commuters edged into his space, and he purposely avoided even the most innocent of eye contact. He irrationally wondered if the weakness he had displayed the past evening was evident from even a single glance at his face. He took a deep breath as he wished for the ability to somehow exhale away his destructive impulses until they would dissolve like the mist over the lake.

He slowed to a walk and felt the fatigue of the last twelve hours seep into his frame. He had built an entire existence on physical duels, but found the emotional struggle for sobriety even more taxing than a hard mile. In this battle he had found there was no sizing up the foe that chose only to whisper in his ear. With a grim satisfaction he acknowledged that so far he had shown the ability to control his aberrant desires, but found the effort left his psyche increasingly drained and weary. When he approached his front steps he vowed to celebrate his small victory of the previous evening by making a hearty breakfast of his own. Soon thereafter the crackle of bacon and eggs on the fry pan soothed his well worn soul.

Chapter 8

An unexpectedly warm day in early March had led Brett to the decision to take a run on his own and enjoy the break in the harsh winter. With the sun shining high overhead he tilted his head back and soaked in the life affirming warmth that had been absent since the fall. A satisfied smile overtook his face when he watched the dual attraction of the weather and lakefront which seemed to draw out an assortment of creatures from hibernation. From the headbangers in their black t-shirts, to other opportunistic aerobic animals, the parkway was alive and thriving. As he stretched on a park bench in preparation for the days' run, he noted with amusement the peaceful coexistence of the variety of life forms.

The mirage of spring-like temperatures rejuvenated him and he planned to hammer out a hard twelve miler. His running had been going well and the workouts with the team added the needed structure to his training. The warm sunshine that lit the air only added to the contentment he currently felt. He looked at the beer being swilled in the surrounding parking lots and once again felt the return of an old craving for a cold beer to celebrate the warm day. But today was not going to be that day he thought when he eased into a slow run.

He drew in a deep breath and reveled in the freshness of the afternoon before beginning a jog up the long hill. He was surrounded by a cast of walkers, rollerbladers, and bicyclists all enjoying the brief respite from another cruel Wisconsin winter. When he finally reached the crest he stopped to reset his watch and begin the timed portion of his run. He was startled by the squeak of hand brakes and when he looked up he noticed a solo bicyclist slowing to a stop. When the cyclist approached the stoplight she turned toward him with a smile that erased all memory of the need of a timed excursion.

"Nice day for a change," Brett said to the biker. "It's about time."

"The winters get so long," she answered as she self-consciously smoothed her tousled blond hair. "Sometimes I wonder why anyone would live here."

When the light changed they both moved slowly into motion and continued on with their journeys. He anxiously hoped for even a simple conversation, but knew the aerobic demands of their chosen sports didn't lead themselves to much dialog. But for as much as he had since his relocation to Milwaukee, he wanted nothing more than a continuation of the discussion to ensue.

"Do you mind if I run with you a bit?" he asked in a voice that belied the tentativeness that he felt.

She smiled shyly before responding: "If you think you can keep up."

Again with the smile he thought. He studied the curves of her almond shaped face and the dance of her blue eyes. But it was the smile that drew him in deeper.

"Look out for the tree!" she shouted.

He jumped aside narrowly missing one of the sturdy maples lining the parkway. "Shit! Ahh, I mean…thanks, I didn't see it," he admitted with a slight blush.

"This isn't your first day running is it?"

He watched her pedal easily and measured the sarcasm in her voice. The apparent playfulness only urged him on for a response. "No. But I guess you couldn't tell by looking. By the way my name is Brett."

"I'm Marie. And actually I can tell you're a runner."

"How's that?" He surmised she had noticed his lean athletic legs and he awaited her reply.

"The windburn. On your nose. It looks like you get outside quite a bit."

"Wow," he said being caught off guard. "I always viewed my face as ruggedly handsome. I guess I got that all wrong."

The pause only allowed her cheeks to flush and she temporarily concentrated on the road ahead.

"Oh no. I didn't mean it that way. You are...," she replied but stopped herself in mid sentence. It suddenly dawned on her that he had an ability to carry on a conversation unimpeded by the effort he expended while running. The smile appeared again as she continued. "How far do you run?"

"About fifteen a day."

"Minutes?"

"Miles," he corrected.

She paused briefly to consider the magnitude of his response. He waited for the typical inane response by the inexperienced as to the breadth of his running, but was surprised when she suddenly braked to a stop. He followed the aim of her finger as she pointed toward the lake and shouted. "Look! Over the cliffs. Can you see the eagle?"

Squinting in the distance, he watched the flight of the majestic bird as it soared over the ridge. He studied the glide of the eagle as it circled the waters in search of its next prey. He admired the wingspan and the perfection of the creature as it floated effortlessly over the horizon. "It's beautiful."

She was surprised by his response and looked at him admiring the swooping bird. Most guys she knew wouldn't give the bird a second thought, and when she turned back to the skies she explained. "They don't usually come in this area of the state, but sometimes they migrate and stay awhile. I used to watch one at my parent's cabin up north and dream I could soar the same way."

He reflected on his own recurring dream and only wished his own life had lead itself to such a comforting image. Maybe there will be a day, he thought before he spoke again. "I hope he stays around a long time," he said as the eagle floated out of sight and they started on their trek again. "Do you bike a lot?"

"When it's not too frozen out. Otherwise I swim and lift weights sometimes. I even do a little yoga."

"Any running?"

"No way, that's much too boring. Well, umm...what I meant was I'd rather do other things. No offense."

"Don't worry about it," he said with a dismissive wave of his hand. "There are days it isn't so exciting to me either. But I still do it."

"How come?"

"I like to run fast and the only way to get faster is to work at it. Everyday and most days twice."

She didn't immediately reply as she thought she must have misunderstood his words. When she realized she had heard him correctly she began again. "Twice? Sorry if my questions are stupid, but is that normal for runners?"

"For some. At least the ones that I'm concerned about." He flashed to that very same morning's internet search for the latest race results. Given his budgetary limitations, he had only the library's computers available for gleaning information on his competitors. He had always found the discovery of his opponent's race times stress producing, yet he had never discovered even the slightest ability to stay away from the latest data. Perhaps one day he would tell her of his dilemma, but he felt fortunate when she simply let the remark drop.

"I take it you go to school too?" she asked.

"I'm in a post-grad program for exercise physiology. I get to learn exciting things like the Krebs Cycle and VO2 Max."

"It sounds like the name of a bad rock band. Better you than me I guess," she commented as she continued her slow pedaling. "I have a year to go before I get degrees in elementary education and art."

"So you can teach all the kiddies the proper technique to finger paint?"

"Touché," she said with an affirmative nod. "Actually, I suspect I'll teach for dough and art for show…something like that anyways."

"I'm sure you'll be great. I can see the little boys having a crush on you already."

She blushed slightly and soaked in the veiled compliment as he sensed the attraction he felt was mutual. With the tour of the lakefront continuing they proceeded to small talk their way through the miles. By the time she led them back to the front of her apartment he was astonished to see a full hour had gone by.

He watched as she climbed off the saddle and paused while contemplating his next move. She beat him to the punch and was the first to speak.

"Here's where I get off," she said. "Thanks, that was nice."

He was not inclined to aggressively seek out female companionship, but found himself blurting out an invitation. "Marie, I'd like to see you again. I promise I clean up real well," he said as he wiped the sweat off of his forehead.

"I'm sure you do," she said as she again self consciously stroked her own windblown hair.

"How about tomorrow? I could come by around six and we could get a bite to eat. It would be a joy not to eat macaroni and cheese by myself again."

She studied him while he fidgeted nervously in anticipation of her response. "I couldn't let you do that to yourself. I'd love to. And look out for trees on your way back."

After exchanging a meeting time they said their final goodbye. When he returned to a slow trot he couldn't erase the memory of a face that had been indelibly burned into his brain. As he carefully heeded her advice his spirit soared and he carefully avoided the maples on his slow trot home.

Chapter 9

He couldn't help but shake his head in disgust when he looked at his aged vehicle and the ravages 150,000 miles had heaped upon its rusting frame. Even after scrubbing clean the windows and picking up the crumpled Power Bar wrappers from the floor, he began to realize the futility of his efforts. He had even taken to hiding the stains on the two back rests by using his best race t-shirts as seat covers, but the observable improvement was minimal. A slow examination of his handiwork ended in a sigh of resignation when he recognized the ultimate futility of his work.

Fully intending to make a better impression than his car, he braved a cool shower and slipped into his lone collared shirt. For years he had resisted any form of fashionable attire in his ongoing quest to avoid the mainstream. But at a time of necessity when an impression finally mattered, he wished he was less the "rebel without a clue" that a past teammate had once anointed him. He sorted through his old running shoes and settled on the least offensive pair from his vast collection. A sudden case of the jitters set in when he realized this was his first true date for as far back as he could remember. His previous dating history was checkered, and he had rarely committed to more than a fortnight of a relationship before ending it abruptly or simply letting it die of apathy. At these times even a shallow amount of soul searching led him to one unmistakable conclusion – that he would leave them before they left on their own. That feeble excuse was further bolstered by the complications that even a platonic relationship had on the inflexibility of his omnipresent running schedule. He stored these uneasy thoughts into the dark recesses of his mind, and continued to ready himself for another likely ill-fated ride on the dating carousel. After a series of pain producing snaps of the rubber band he found himself pulling up to her apartment where he noticed her peeking out from the second story window. He had barely gotten out of the car when she stepped out the front door to meet him on the steps.

"Hi, Brett," she said. "You sure look nice."

He momentarily had forgotten the previous day's promise until it dawned on him. "I did my best. I even powdered my nose." He nearly commented on her own comely looks, but withheld the words of praise that he knew were bound to come out as overly saccharine. In a quick change of topics he deftly re-directed the conversation toward that evening's final destination. "I thought we'd go to the legendary Hooligans before it gets too crowded. I haven't even gone there yet because I've been so busy."

"My girlfriends and I stop in there sometimes," she said as he opened the car door for her. "It can get crazy in there. One time this little guy did a beer slide on his belly across the whole floor and knocked himself out when he hit the wall. Someone said he was a runner too."

"I wouldn't doubt it. I'll ask around," he said knowing full well the prime suspect. As he circled around the car to the driver's side he was embarrassed by the state of his vehicle and the scattered rust spots that dotted the exterior. "Sorry about the car. It does get me around pretty good though."

"I've never worried much about cars. I come from a family of ten and when we traveled to my grandparents, sometimes my dad would threaten that he needed to strap me on the top. Really, I think it's quite unique."

"And in a few years maybe even 'antique'," he replied as he maneuvered the small car through the quiet streets. They continued to engage in idle chatter as they reacquainted themselves with the banter of the previous day. "Ahh…in the front row," he said pulling up to the curb directly in front of the pub.

When he opened the thick oak door his mind flashed back to the countless bars of his past. He had avoided them so as not to tempt himself and hadn't been in one for months, not even just to socialize. A sad smile crossed his face when he thought of his ironic choice of pub-happy Milwaukee as his latest educational venue. Once proudly nicknamed "Beertown, USA", he considered the tease of the neon beer signs adorning the walls to be one more test he would have to pass. But with his own innate stubbornness leading the way, he fully intended to achieve nothing short of a victory over his own personal demon. Even with his senses being bombarded with the dual odors of smoke and stale beer, he refocused on Marie in an attempt to once again bury his own weakness.

"Thank you," she said in acknowledgment of his gentlemanly ways.

"I think I used to be doorman in a past life. But I do aspire to greater heights this time."

"Perhaps a butler?"

"If it pays well enough, I can be bought," he replied. "Follow me, Marie, I'll find us a nice view for the night."

He located a choice table by the window and was surprised to see a well maintained walnut décor that had held up well in spite of the weekly assault of the collegiate crowd. Just as he had hoped, the crowd was still light at this early hour and the waitress came by and greeted them amiably. "Can I start you with a drink?"

"Just a coke," Marie said.

"I'll have the same," he told the waitress.

When she went to fill their order they again concentrated on each other. His thoughts stagnated when he looked across the small table and suddenly felt as if he was in over his head. This is the real deal, he thought to himself after remembering the many plastic relationships he had involved himself with over the many years. Say something you loser, cried a tiny voice from deep inside. "I'm really impressed you have a double major," he said finally as he played with a napkin.

"It's not as hard as you'd think, "she said as she ran her fingers on the grain of the old table. "I look forward to being a teacher, but I really love the art classes. Fortunately, an art major is a little easier and doesn't really take that much time. But since

I would be drawing on my own anyways, it's almost like getting credits for what I like to do."

"Do you paint?"

"Some. But primarily I sketch with pencil. Wildlife mostly."

"I admire people with artistic talent. I remember once in grade school I brought home a turtle made out of clay. I gave it to my dad and he put it on the table upside down as if it was an ashtray. The problem was it looked better his way than mine. If I remember right, that was about my last foray into art."

"I'm sure it wasn't that bad," she said as her laugh trickled across the small table.

"Maybe I could sneak you into the art lab and see if you've improved. If not, we can donate all your ashtrays to Hooligans."

"I doubt they are that desperate. Have you ever sold any of your work?"

He watched as she paused before answering. Unknowingly he had hit a button and she seemed briefly to be at a loss for words. As she continued to trace the grain of the wooden table she finally replied. "God, no. I barely even show anyone my work much less put it up for sale. That's why I met you outside my apartment tonight. I'm not ready to show anyone my work yet."

"I'm sure your drawings are great. I bet the talent is there but you just need some confidence."

"That and some rich art lover with bad eyesight. Like a millionaire Mr. Magoo."

"Road hog!" he blurted out in an attempt to imitate the bespectacled cartoon character. "Do you think you could ever draw something for a poor boy's wall?"

She looked at him and paused while she contemplated the question. "Don't hold your breath. It's such a personal thing to me that I'm kind of embarrassed to have them out there in the public. It's like I'm opening myself up for the entire world to see. But maybe I'll draw something for you if you become one of the chosen few."

"Let me know if you ever choose me, okay?"

"You'll know," she said as she returned to looking him squarely in the eye.

When the waitress returned with their drinks an awkward pause again presented itself. He knew instinctively that he wanted to become closer to this girl than he had ever been to anyone. But remembering the smothering sensation of the clinging groupies that had pursued him at his previous collegiate stops, he knew better than to demonstrate even a trace of vulnerability. He returned his attention to the drink in front of him and after they both took a sip, Marie broke the uncomfortable silence. "Do you play darts? They have a nice board in back."

"I played in a few leagues back east. I'll be glad to give you a game if you think you can keep up," he said remembering her bicycling comment from the previous day.

"Bring it on," she said more than game to take up the challenge.

They moved to the board and each gathered up a handful of the brightly covered darts. He waved her toward the white line in the floor and with a magnanimous sweep of his arm the contest began. When she moved forward he recognized how curiously comfortable he felt with her in spite of the limited time they had known each other. Even more surprising was the quick flash of possessiveness he experienced when he noticed a duo of collegians admiring her more obvious attributes. His threatening glare quickly ended their bar-room peep-show at the same time Marie made her first attempt at the circular target.

"Bull's-eye!" he shouted after her first dart found the mark. "I'm a dead man."

"That you are," she agreed.

They threw the darts and the talk flowed as well as an effortless run. With one final groan Brett raised his hands in the air. "I surrender. Bloodied and beaten. Let's go sit for awhile. Tell me more about your family," he asked as he watched the glowing signs blinking in the background.

"Well, nine brothers and sisters in a house with five bedrooms explains some of it. For better or worse you get to know everybody real well. But we're still close and all I can remember are good times."

"And your folks?"

"My dad is a plumber. And yes he keeps his pants pulled up. He had to work hard to support our family, but I never remember him complaining or us wanting for anything. My mom stayed home and took care of us and never seemed to run out of energy."

"Sounds perfect."

"Close to it I guess. How about you?"

A flurry of emotions confronted him unexpectedly as he weighed her question. He had spent years fiercely protecting his privacy from the bevy of acquaintances that had crossed his path. Yet her open and accepting face lent itself towards one slight step back into the past. "My life hasn't been quite so idyllic. Dad passed away about six years ago and my mom sort of died before that."

"Sort of?"

"She started to drink and we've kind of lost touch lately. She lives in Ohio now and I don't see her much."

"I'm sorry, Brett. But you seem like you're doing okay for yourself," she said in an attempt to reassure him.

"You haven't seen my apartment yet so I'd withhold judgment on that. But, I guess I've managed. 'Adapt or perish' a wise man once said. I didn't want the latter."

"Here's to adapting," she said raising her glass in a toast.

"To adapting," he echoed as he looked at her while being drawn deeper into the charms of her blue eyes.

The burger went down easy and they talked of the hopes and dreams of the future. The track seemed miles away and it dawned on him he could not remember the last time he had been on a date where alcohol had not greased his wit. This one was different he thought... and somehow better than the rest. When the night ended he walked her to her door. He softly grasped her hand as he faced her and said, "I had a great night."

So did I," she replied.

He leaned forward and gave her a soft kiss as they promised to see each other again. And walking away he realized it was now his turn to smile.

Chapter 10

The tease of the premature warm spell faded quickly from Brett's memory, but the bonding he had felt with Marie was foremost in his mind. He had not mentioned his successful date with her to his friends and fully intended to keep their relationship under wraps as long as he could. He knew the post-date harassment he would experience from the other runners was inevitable, and when they gathered together at Logan's apartment he was purposely tight lipped. When the group settled back into his mismatched furniture they came to an agreement that the roomful of barren pockets had left only the choice of free entertainment as a viable alternative. When Logan waved his favorite DVD in the air he got a quick response from Hollywood. "I'm not going to watch that stupid movie again," he shouted with contempt. "We must have seen it twenty times."

"What's wrong with you? This is a classic. Don't you realize 'Gladiator' is the ultimate running movie? Maximus kicks butt and takes names just like me."

Hollywood snatched the DVD from his friend's hands and offered a terse statement that spoke for the group: "You so need a life."

"If you two girls would stop arguing, maybe we could figure out something to do," said Brett from the ratty couch. "Or we could all leave and let dirtball here clean this place." He surveyed the front room and measured the assortment of clothes and dirty kitchenware scattered about the small room. The requisite assortment of running shoes was heaped carelessly in the corner where they added to the already murky smell of the apartment. It was only the line of well-tended picture frames containing family photos that added even a hint of decorum to the living quarters.

Rip digested Brett's comment and shook his head woefully. "This place actually looks better than our apartment did last year. The three of us had a flat on Oakland Avenue right next to the 'Pizza Man' restaurant. But Logan was such a pig that we got evicted by the landlord when he did a spot check and almost keeled over from what he saw."

Hollywood hopped to his feet as he warmed to the topic of conversation. "Rip and I went on strike and refused to do dishes for Logan and he just kept on piling things up in the kitchen. It got so bad we had nothing left to eat on so Rip and I went to plastic forks and paper plates. When Logan ran out of cookware he just started ordering pizza from next door until he had probably twenty boxes lying all over the place."

The three waited for Logan to defend himself and he didn't disappoint them when he raised his own index finger in the air. "While I'll agree things stacked up for a bit, you do remember that I eventually cleaned up the place, right?"

"You brought in that plastic Mickey Mouse wading pool into the kitchen and piled all the dirty dishes into it," Rip said in exasperation. "Then you threw in some car wash detergent and let them soak for a week. The dishes eventually molded over and we had to throw them all out."

"I admit I might have messed up…a little." Logan agreed when he finally owned up to his past failure. "But at least before we got kicked out we had one hell of an eviction party."

"From what I remember you hooked up with that girl that looked like Shrek's troll girlfriend," added Hollywood. "And you could barely get her to leave the next morning."

"Don't remind me about that one. I think she only left because I ran out of frozen waffles."

Rip stirred restlessly when the reminiscing dwindled and brought them full circle to Brett's initial observations. "Someday maybe you'll find a girl who will take care of you. But for now it's just pathetic."

"It makes chicks think I'm helpless and brings out the mothering instinct in them," said Logan. "And I love to be mothered."

"Run, Oedipus…run," said Brett.

"Are you calling me a homo?"

"Never mind," said Brett with resignation over the missed joke. In further study of the disheveled surroundings he couldn't help but notice the flashing antique beer signs decorating the walls. It seemed that everywhere he went he was bombarded by both reminders of his past and the temptations of the future. He closed off the thoughts and attempted to continue hiding his personal flaw by asking a simple question even though he was quite aware of the likely answer. "Hey Logan, what's 'Blatz' and 'Pabst'?"

"You're such an easterner," he replied with a shake of his head. "They're both good old Milwaukee swill…born and brewed in Wisconsin."

"Signs from your dad's tavern, ay Logan?" asked Rip.

His eyes shined and a proud look overtook his face. "Yup, 'Ed's Place'.

"'Ay'… 'yup'… 'Ed's Place'? You're all a bunch of goobers," mocked Hollywood. When he stood up with an animated demonstration of pelvic thrusts he continued. "Someday I'll go to your hometown and take 'Daisy Mae' out to the corn field to show her a good time."

"Two Rivers was a great place to grow up in," said Logan stubbornly as he ignored the taunt. "For awhile my folks lived above the bar until mom got a job at the cheese factory."

"That is just too Wisconsin!" snorted Hollywood as he could scarcely contain his excitement. "I bet she squirted out her cute little eight pound cheese curd during a polka."

Logan rose up and with balled fists threatened the taller runner. "Don't make me hurt you. Ed and I will both kick your ass all the way back to Illinois."

With Hollywood sniggering in the background Brett examined the multitude of photos before speaking up again. "Does your dad run too?"

"Naw, he gets out of breath watching the Packer's games," Logan exaggerated as he looked toward the photos. "Golf is his game...hey, that gives me an idea." They all watched in curiosity when he scooted to the hall closet and listened to the clatter of belongings fall from the overstuffed shelves. Rip shook his head and rolled his eyes in fearful anticipation of the latest unveiling of another of his friend's "ideas".

"Are you okay in there?"

"Yes," came the cry a second later. "I knew I still had them." When he re-entered the room he proudly displayed a tattered golf bag filled with mismatched clubs and hoisted them overhead as if they were an offering to a king. The other runners looked on uncomprehendingly and waited for an explanation.

"What are we going to do with those?" asked Hollywood. "Have a coliseum fight like 'Maxipad' would?"

"It's 'Maximus'," replied Logan sounding slightly offended. "Actually that's not a bad idea, but it's not exactly what I had in mind." After pulling out an old woodenheaded driver he waved it menacingly at his friend. "I was thinking we could play a little 'speed golf'."

"What the heck is that?" asked Rip.

"Eighteen holes as fast as you can play. The course is still closed because it's too cold, but we could sneak on. We each get to pick out one club to use and the first man in wins. Strokes be damned."

"It's got possibilities," said Brett as he nodded in understanding. "I heard of Steve Scott doing that once."

"The *Terminator* director?" asked Hollywood.

"Not Ridley Scott. Steve Scott, the miler," he said with eyes wide open in disbelief. "You watch too many movies."

"Tony says golf is for 'limp noodles'," chimed in Rip while he slid an iron out of the bag. He proceeded to waggle the club as he addressed an imaginary ball and released a slow-motion swing. "But then again he has gotten more crotchety than a ten year old pair of Wickers' boxers," he reconsidered while he pretended to peer at a ball flying into the distance.

"I've been learning that depending upon the day Tony hates just about everyone...and everything," reminded Brett.

"I haven't golfed since I was a kid but how hard could it be beating you hosers?" questioned Hollywood. "And at least it would save me from watching that Grade B flick again. But Logan will have to loan me some shoes to wear because I'm not going to wreck my new boots."

"I wouldn't want you to ruin your prairie dog leather or whatever they are," replied Logan. "Maybe you could wear an old pair of my running spikes and pretend you are a real golfer."

"I'm in," said Brett with finality in his voice. "I vote we go grip it and rip it." As usual the runner was game for any sort of competition that crossed his path. "Last man in makes dinner."

They all agreed to the bet and selected their favorite club before divvying up the well traveled golf balls as equally as possible. They bundled up in an assortment of baggy clothes and soon headed out to the nearby campus course. The foursome jogged at an easy pace until they reached the first tee and viewed the frozen ground of the abandoned holes. The flattened and yellowed grass held little aesthetic appeal, but the dream of golfing glory was foremost in their minds.

"Remember fastest man in wins," said Logan. After spreading out the balls on the hard plains they all loosened up with an assortment of amateurish swings. Brett himself could hardly remember the last time he had traversed the links, but had suspected it had been somewhere in his home state of Connecticut. But he knew wherever it had occurred, it had surely been under different circumstances than he was about to partake in. Along with the other runners he waited patiently until Logan pierced the air with his index finger and let loose a final decree. "Gentlemen on my order...unleash hell!"

The clubs slashed through the cold air and the "pock" of the ball strikes echoed clearly over the terrain. The flight of the balls was followed by watchful eyes and their eager steps quickly followed in the hunt. The crunch of the grass echoed under their feet as the game lurched to an uneven start.

"What the hell?" shouted Hollywood from the tee box. "Mine didn't go anywhere."

"Must be a bad ball," called Rip from over his shoulder. "Try to concentrate."

The leaders battled over the hilly terrain and attacked the ball with a vengeance. Style was instantly forgotten as they raked the ball over the course hole after hole. As they slid over the frozen ground they battled the winter barriers that only added to the game's inherent degree of difficulty.

"The sand trap has snow in it," complained Logan as he struggled to locate his ball.

"Play the ball where it lies," advised Brett when he sprinted on by. He turned back to check on his adversaries and watched Rip methodically preparing to putt at the previous hole. Brett shook his head in the realization that his friend's mental make-up was unlikely to change notwithstanding the urgent need for recklessness. Hollywood was nowhere in sight and the battle for the championship narrowed to Logan and himself. "Tiger Woods you ain't," he taunted after watching his closest competitor flail away in the sand trap.

"My hands are frozen," complained Logan. "I can't even grip the club."

"Real gladiators don't whine," he reminded his friend as he hurriedly lined up his own putt.

"You're right," Logan replied when he rocketed a shot from the trap. Brett howled as he felt a smack in his thigh from the errant ball. Logan nearly danced in glee when he saw his ball settle only inches from the cup. "You da man!"

"Lucky shot," said Brett as he sprinted to the last tee. "It's time to piss on the fire and call in the dogs 'cause this baby's over." He hammered at the ball and groaned at the sight of it careening into the barren woods that lined the last hole. With Logan sniffing hotly at his heels he crashed through the thick bramble in search of his ball. He frantically tore at the tangle of branches in a last ditch effort to locate the missing white ball. "It's under the ice," he protested when he finally found it resting beneath the frozen cover in a small creek.

"Play the ball where it lies," reminded Logan unsympathetically as he teed up his ball for the last time.

Brett proceeded to chop at the ball in the hopes of freeing it from its icy home, but only succeeded in splattering frozen shards into his face when they exploded from the attempts. His stroke quickly degraded into a series of hacks and his panic over a potential loss escalated to unprecedented heights.

"Strength and honor," called the new leader when he strode down the last fairway.

Brett's frustration deepened when he saw Rip also approaching from the rear. His attempts to free his ball had forced it deeper under a thick plate of ice and he knew it would take an ax to eventually free it. When Rip ran on by he realized he would have the first "Did Not Finish" of his career, and he watched his ball settle into a haven that would be safe until the spring thaw. When he trudged dejectedly to the final green he saw Logan doing what passed for a victory dance.

"Thank you…thank you," he mouthed to the imaginary crowd as he blew them kisses. "I just want to say I owe it all to the girls at 'The Meatlocker' for their undying support."

Brett couldn't help but laugh when he noticed an elderly driver look quizzically at his impaired friend.

"Anybody seen Hollywood?" asked Rip as he sealed second place by tapping in his final putt.

"Just watch out," warned Logan. "He's not a good loser. Last year after a bad race, he threw a javelin into a pond and almost speared a goose. Wickers made him wade into the sludge to find it and then sit in his own slime the whole way home."

Almost as if on cue he marched up the fairway and they watched in surprise when he suddenly flung his club toward the green where it landed with a muffled "thunk". They all recognized the likely agitated state of their friend and withheld comments as he approached the final green. Hollywood broke the quiet by offering his own frustration filled dialog.

"Stupid freakin' sport!" he screamed as he threw his Titelist to the ground and glared at it. "You think that was funny?" He gleefully drove his spikes into the ball and laughed while he twisted his foot back and forth. "Does that feel good you dimpled mutant? I'll teach your sorry ass to screw with me. How does it feel with a spike on your throat? You want some more? Well, here's some more," he called as he answered his own question. With the ball embedded into the earth he then focused his rage on the nearby club. "And you," he said picking up the old five iron.

"You think you're getting off so easy? How about a little sand in your grill?" He slammed the face of the iron into the frozen sand trap while the other runners watched in amazement. "Ahhh!" he screamed as he unexpectedly charged towards a tree with the offending club. The sound of the impact echoed in the air as he beat the shaft against the trunk and marched off leaving the club looking like an oversized horseshoe on a stake.

"Are you done yet?" asked Brett bravely when it looked as if Hollywood's anger had run its course.

"Tony was right," he called back without acknowledging the question. "You're limp noodles all of you!"

Brett couldn't resist one final jab at his frustrated friend as he stormed away from the threesome. "Pasta does sound good, doesn't it boys?" The remaining golfers seconded his menu choice and from a safe distance followed Hollywood to collect on the free meal they had earned on the eighteen holes of frozen tundra.

Chapter 11

With school hitting hard, the student-athletes were struggling to maintain balance as the scale tipped ever so slightly toward academics. Brett had been able to keep a solid "B" average even though he found the midwestern school substantially more difficult than he had ever imagined. In addition to the mid-terms demanded of all students, he had the additional burden of conducting a controlled experiment on live subjects as a requirement to pass the laboratory portion of the physiology program. Fortunately, he had a team full of aerobic lab rats as prospective candidates for his study. As he puttered about in the crowded physiology laboratory, he carefully calibrated the necessary instruments in preparation for the next test subject he had secured. When he was comfortable with the settings, he taped the monitoring electrodes to the athlete's chest, and ignored the attitude of the current runner on the treadmill.

"The experiment is called 'The Effects of Visual Stimuli on the Aerobic Threshold'," he explained again to Hollywood. "Like I told you before, when you're on the treadmill I'm trying to see if I can manipulate your heart rate by forcing you to look at thirty different photos for one minute a piece. You'll run at 6:30 pace and the blinders will make you concentrate solely on the projection screen. During the test I'll use a monitor to measure the changes in your heart rate."

"And what's the point?" he asked with a look of disdain on his face.

"To see if I can mess with your heart by playing with your head. Or in other words I want to calculate if sights you see on the road or track can affect your running performance."

"Sounds stupid," said his subject as he boarded the platform.

He had to fight back the urge to run his friend off of the platform with an unexpected accelerated start-up. But after regaining his composure he began the experiment and the runner started into a slow trot. Hollywood was among the test subjects who had completed the first thirty minute "baseline" run a week ago with the use of only a blank screen. Those runners that had managed to keep their heart rate under the allowable maximum for the entire period were able to continue on to the second and most important test. With the treadmill motor purring softly, he watched his friend stride easily into action. He tried to ignore his personal disdain for treadmill running and noticed the runner's breathing elevate slightly as he settled into the required pace. The thirty minutes flew by without any visible signs of discomfort on the test subject's countenance, but he stepped off the treadmill with a scowl crossing his face.

"I hate these damn blinders," he complained upon finishing his second timed run. "I felt like a plow horse in a field." He ripped off the leads from his gleaming chest and tossed them towards a nearby wastebasket. "And these things make me feel like you're checking me for a heart attack or something."

"Just remember you did science a great favor. Maybe someday I'll let you tour with me when I discuss my findings at symposiums around the world."

"I can hardly wait," he responded as he toweled the sweat from his face. "But what the hell do pictures of 'Gumby' and 'two screwing cows' have to do with science? I think maybe *you* should be the one being studied and not me."

Brett smiled and tried to maintain his professional decorum. "Yours is not to question. And I would appreciate it if you do not discuss the visual stimuli with the next subject when you send him in. Your five dollar check for participation will be sent in the mail after you complete the post-study survey."

"For five bucks maybe I can buy a few cans of 'cream corn' just like the ones on the screen," Hollywood said in disgust just before he slammed the laboratory door behind him.

Brett shook his head in resignation after being on the receiving end of a small dose of the runner's hair trigger temper. Unlike his other two friends who freely talked of their past, Hollywood had always maintained a sense of secrecy regarding his background. Logan had gleaned that Hollywood came from a wealthy Illinois family that for generations had festered in dysfunction. The blond runner had once even admitted to his friend that the acceptance of a track scholarship to the small Wisconsin school had disgusted his Harvard educated father's upper crust mentalities. Logan had gotten the distinct impression that this single fact gave their friend a daily sense of liberation that he had found unattainable from other means. But Hollywood had also admitted that the resulting freedom had led to a wide and seemingly irreparable chasm in the day to day contact with his family. Brett himself had sensed that success had come easily to the runner, but also suspected he was destined to forever become a chronic underachiever. A sliver of his own battle with self-actualization entered his thoughts as the newly collected experimental data noisily completed the printing process. After carefully procuring Hollywood's results, he consciously vowed to distance himself from the runner's personal life in what he regarded as an even exchange for his own ongoing privacy.

He quickly re-focused his thoughts and smiled cordially when Rip entered the cluttered lab with a look of anticipation on his face. Brett knew he would have to settle down his friend's competitive nature for even the simplest of runs. He recalled the recent Friday night get together in which a casual game of Texas Hold'em had nearly degraded into a world class Texas free-for-all.

"Remember this is just an experiment to test a theory."

"I know," he replied. "But this is kind of fun…like I'm in the Olympic Training Center being tested for my freakish world class abilities."

Brett hated to burst his bubble as he positioned the blinders on his enthusiastic subject. After securing the heart monitor. he allowed for a slow ten minute warm-up to help accustom Rip to the treadmill. Once again he had to repeat the instructions to ensure the consistency of the testing.

"Now I'll be increasing the pace to 6:30 per mile just like last time. Try to focus on the pictures and enjoy the run."

"You can crank it up if you want to. Let's see what this baby can do."

"It's not a race," he reminded him again. "No more talking please!"

He watched his friend stride easily at the prescribed pace and watched him stare intently at the screen. Even though Rip's muscular back slowly glistened with sweat, Brett saw no observable difference in the subject's breathing. In admiration he studied the lean runner's stripped down musculature and when each muscle contracted he mentally recited them one by one. While he sat and watched Rip concentrate on the images flashing before him, he had no doubt his friend would be a natural in his stated career goal of becoming a high school teacher. He found himself swallowing a hint of jealousy knowing that Rip's stable upbringing led itself to a likely foundation of future success. The time slid by quickly but after completing the required interval his friend stepped off the treadmill with a dismayed look on his face.

"That was too easy. And too weird." After handing the eye shield to Brett he continued to echo Hollywood's theme. "Someday you can explain to me what pictures of 'Pee Wee Hermann' and 'drunken Shriners' have to do with running. Just don't tell Wickers what you're doing or he'll think you're nuts."

"I'll reveal the method to my madness after I collect and analyze the data. Until then consider yourself sequestered."

"I hope you don't turn into a scientific egghead on me," Rip said with a shake of his head. "If you think too much, it will slow you down on the track."

"I wouldn't worry too much about that. I leave my gray matter at home when I run." He made one final request as the sweaty runner made his way towards the door. "Now please do me a favor and send in subject number twenty three."

He checked the printout of Rip's heart rate and waited for the last participant in his experiment. As dry as academic research might be, he felt fortunate that at least he was able to tie it into his passion, and only hoped the accumulated numbers would lead to a relevant conclusion. He knew it was inevitable that he would eventually finish his class work graduate, but it was the uncertainty of the future that had become a constant source of anxiety. The onrushing march of time only heightened his mental fatigue as he waited patiently for the final set of data from the old printer.

The door to the cramped quarters swung open and Logan strode in confidently with a wig of Rastafarian dreadlocks adorning his head. Brett was momentarily speechless as he studied the small runner. "Thanks for coming Mr. Marley. However, you will have to remove your hairpiece to truly replicate your first run."

"But I feel so naked without my 'dreads. But in the name of science I'll do my duty." He looked around the room at the mass of electrical equipment and tangle of wires before continuing. "C'mon, Dr. Frankenstein…let's get this party started."

Brett marveled at the personality differences between each of his three friends. He had taken to calling the threesome "the good, the bad, and the ugly" and left it entirely up to them to attach the most fitting moniker. Logan's infusion of energy helped him fight through his dwindling enthusiasm and he was happy to be harnessing the leads to the last of his three friends. After securing the heart monitor he gave the hyperactive runner the usual instructions of how to complete the test. "Any final questions?"

"Just a request. If you fry me with these electrodes, just scatter my ashes over Lake Michigan," he said wiping a bogus tear from his eye. "And tell my Mammy and Pappy I'm sorry for what I done wrong."

"I promise I'll give you a proper send off. Now shut up and run," Brett demanded as the treadmill sped into action. He laughed to himself when he spied the runner's wig lying in a heap in the corner of the lab. Logan's imaginative nature had often carried the group through a tough workout where the sheer force of his personality lightened even the most taxing of efforts. The little runner's kinetic personality was on display during the run as he pranced on the treadmill like a puppy in the throes of an animated playtime. Brett had no doubt he would find a way to rise above his 2.5 GPA and become the "big bidnissman" his friend had bragged would become his occupational destiny.

After a surprisingly uneventful final test Brett looked forward to the normalcy of the day's practice. That illusion was shattered a few hours later when he was accosted by his friends as he entered the locker room. After a discussion of the experiment the threesome were anxious to hear the results of the study and quickly peppered him with questions.

"So what did you find out?" asked Logan. "That my concentration is incapable of being affected like normal men? Or maybe that I'm a genetic superman who should be set out to stud like Secretariat."

"I'm not sure I should divulge the preliminary data yet," said Brett. "I need to analyze it some more."

"C'mon," protested Hollywood. "You owe us after subjecting us to that nonsense."

Brett contemplated the three runners and overruled his better judgment in keeping the results confidential. With a sigh and a shrug he began to speak. "All three of you are obviously very fit because your heart rates never reached over one hundred and sixty beats per minute. You each averaged about one hundred and forty five, but specifically hit your maximum with very different pictures." He paused again as if somehow he had revealed too much.

"Spill your guts, Mr. Science," urged Hollywood with Rip nodding in agreement. "We deserve to know what's going on in our own heads."

"A little knowledge is a dangerous thing," Brett cautioned as he repeated a favorite quotation. He went against his better judgment by continuing on with his dissertation.

"Rip...you were extremely stable in your measurements except for one picture."

"And that was...?" Rip asked as he waved the answer on.

"A waffle iron," said Brett as Logan and Hollywood burst into laughter. Rip looked on quizzically as Brett continued. "And

Hollywood, although you fluctuated a bit more in your heart rate you definitely maxed out on a picture of 'Peter Pan'."

"Boys in tights…I knew it," taunted Logan.

Brett worried about Hollywood's legendary temper and quickly spoke again. "I wouldn't get on him too much, Logan. You had an unusual finding also."

"I'm not worried. I'm sure it was some babe picture."

"Something like that. Your pulse hit one hundred and fifty nine at a picture of Queen Elizabeth waving to her royal subjects."

"You're hot on the Queen Mum. Mom…ma," Hollywood teased as he made a series of sucking noises that echoed through the locker room.

"So what does it all mean?" asked Rip.

"It means you guys probably need counseling and I'll be damn lucky to pass the course. Then again maybe I should re-do the test to check for the reliability of the findings."

"Not a chance in hell," said Rip offering what was probably a common sentiment. But with the other runners still nodding in agreement he offered his own final advice to the group. "I think before Brett gets any other bright ideas to waste our time we better get out there before Wickers takes a paddle to Tinkerbell or Princess Dangle for being late."

"Watch it waffle-boy," said Logan as he launched a shoe at the back of the suddenly retreating runner.

As they banged against the lockers in their chase down the narrow aisle Brett shook his head in resignation. He heard the noisy horseplay and the slamming of the door when his ex-lab rats scattered toward the gym. At that very instant he formulated his next experiment and quickly assigned it the working title of "IQ and the Distance Runner – Nothing but Oxymoron's?"

Chapter 12

Although it was one more obligation that he had to fulfill, Brett looked forward to his hours at the store. He had come to find the work a simple diversion from the never ending stress of school and training. When business was especially slow he often found himself staring out the front window lost in thought visualizing the challenge of upcoming races. Tony called him "Ozone" when the store owner noticed him doing it, but the daydreaming runner had never revealed the visions filtering through his head. He still hadn't told anyone that he had qualified for the trials, and true to his promise so far Coach Wickers had not said a word. Once again he was lost in an imaginary race until the jangle of bells at the front door jarred his daydreaming and alerted him to a potential customer. When a sun-streaked brunette entered she smiled at him before slipping a pair of stylish sunglasses to the top of her head.

"Good morning," he said. "Take a look around and I'll be with you in a minute."

He eyed up the customer and automatically began to categorize her. He had taken great pride in developing his own system of placing all who entered the store into one of five pre-determined slots. Not a "newbie" he thought to himself when she strode into the store with confidence. He truly enjoyed working with those virgin runners who were starved for information on how to get started, and he knew they appreciated his advice as he guided them in their change of lifestyle. Perhaps a "rec" he thought after studying her lean body which he used as an indication that she might run for recreation or occasionally participate in a mass race. He was mulling it over when she impatiently waved him down with a frown on her face.

"Do these come in powder blue?" she asked picking up a shoe off the wall. "They would match a cute top I have at home."

He paused before answering and immediately ruled out the third category of "trophy hound". Those were the runners that helped fund Tony's retirement plan by buying anything that promised a faster race time or would aid in the attainment of a coveted age group award. He knew those runners would buy Chinese ear wax and rub it on their calves if it would shave a few seconds from their finishing time.

"No ma'am, only what's on display."

"Darn, they would be so perfect."

He quickly closed off category number four and knew she was definitely not a "throwback". He placed himself in the blood and guts group of runners that knew it was the work that held the key to success. But after remembering his real purpose for being employed he delved into his retail mode. "However, I think I have some shorts over here that would go very well with them."

She shrugged in what he perceived as a non-verbal acknowledgement of her low expectations of the innate male fashion sense. Yet without comment she accepted the shorts and slipped behind the curtains of the cubby-hole that served as a changing room. Within minutes he watched as she pranced around and admired herself in the coordinated gear that he had suggested. Definitely a "disco runner" he calculated assuredly and wished the store had a mirrored ball to heighten the effect. A perfect match for Rex he thought silently…they could be the undisputed king and queen of the track.

"I'll take them. You have a good eye for a man," she noted emphatically as she slid her sunglasses back firmly onto the bridge of her nose. "I pride myself on it." When he rung up the final purchase he heard the faint sounds of KC and the Sunshine Band drift through his head. "Come back soon," he said as he handed her the receipt.

She left promptly and while watching the door close behind her felt a vague sensation of satisfaction in a job well done. He observed the empty store and enjoyed the temporary quiet before his peace was again interrupted by the jingle of the door. He automatically cleared the counter when the mailman struggled through the entrance with an unusually heavy load. The uniformed carrier flashed a plastic smile while he carried out his daily mind-numbing routine. The carrier walked briskly toward the counter and carefully set down a stack of envelopes followed by a thick package of magazines.

"Have a good one," said the postal worker with half a wave.

Like many runners Brett regularly scoured the internet for the latest race results. Yet it was the hard copy that made it seem more real to him, and he carefully broke the bond on the stack. He felt stress immediately flow through his body and he braced himself for the emotional response he invariably experienced after viewing his opponents latest efforts. The race results of the world's finest runners were a fundamental and unyielding measuring stick that he both embraced and dreaded. No matter how obscure the competition, or how unrecognized the name, the final tick of the clock listed within the pages was a cold, hard fact that became indisputable. In his mind the runner soon found himself either the pursued or pursuer after inserting an estimation of his own current racing abilities. The magazine added additional fuel for his collection of emotional frailties with a scattering of "up close and personal" vignettes that documented the training diaries of the latest and greatest of the world's runners. After he reviewed their typically massive training regimens, he found himself once again questioning his own level of commitment towards the all-consuming sport he had chosen. As he lifted a copy of the latest *Track and Field News* he reddened when he saw the smiling visage of Lance Shelton again gracing the cover. He studied the lines of the sinewy athlete, but focused mostly on the confidence set deep within the runner's dark eyes.

"The Kid," he said bitterly using the moniker the press had anointed him with. "Lance Pierces Another Record!" read the headline under the picture of the celebrating runner holding his index finger in the air. He looked at the photo of the current young lion of American distance runners with more than a bit of envy. Being the present American record holder in the 5000 meters, Shelton's reputation was not altogether undeserved, but it was the style in which he performed that drew Brett's ire. The Kid's winks to the cameramen and waves to the crowd while racing were incomprehensible to him. Yet, he knew more than anything it was the ease of which the Kid had attained success that truly fueled his disgust. Even though he was loath to admit it, the fact that he had also been in that position himself somehow made it even more indigestible.

He thought back to the ESPN special entitled "On the Road with the Kid" during its inevitable pre-Olympic year hype. In it the Kid had arrogantly belittled the performance of the other American runners as "the second tier" of which he had little to be concerned with. He had "bigger fish to fry" which referred to the multitude of foreign challengers that inhabited the far corners of the earth. The American track public was so starved for a champion that it had swallowed the rambling of the phenom wholeheartedly. Because of the Kid's current west coast home of Washington State, the comparisons to a young Prefontaine were inevitable.

He had seen the Kid race before in person. The previous winter he had witnessed him demolishing an international field indoors at the Millrose games. Like a World Wrestling Federation wrestler, the Kid cupped his ear during the final lap and stirred the crowd into a frenzy. He hated the showboating but could not deny the talent of the collegiate sophomore. When he had watched the talented runner he remembered what his father had taught him about racing. Study your opponent, find a weakness, and strike when the opportunity arose – "Study and strike" he had called it. It disturbed Brett that so far he was unable to find even a single flaw in the cocky runner, but he knew he was most shaken by the unwavering confidence he saw in the Kid's dark orbs. Even from a distance he could see the cold blooded disdain the runner's eyes held during the race. The "eyes reveal the mysteries of the soul" he once read, and on this night the Kid was soulless.

He remembered sitting in the cheap seats that night sipping a five dollar beer with his self loathing at an all-time high. He had long since accepted that his own self-identity was wrapped tightly into his current achievements as a runner. When he peered from the rafters of the once great sports arena, he felt his anxiety only slightly dulled by the beer-buzz swirling throughout his system. He knew that his fitness level was thousands of miles behind that of the athletes below, and he felt like a fraud in his old U-Conn windbreaker that only served to magnify his previous failures. Still, somewhere deep inside his gut he felt the smoldering heat of competitive embers glow as he watched the Kid completing his victory lap. After putting down his beer he vowed in silence to one day take his shot at the smug athlete that was blowing kisses to the adoring crowd.

"Ozone!" called Tony when he strode through the stock room door. "Are you okay? You look like you just found out somebody took a shit in your favorite racing shoes."

"No, I'm fine, I'm just thinking about a gift I have to deliver. I only hope I can get it there in time."

"That sounds nice of you," the owner replied as he sorted through the mail.

No, thought Brett, I hope it's anything but nice.

Chapter 13

He found his thoughts meandering again when he waited with dozens of other anxious runners for that afternoon's workout. After another brief rendezvous in the gym, he self-consciously matched goodbye waves with Marie and absently smiled to her as she made her way through a far set of doors. When the thick door shut behind her he dimly recognized it as an ironic commentary on the current standing of their relationship. He had been able to squeeze in a few dates with her after the initial hours spent at Hooligans, and he fully acknowledged the immediate gut level attraction. Despite an undeniable need for her that increased daily, he had so far slammed the door on his own secrets and allowed her nary a glimpse into his fractured past. Trust had not come easy for him since his own family's breakdown, and he nearly resented the vulnerable state she had unknowingly put him into. After tightening his shoelaces to the breaking point he welcomed the impending workout where his powerful stride would help him regain control of his fragile psyche and force the emotional scars deeper into the black hole of his sub-consciousness. Upon closing his eyes for a few minutes of pre-practice solitude, he was interrupted when a group of undergrads settled in nearby.

"Mr. Rodgers?" said one runner with hesitation in his voice.

"Call me Brett, please," he responded with a tired smirk. "The TV show is my other job."

"Sorry sir. I mean Brett. It's just that we were all wondering what it's like. To run as fast as you have," the runner asked in broken sentences. "And how we can get there too."

He knew they would wait in breathless anticipation for his words of wisdom as if he was Moses returning from the mountaintop. He had long ago understood the mindset of the runner and the undeniable fascination each competitor had with anyone that had turned in a faster time than they had been able to register. It was as if a more accomplished runner had discovered some elusive kernel of truth that had resulted in an experience of esoteric enlightenment. He looked at their eager faces as he once again considered the question.

"How did I get there?" he repeated aloud. "I'll tell you all what I've learned only if you promise to keep it to yourselves. I still remember when my first coach sat me down and tried to answer the very same question that I asked of him." He paused as their breathing slowed and the group quieted to an eerie silence. He felt his own face redden when he looked at their expectant faces and remembered the days of his own youthful naiveté that the group had been able to dredge up so unexpectedly. God, I was so stupid back then, he cursed silently. Just like these guys! The poison that instantaneously coursed through his system elicited an unusual anger tinged outburst. "There is no goddamn magic to being fast," he spewed out menacingly. "And there sure as hell is no secret potion that will lead you to fame and glory. And the sooner you understand that, the sooner you have a chance at greatness." He studied their blank faces and part of him felt suddenly cruel in his blunt discourse, but he knew they all would be better in the long run if he hammered his point home.

He settled into his anointed position as their role model and listened to their now rapid collective breathing before beginning again. "Sorry about that. But I wanted you all to remember there is no magic elixir in running. It's not about some 'special workout' or 'system' that will guarantee you success. Any of you that are willing to pay the price month after month and year after year has a chance to surpass anything I've ever done. Running isn't a sport for pretty boys with visions of grandeur. It's about the sweat in your hair and the blisters on your feet. It's about the frozen spit on your chin and the nausea in your gut. It's about throbbing calves and cramps in the dead of night that are strong enough to wake the dead. It's about getting out the door and running when the rest of the world is dreaming about having the passion that you need to live each and every day with. It's about being on a lonely road and running like a champion when there's not a single soul in sight to cheer you on." He took a breath and felt the pounding in his temples and the sweat trickling in his armpits while he completed his soliloquy. "Running is all about having the desire to train and persevere until every individual fiber in your legs, heart, and mind is turned to steel. And when you're finally forged hard enough, you will have become the best runner you can be. And that's all that you can ask for."

They looked at him respectfully before an enraptured runner asked one last question. "What does it feel when you get there?"

He paused again and looked over the expectant faces. How to explain the power of the perfect race? he asked himself. He flashed back to those all too rare moments of omnipotence he had experienced over the course of his career. "It's like a power is unleashed from your very core," he finally replied. "And that somehow you've been allowed to hold the hand of God." The heaviness of the statement hung in the air like a thick band of smoke from a cigar and he took a deep breath before he began again. "But remember, if you ever reach your dreams, you have to savor it and take the victory lap. The problem is sometimes it's hard to know that you are there until it's already passed you by. Maybe next time I'll know. Sometime soon preferably."

They all considered his words as if they were gospel but quickly quieted when Rex approached them from the front of the gym. Brett braced for a confrontation and wondered if the assistant coach had overheard the content of his speech to the young runners. He realized the last thing he needed was a public argument with the ego driven assistant and was relieved when he saw the head coach preparing to speak.

"Quiet, Brent," whispered Rex

"It's Brett. Two t's. Try to remember next time," he snarled back.

They glared at each other as a loud voice sounded from the front. "Gentlemen," the coach called as he tapped his pen on the clipboard that held their fate. Coach Wickers had warned them to rest well as today's effort was a "special treat" for all of them. He looked at his charges and surveyed their faces when a sufficient silence had been reached. The Milwaukee Meat," he stated, "I'll see you at the hill."

The distance runners groaned as his words echoed in the air and Wickers only smiled at their response. The "Meat" had been so named for over a decade by previous runners who complained that after its completion they felt like flesh hanging in a slaughterhouse. Brett had been warned of the workout but had yet to experience its particular pleasures. Yet, characteristically he was more than ready to attack the workout and release the steam that he had stored for that afternoon's challenge.

As usual Rex wasted little time before he threw in his own contribution to motivating the team. "Nine loops is the record, boys. Set by a particularly talented runner a few years ago," he said with a smug look.

Brett wished right then he could take on the record holder, but realized their duel would have to wait for another day. With a deep sigh he watched as Wickers woodenly studied the emotional interaction between the runners and his assistant coach. "Let's go," said Brett before they started into the twenty minute jog to the hill.

The hill glistened with the remnants of that morning's rain and the still remaining gray clouds dampened the mood even further. The runners stood at the base and examined the steep incline as if a careful analysis might lead to a less taxing route to its crest. After they recognized the futility of the thinking, the group began a series of eighty meter striders to prepare for the assault on the infamous hill. The wet grounds were more precarious than they had expected, and the rain-soaked turf did little to support the tentative footstrikes of the pack. Anticipating their concern, Wickers spoke to his anxious charges: "This ain't no 'Candyland' and I sure as hell ain't no Willie Wonka. Line up at the base and let's go to work."

As the group followed his orders it seemed only appropriate that a cool drizzle started to fall over the already bleak landscape. Wickers' only acknowledgement of the precipitation was a firmer tug on his cap that signaled his intention to begin the day's workout. Wickers' workout menu included a one mile circuit repeated until the coach was satisfied the desired threshold of pain had been reached. Under his critical eye the runners were instructed to bound up six hundred yards of steep climb before looping back and striding down the incline at race pace. It was only the three hundred yard section at the bottom of the hill that allowed for any recovery time whatsoever. At the sound of the whistle they started the repetitions and worked through the first few loops until the sweat started to pour out as fast as did the increase in their breathing.

"On my whistle, gentlemen," he commanded. And as the shrill sound pierced the air the runners obediently sprang into the required action. Tufts of grass kicked into the air as the pack pushed off the balls of their feet and began their attack of the hill. The runners concentrated on their form and drove their arms forward in an exaggerated fashion best suited to assist their legs in the fight up the incline.

"Again," the head coach called out succinctly after he watched them complete the fourth of their recovery jogs.

"Come on you guys," Brett called to the group. "Let's stay together. We can't let this little mound of dirt beat us."

"Damn straight," barked Rip as he pushed harder up the hill. "Nobody drops."

The runners felt the twitch of their fatiguing calves as they bounded up the hills. Their relief at reaching the top was short-lived when the speed of the downhill was only slightly less of a burden on their burning quadriceps. "Embrace pain, love suffering," Brett whispered under his lips as he quoted the words his father had borrowed from a coach of years gone by.

"Again," Wickers demanded as they rounded the circuit. The coach smiled as he watched the runners continue their assault of the hill and he admired their spirit and pluck. Even his self named twin hemorrhoids, Logan and Hollywood, battled their way to the muddy top and he happily observed the change that had overtaken the group since the Connecticut runner had joined on. The distance runners' focus had been ratcheted to a new level in their workouts and he was anxious to eventually see the results manifest themselves on the track. Over and over he watched them stride by as their fatigue deepened until he finally raised his index finger with conviction. "Money time," he stated with finality.

They wholeheartedly welcomed Coach Wickers' favorite shorthand for the final lap of a race because it meant their efforts were nearing an end. With a pained expression the runners began their climb for the record breaking tenth time. At its completion Brett sucked hard on the lake air and noted the conspicuous absence of the previously condescending assistant coach. When the remaining mud-splattered runners straggled in, Wickers rounded them up and listened to their ragged breathing.

"You'll love me someday," he said in anticipation of their displeasure.

"Forgive me if my lips are too tired to pucker up right now," said Logan. "Maybe later."

"Ease it in and shower up," he said ignoring the sarcastic remark. "You've done well."

They jogged in through the light drizzle and Brett hoped the old adage "if it doesn't kill you, it will make you stronger" to be true. Otherwise he could make no rational sense of the pain he had absorbed the last ninety minutes of his life. He was relieved when he could finally sit on the hard benches of the locker room and ruefully observe the fibers of his calf's fasciculate in a series of random contractions.

"Wickers is a cruel bastard," said Hollywood. "I saw him smiling halfway through the workout."

"The Marquis de Sade had nothing on him," added Logan as he stripped off his soaking socks. "Actually, I'd bet the Marquis himself would have stopped us after five repeats."

"He just wanted to spend a little quality time with you," offered Brett.

"If that's all he wants, I'll invite him over for cheese and crackers," said Logan. "Hell, I'd even wax his hairy back if it would keep me off that hill."

"You do realize we could barely finish seven reps last year," said Rip. "We're getting stronger."

Rip's perspective quieted the locker room as they considered the importance of his remark. A thirty percent improvement was a measurable mark the statistically oriented runners could relate to. Step by step, mile by mile, and year by year the veteran runners knew the importance of building their fitness incrementally.

"If we hit twelve next time, I'll consider it having beaten the 'Meat'," quipped Logan as he limped to the shower.

Brett smiled at the remark while he flicked at his series of blackened toenails. With the usual contented exhaustion of a hard workout replaying in his mind, he got up with a groan certain that the famous workout had left his thighs with only the gristle still remaining on his bones.

Chapter 14

The next day was a scheduled easy run that allowed them to recover from the beating they had sustained twenty four hours earlier. None of the runners could handle a steady diet of hard work like they had performed the day before, but they had long ago accepted its necessity. Brett himself had often played the mind game of "getting through the hard day" with the savory thought of the easy day that typically followed. He was just as pleased as the other runners when he found out they had to complete only an easy seven miles followed by light weight work and a dip in the pool. To the runners accustomed to a daily pounding, the well deserved break in the daily routine seemed a veritable vacation.

"Watch this!" shouted Logan as he dove off the springboard into the university pool. Brett watched the runner as he arched toward the ceiling in an awkward attempt at performing a jackknife. He joined the rest of the team in an audible groan when the diver met the water with a resounding splat that reverberated off of the faded blue walls.

"Ooh," said Brett. "A mangled dangle."

When he rose from the water they all admired the instantaneous reddening of his puny chest. After hiking up his shorts he stood on the deck of the pool and performed a mock bodybuilder's pose complete with a narcissistic smile.

"You look like an emaciated robin," said Hollywood from the edge of the pool.

"But as graceful as a swan," countered Logan.

The runners all took turns doing easy laps and let the cool water wash out the aches of the previous day. They enjoyed the few moments of freedom that they had been granted from the strictness of the routine. The buoyancy and natural massage of the water helped the grind of the yesterdays "Meat" workout slowly fade into memory. As cruel as the workout had seemed to the team, Wickers knew the proper buttons to push in order to peak his runners at the right time. But through his vast experience he understood that there was a risk in breaking down unless he eased up on the whip occasionally.

"Ahh, this is the life," said Brett as he floated towards Rip. "Maybe I ought to try out for synchronized swimming. It would sure make life a bit easier."

"If you had wanted the easy way out, you would have picked something besides running years ago," suggested Rip. "Anyways, even my mom's water aerobics class would laugh you out of the pool after seeing your pathetic body."

"Nothing but prime beef here, baby. And actually I'm rather proud of my exquisite muscular definition. Marie says my chiseled in stone physique is one of her favorite things about me."

"I'm sure I don't want to hear about that," said Rip as he backstroked lazily through the water. "For being as smart and pretty as she is, she sure seems rather easily pleased. Heck, even Logan has bigger 'pec's' than you and he's flatter than the diving board."

"She must be attracted to my sparkling wit then. But I'll agree that with my body I'll probably never win a bar fight." He suddenly blushed as he thought of his hidden past.

"The odds wouldn't favor you," Rip replied. "C'mon, I'll take you on for a few laps. It's about the only time I'll get a chance to beat you."

The two runners pushed off of the pool wall and chopped wildly through the cool water. Even without any true meaning the two competitors battled between the floating lane markers for bragging rights to the irrelevant contest. They proceeded to flounder like water-soaked dogs and struggled mightily to complete even a full lap. The absence of body fat and the lack of proper swimming technique hampered the two competitors as they flailed through the pool. After gulping in the chlorinated air with raspy breaths, the event quickly deteriorated when both runners admitted defeat after fifty meters and hung on securely to the edge of the pool.

"Maybe I'll stick to running," sputtered Brett. "At least I won't drown."

"You got that right," agreed Rip in between his own sharp breaths. "I feel like I just did a hard mile. Even so it sure is nice to whup on you for a change."

The two runners drifted apart and proceeded to float contentedly through the pool. Brett dove under the surface and kicked lazily while he propelled himself through the tinted water. The sensation triggered the memory of the many times he had dived into his old backyard pool in an attempt to escape the turmoil of his family life. The water always served to muffle the arguments of his parents in their ongoing fights over the unkempt house or his mother's liquor consumption of the day. When he had flutter kicked through the water, he had always hoped if he stayed under long enough that somehow the argument would be over when he resurfaced. But invariably upon returning from the depths of the water, the angry shouts continued and shattered his underwater dream faster than a crash of thunder in the night. When he reached the surface of the collegiate waters his unexpected recollections were interrupted when another runner swam over and whispered discretely in his ear.

"I found a bird for the bath," Logan said under his breath. "She's going to meet me there in ten minutes."

He knew immediately what his friend was proposing. "The old whirlpool?" he asked. "Wickers will kill you." But of more interest to him was the next potential conquest.

"By the way...who is she?"

"Lara, the high jumper. Did you ever watch the way she straddles the bar? She's Swedish for god sake," he said dreamily. "Her coach gave her a key for the whirlpool so that she could soak her knees and I promised I'd be more than willing to massage away the aches for her."

Brett knew that the old steel pool was located in the trainer's room and was always considered strictly off limits to the male runners. Wickers professed his disdain for the antiquated unit because he felt the runners would develop an affinity for its comfort, and they got his standard "not a chance" when they asked him about using it. They knew that for years it was primarily utilized by their old trainer "Dog" as his own private Jacuzzi, but to the runners it still contained an unexplainable mystique that seemed as tempting as looking behind the curtain in the Land of Oz. Brett wondered about the logistics of the encounter, but he had learned to never doubt his teammate's ingenuity when it involved the pursuit of the fairer sex. Along with many other team members he had been living vicariously through his hormonal-driven friend's seemingly plentiful adventures. He was loath to admit it to himself that the closest he had been to a sexual encounter in recent memory was an inadvertent eavesdropping on his downstairs neighbor's latest bar-time delight.

"What about Dog?" he asked as he again focused on the impending escapade.

"He's at a seminar and Wickers and Rexy are working with the sprinters. It's perfect!"

Brett couldn't help but think of the potential consequences of his friend's upcoming dalliance. "Remember Rocky Balboa's trainer?" he said recollecting his favorite movie. "Women weaken legs."

"It ain't my legs I'm thinking about," Logan called when he climbed out of the pool. Nimbly slipping on his corroded flip-flops, he proceeded to do an impromptu shadow boxing exhibition for his friend as the beads of water flew from his hair.

Brett continued in the raspy voice of Rocky's trainer and gave his newest charge further instructions. "Remember it ain't gonna be no cakewalk in there. I met a man-eatin' Swede like her back in fifty-two that left my 'twizzler' looking worse than a piece of Spam on a stick. Took me three weeks before I could pee straight."

Logan giggled as he toweled off. "So what do you suggest?"

"Beat her at her own game," he continued in a growl. "Those blonde 'Laplanders' are nothing but dream stealin' ice queens. She'll be coming at you with a silvery tongue stuck in your ear just trying to slow you down. But you gotta use your speed and take care of bidness before she knows what hit her. Now get in there and do it for the old U.S. of A!"

Logan pranced in place while he pumped his knees and raised his arms in an impromptu *Rocky* victory dance. He blew farewell kisses to the runners in the pool and bid them an overblown farewell before he headed out towards the exit. After creeping down the back hallway, he made his way to the nearby trainer's office and smiled when he saw the door open a crack.

"A lively one," he whispered in an anxious voice.

He eased the door open further and tiptoed into the darkened room. The low rumble of the whirlpool dominated the small space and he breathed hard in anticipation. With the steam rising from the tank and clouding the mirror covered walls he could scarcely believe his good fortune. He made out a shadow in the whirlpool and tip-toed towards the groan that was emitted from the inside of the enclosure.

He deftly climbed over the side and lowered himself into the oversize tub before sliding his hand through the water in a search for the downy fur of his desire. When he hit the jackpot he stroked at its softness and his pulse raced uncontrollably. "You don't know how long I've waited for this," he crooned softly as the gurgling of the waters only intensified his mood.

"You better get your hand off my ass or you'll be feeling more than you ever thought possible," he heard a raspy voice demand in return.

"I...I never..." Logan stammered as he drew back in astonishment.

"And if I neuter you tonight, you just might never again."

Coach Wickers couldn't help but laugh softly to himself as he made out the skinny runner slipping over the tile floor and scampering frantically for the door. "Twenty years," he said aloud wistfully. Until a few minutes ago he had thought he had seen just about everything, but he was pleasantly surprised there was still room for a few firsts. He smiled as he sank back into the bubbling water and privately hoped for the chance to have at least a few years more.

Chapter 15

The sound of Metallica throbbed in the background as a cloud of steam billowed from an oversized pot. When Brett rushed toward the stove with a pair of flowered oven mitts on his hands, Marie was barely able to suppress a laugh. She covered the smile with her hands and settled back in the wobbly kitchen chair while perusing the rest of his humble dwelling. The black and white TV was nestled on a cardboard box in the corner with the rummage sale sticker price still adorning its side. Worse off was the ragged love seat that had the look of a dumpster reclamation project that she was hesitant to learn the full truth about. Even the ceiling added to the overall effects when the water stains dotting the overhead surface reminded her of an unintended Rorschach test. With a wry smile she returned her attention to his fiddling in the sink and she could only admire the earnestness of his efforts in preparing their mid-day meal.

"Don't burn yourself big boy. I doubt you have any insurance if I have to take you to the E.R."

"Are you doubting my skills?" he replied in a phony French accent. "I am an expert at boiling this magnificent pile of pasta to just zee' correct tenderness. And now as I add zee' proper garnishments my entrée is complete."

Marie smiled when he set the heaping plate of macaroni and cheese in front of her. She knew he had a no-frills diet that stressed economy over balance, but couldn't help but admire the diligence he displayed in the preparation process. "The slice of cheese and the hot dogs are a nice touch," she said. "But I doubt if there will be a book about your culinary talents any time soon."

"You're dead wrong," he replied as he sidled up to her at the table. "The 'Destitute Gourmet' will be on every collegians bookshelf someday. You should see what I can do with fried bologna and salsa. It's destined to become a classic."

She knew his limited budget prohibited the purchase of even moderately priced food stuffs and she decided to take a forkful before giving an unbridled review. "It's not too bad actually. Each day I get more impressed by your vast array of talents."

"Why, thank you. And as tasty as it is I'm also expecting this pile of carbo's on my plate to get me a good twelve miles or so. All for under a dollar."

"Quite an accomplishment," she complimented him as she continued to eat. She looked beyond him and for the first time noticed a small picture frame set on top of the antiquated refrigerator. She knew in an instant it was a photo of him and his parents captured at a time of innocence long since forgotten. She estimated he must have been six or seven at the time the photo was shot; likely old enough to remember the moment even to this day. While she studied the trio of happy faces she wondered how his family life could have deteriorated to its current status. Although she wanted nothing more than to ask him that very question, she felt it was neither the time nor the place to pry open an old wound. Perhaps there will be a day, she thought. She snuck a glance at him fully aware of how he had only allowed her peeks into his past life much like an eye to a keyhole, but for now she accepted the surface level communication they had become accustomed to in the early stages of their relationship. She refocused her gaze and turned her attention to the curious running poster decorating the center of his living room wall. By nature of it being the largest decoration in the tiny apartment it couldn't have been more conspicuous. She had often sensed he was relieved she had such little knowledge about his running, but the singular wall mounting peaked her interest. "Tell me about Steve Prefontaine," she said.

He immediately focused on the image and felt flooded by a heavy array of emotions. Part of him held tightly to the privacy of the poster, while the other side wanted to shout at the world. She noted the pause and looked at him curiously.

"Did you hear me?"

"Yes…I was just thinking of how to answer you," he responded as the words came slowly to him. He had often wondered how the general public could be so ignorant of the icon that he held so deep inside. He thought of his dog eared copy of the biography *Pre* and recognized the different world Marie had come from. But when he stared at the poster he found the words gushing forth as if a dam had finally given way to the insistent pressure behind its moorings.

"Prefontaine was a runner for Oregon in the early seventies and he literally dominated USA running. Most runners still can't touch his times even thirty years later. Unfortunately he died in a car crash far too young to reach his potential. Even so, it's really not his times he's famous for as much as his heart. It's kind of like his refusal to lose and the ability to bare his soul on the track still lives on as a goal for every runner to shoot for. It's that way for me anyway," he finished breathlessly.

"And what is the 'Gift'?"

He paused and carefully measured the words that were about to expose the truth of his current motivation. With her eyes silently urging him on he sputtered to a start. "I…I think it's the idea that we all have a certain amount of talent that needs to be nurtured and fully developed. And if we waste that talent, it's like we're spitting on the very blueprint of our being." He quieted as he let the words drift like a cloud across the table. "Umm…sorry if that sounds kind of weird. I just get going sometimes."

It was her turn to pause and before responding she considered the growing redness that had spread throughout his face. "Please don't feel bad about believing in someone…or something," she replied with a firm shake of her head. "I probably wouldn't even be here with you if you didn't." She again looked at the wall and marveled at the meticulous writing that documented the accumulation of his daily travels. The sheer totals of the recorded miles surprised even her and fully explained the veil of fatigue often hidden deep behind his playful smile. "I still can't believe you run so much," she said gesturing to his open running log. "It's amazing."

"The miles just sort of add up. And after a while the numbers become just that –simple numbers."

"I guess. But I can't even imagine how many hours you put in to run that far. What does the letter inside of the parentheses stand for?"

A crinkled smile crossed his face and he seemed to uncharacteristically be at a temporary loss of words. She let him take his time while he slowly formed an answer. "It's my own grading system for how I ran that day. Kind of like a report card I keep on myself."

"So what do they stand for?" she questioned again.

"Well 'S' is for 'sucked'. Some days you just don't have it," he explained while pounding in another forkful of food.

"And 'E'?"

"For 'easy'. Those are usually my rest days."

"What about 'C'?"

"That stands for 'cruising'. A medium tempo."

"H?"

"That means I 'hammered' it. A good hard run."

"And 'T'?" she asked.

"Ahh…I sort of stole that one from Logan," he said as he turned a shade of red one more time. "It's what he says to himself whenever he spots a big set of…um, a well endowed woman."

"I take it that's a good run?"

"A very good run," he admitted through an embarrassed smile.

"I noticed those don't happen too often."

"Not enough for my tastes," he said with a smirk.

She considered his reaction and took a drink of her bottled water. Realizing the futility of addressing the overt sexism of the final category, she chose to focus on the undeniable influence of his small circle of friends. "You guys are pretty twisted aren't you?"

"We do seem to bring out the least in each other," he agreed as he settled his fork onto the empty plate. "But occasionally the best too."

"Does every runner keep track of their miles like this?"

"On a wall I seriously doubt it," he said with a laugh, "but probably in one form or another. I was reading about the 'Kid' and he's got it all computerized. He even records his daily weight, pulse, and caloric intake and then graphs it. And you thought I was obsessed?"

"Are you?"

"I think of it as being intensely devoted."

"Sort of like a running Moonie?"

"Very funny."

"Brett, do you really think you can make the Olympic team?" she asked more seriously. She sensed she had hit a bull's-eye in her casual probing of his mile-hardened beliefs when a sudden laser-like penetration emanated from his dark eyes.

"Yes I do," he replied in an even tone.

"And if you don't?"

He felt a sudden anger well up from deep inside and he had to concentrate hard to subdue it. How dare she even ask that question, he thought? He took a few deep breaths before answering. "I don't even consider that as a possibility. Thoughts like that get a snap from my rubber band. And lately I haven't had to use it."

"I noticed. When I first met you I thought you were some sort of weird masochist who just enjoyed bruising his own wrist." She paused before asking one final question. "Won't all the runners think they will make it?"

"Probably. And I'm sure most will go home disappointed. I won't."

She watched the steel set into his jaw and prudently chose to let the tension thaw. She knew she had been allowed a peek into his closely guarded world that until now he had kept under lock and key. When he stood up and started to clear the table she memorized the far away look in his eyes that demanded silence. I hope he's right, she thought, for both our sakes.

Chapter 16

The student lounge was the runners' normal meeting place during their breaks between classes. They had all gained an appreciation for the comfort of the worn sofas broken in by the tens of thousands of students that had passed through the college. Dozens of collegians were stretched out in various stages of alertness as they relaxed between the demands of the day. Brett himself was in a state of slumber as he dozed on the cracked vinyl in an attempt to recover from the trials of another exam. His well deserved sleep was disrupted when he was startled by a shaking of the couch and the faces that loomed overhead.

"What the hell?" he exclaimed through sleepy eyes.

"Wake up, girlfriend," said Logan. "No rest for the wicked."

"I was up half the night studying," he explained. "I think I'm more than deserving."

"Aren't we all," added Hollywood. "But if you were smart like me you would have picked an easier major."

"Yeah, with that sociology degree you'll be a crew chief at McDonald's before you know it," said Rip joining in the conversation. "I can see you looking pretty in that hair net already."

"Mmm...I'd be in charge of all the high school honeys," said Hollywood with a leer. "Tasty as pork chops and applesauce."

"And young enough to get you twenty," cautioned Brett knowing that he was probably only half kidding. "We'll be glad to sneak you some smokes in the big house."

The group slumped into the cushions and enjoyed the well-earned respite from the pace of their usual frenetic activities. The runners had taken Wickers' early scholastic warning to heart and had all fought hard to maintain the necessary grade point. Although they rarely had the chance to meet during the day, the unplanned gathering of the foursome was a welcome break from the competitiveness of the daily practices. They casually watched the crowd of students drift in and out of the commons and with the lunch hour soon approaching, they smelled the scent of the usual marketplace wares wafting in the air.

"Man, I'm starving," said Logan. "I could go for a couple dozen Krispy Kremes."

"Those things are gut bombs," warned Hollywood. "I ate six once and ended up sitting on the can for an hour."

"That's 'cause you're a wuss. I could do two dozen at a four minute pace and not even break a sweat," bragged Logan.

The group had gotten used to his elevated sense of braggadocio, but on this particular day they considered the unexpected line that had been drawn in the sand. Rip was the first to toe it up and he challenged the statement aloud. "Logan, are you serious?"

"Do monkeys like to hump?"

"Twenty-four in four minutes?" questioned Brett. "For once I'd like to see you put your money where your mouth is. But if you don't finish them, you'll double the money back and do our laundry for a week. Deal?"

"Absolutely," he promised. "Get the goods and a couple of milks and let's get it on."

The little runner stared at them defiantly and jutted out his chin as if he was daring them to take a shot. Brett could scarcely contain his glee and quickly pulled out his wallet from his back pocket. "Boys, today he goes down. And for five bucks apiece it'll be worth it."

They whooped it up as they collected the necessary funds for the donuts. When Rip ran off to bring back the supplies Logan crouched on the fraying carpet and began his spontaneous preparation. "Crunches to firm up the old stomach," he said performing his daily abdominal work. "Just getting myself ready for a little free lunch."

Brett and Hollywood shook their heads while watching him display his usual bravado. A bevy of onlookers peered curiously towards the little runner as he completed his preparatory calisthenics. Right on cue Rip reappeared with two donut boxes balanced carefully under his arm and tossed the cartons of milk from his free hand to the runner on the floor. "Time to get up and eat fat boy."

Logan settled into the oversized couch and spread out a box on either side. Next he methodically opened the containers of milk and set them between his legs. "Preparation is everything."

"Preparation H is more like it," warned Hollywood. "You're going to need it after you crap out an intestine."

"Yeah, right. Who's the timer?"

"Me," volunteered Brett. "Are you ready?"

"Like a dog in heat."

A small crowd started to form as they heard the commotion for the upcoming event. A murmur rippled throughout the commons when the strange nature of the event revealed itself to the curious bystanders. Logan didn't seem to notice the extraneous buzzing as his eyes glazed over in concentration and he licked at his lips in anticipation.

"Glutton on your mark…get set…go!" Brett shouted.

He wolfed down the first donut with scarcely a breath and dug smoothly into the second. He packed it in effortlessly when Brett began an unexpected commentary on the contest.

"He's a natural this one is…the likes of which we may not see again for quite some time. As he pounds down donut after donut he looks as happy as a boy discovering his first *Playboy*. At forty seconds he's right on pace to challenge El Guerrouj's current World standard. There's a buzz among the onlookers as this young phenom seems oblivious to the taxing pace he's setting for himself. Has he started out too fast for his own good? Only time will tell if the crowd favorite can complete his divine mission or puke trying."

"Shut the hell up!" the contestant mumbled with a mouthful of dough and milk dripping from his lips.

"He speaks and wastes valuable time," Brett continued as he brushed off his friend's complaints. "One can only hope he won't go into oxygen debt and get lockjaw. Choking down his eleventh Krusty Kreme, he's fallen off the pace as he approaches the two minute mark. Is he just another pretender not quite ready for prime time? Or does he have the esophagus of a champion and the guts to slide down thirteen more gooey nuggets of gold? The crowd has begun to call his name as he continues his heroic quest for immortality. 'Logan...Logan...Logan' they chant as if one. One gets hard nipples just feeling the excitement in the air."

"Shut up," he begged as he jammed another ball of dough in his mouth.

The crowd was three deep by the time he bit into his seventeenth donut. His complexion had slowly turned a murky green due to the mixture of oil and sugar that was pouring into his bloodstream. He had found the simple act of swallowing becoming more laborious as the effort to finish increased exponentially. The noise of the break area reached a peak when Hollywood and Rip fell to their knees in helpless laughter.

"Money time!" shouted Brett as the crowd clapped in rhythm. "One minute to go for the young swine. Not since Rosie O'Donnell has a stomach so inflated been as beloved. Can the crowd will him to a victory? Or is America's latest hope just more media hype? As he stuffs in his twenty-first donut can he still maintain his form and swallow three more disgusting rings of sugary waste? In this man's opinion only the legendary Roger Bannister attacked the four minute barrier with such fervor. Fifteen seconds to go! Can he do it?"

The lounge erupted into pandemonium and the crowd dramatically counted down the final ten seconds aloud. When Logan forced in the last of the twenty four donuts his eyes rolled into the back of his head as if he was overcome by the intensity of the effort. At the designated time Brett lurched forward to pry open his mouth and check for any unauthorized remains. Because of his role as the timer it was accepted he would have the final say on the legitimacy of the outcome.

"Ladies and gentlemen we have the judge's decision," he cried. "After reviewing the evidence it is determined the young swine from the University of Milwaukee is indeed the winner of this year's 'Obesity Cup'. We can only hope he has been an inspiration to all of you in striving to be as stupid as you can be. Mr. Logan, do you have any words for our young crowd?"

"I think I'm gonna be sick." He wobbled up from the couch and slowly staggered toward the men's room while the crowd gave him a well-deserved standing ovation.

"And off he goes to take his victory crap to celebrate an effort for the ages," said Brett as he finished his short but animated announcing career. "Across the land milkshakes are being raised in honor of the young overeater."

When the crowd thinned the three remaining runners settled back into the soft backed sofas. "That was worth every penny," said Rip. "I thought I was going to piss myself laughing."

"Just wait till he tries to run today," warned Hollywood. "He's going to be so messed up."

Brett watched as Logan disappeared from his view. "Knowing him he'll probably be okay. Like they say: never underestimate the heart of a champion... or the stomach either."

They laid back in the chairs secure in the knowledge that at the moment they were feeling better than their compatriot. And they were just as sure they would never be able to view even a single donut in quite the same way.

Chapter 17

When the runners gathered in the gym that same day they began the usual preparatory contortions that had long ago become engrained in their flesh. The personal experience of each of the runners led them to boil down the stretches to the bare essentials needed to remain injury free. Most of the runners were perpetually assessing the state of their legs and the various aches and pains the daily miles created. While Brett stretched out his hamstrings he counted no less than six runners bearing the mark of the revered trainer's taping techniques in Dog's ongoing effort to support their injured tissues. He had so far been able to avoid any substantial setbacks of his own, which he attributed to both proper training and his own increasingly precautionary measures. Marie had even called him "paranoid" in his refusal to sit in a cramped movie theater due to his fear of "tightening up" for the next day. When he finally finished up his set of core stretches he relaxed and listened to the other team members' playful dialog that he had come to enjoy nearly as much as a successful run.

"How ya feeling, Logan?" Hollywood asked when he spotted his friend.

"The joints are greased and I'm carbo-loaded to the max," he replied as he gingerly sat down on the gym floor. "Aside from a little 'monkey-butt' I think I'll make it."

Hollywood shook his head in disappointment at the gastrointestinal fortitude of the runner. "I can't believe it. I was sure you'd be out of commission today."

"It'll take more than a few sliders to bring me down," he bragged as he shifted uncomfortably.

"Rex will be glad to do that for you," said Rip with a shake of his head. The group turned and stared at the assistant coach who chose this particular day to model his burnt orange outfit topped off with the do-rag that accentuated his flowing locks. "He's such a douche bag."

"Watch you mouth altar boy. What would your momma say?" asked Hollywood as he reminded his friend of his strict Catholic upbringing.

"She'd say I was being too easy on him."

"Why do you think he's such an a-hole?" Brett asked his friends seriously. "Most runners I know are pretty cool."

"Good question," replied Rip. "But I heard he was a jag from day one. A couple of older guys I know said they used to crush him in practice his first two years. But as he got better they said it was harder to beat him and he became insufferable."

"Yeah," chimed in Logan, "and he was a real jerk too."

Brett and Rip looked at each other and smiled in acknowledgement of Logan's limited command of the English language. They decided to let it drop and Brett added his own thoughts as he watched Rex stroll in the distance. "Usually all the demands of running humble a guy. I think once you realize you probably won't win them all you gain a little respect for your opponents. It's gotten that way for me anyways."

"Once a dick, always a …," summarized Rip as he left them to fill in the blank.

"Careful big-man," warned Hollywood, "don't let him hear you. By the way do you know what he did to the freshmen yesterday?" When a blank look covered their faces it was obvious they were clueless. "He took them on a ten miler over the trails and dropped them faster than Logan popped his cork the first time out. The rookies got so lost they ran at least fifteen." The group took to studying the drawn faces of the underclassmen and they all resented the recklessness of Rex's deed.

"Bastard," said Rip breaking his deeply held code of decorum one more time.

"I've had an idea for quite awhile," interjected Logan. "Somehow today seems like a nice day to break it out."

The Gift – A Runner's Story

Rex was seemingly drawn in by their conversation and they watched in silence as he sauntered over to the four runners. "Hey ladies," he called to them as he started into taunting the disinterested runners. "Ready for a nice workout like the little cretins had yesterday? It seems as if I might have to leave a trail of bread crumbs next time so the young-uns can find their way home."

Brett glared at the assistant coach and stood up for the fledgling runners. "We were all young once, remember?"

"Youth is no excuse," spat back the assistant coach as he measured the mood of the group. He focused his glare at Brett and a mocking smile crossed his face before he spoke again in a hushed tone. "And I've been following a youngster by the name of Lance Shelton who seems to be catching on pretty quick. Don'tcha think, Brent?" Brett ignored the baiting but couldn't control the heat that flushed his face. "Have you had the chance to run against him yet, wonderboy?"

He felt his hairs stand on edge as he stood to challenge the statement and stood nose to nose with the assistant coach. He was used to confrontation on the track, but Rex had laid out the gauntlet in a very different venue. He did not dare mention his one public viewing of the skilled runner at the Millrose Games where he had bitterly promised himself the very chance Rex chided him about. "I haven't had the opportunity, but I'd welcome it." He felt his fists ball up as the white teeth of a self-satisfied smile lit up Rex's face. Not a moment too soon Brett felt an arm around his shoulder as Logan played peacemaker to the two rivals.

"Someday we may all get the chance we're waiting for. But until then let's just be happy little runners," he said calmly in an attempt to defuse the situation. "Rex," he continued as Brett noticed a glint in his friend's eyes, "the grapevine says Wickers is thinking of stepping down soon. And I heard him telling Dog the only thing he's really afraid of is turning over his program to some 'pantywaist yes-man'."

"Yeah," pitched in Hollywood, "only yesterday he told me to 'stand up to stand out'."

They could almost see the wheels churning in Rex's head while he processed the new bit of information. It was no secret to any of the runners that the recent Milwaukee graduate desired to be the next head coach, but they all held out hope that Wickers would be the front man for at least a few years longer. Brett's anger began to fade with the change of topics and he was further subdued when he heard the familiar rapping coming from the front. Like a well-trained pup Rex obediently made his way towards Wickers and the usually even-tempered Rip couldn't resist one final parting shot. "He looks like a freakin' pumpkin."

Rex seemed oblivious to the comment and as usual he was soon perched at Wickers side while the head coach barked out the day's agenda. The mass of runners silently nodded their heads in understanding or groaned at the thought of the upcoming intensity of the workout. After completing the instructions he boomed out his usual closing. "Any questions?"

The typical silence was broken when Rex puffed out his chest and piped in an unexpected suggestion for an alteration to the planned workout. "Coach, I think you may have overlooked the fact that the freshmen distance men need a little more speedwork today. I think we should see how they adapt to two hard days in a row."

Brett watched bug-eyed and felt Logan squeeze his arm from behind. The gym was eerily silent as Wickers' distended carotid arteries pulsated violently in his neck. When the crimson flowed into his face he turned toward his assistant and raised his thick index finger in a silent call for a timeout. With a nod of his head he walked to the far corner of the gym with Rex following close behind carrying a confused look on his face. The four runners couldn't help but smile as they strained to hear the choice words that flew out of the old coach's mouth, each punctuated by a small fleck of spittle. Brett repeated them aloud to his amused friends as they enjoyed the spectacle from afar. "Pimple faced...my authority...you think...overlooked...thirty years coaching...in charge!" When Wickers spun and lumbered back to the athletes Brett nearly felt sorry for the assistant coach who quickly took up the menial task of dragging the hurdles from the corner of the gym.

Logan whispered to Hollywood as the assistant coach continued to isolate himself in the distance. "Stand up to stand out? What's that all about?"

"I made something up just like you did, moron," he whispered back. "And Rex sucked up the bait like a blowfish."

At the sound of the whistle they automatically started into a slow jog in preparation for the day's work. They all felt the tension still flowing from Coach Wickers as he paced alongside of the track and wisely chose to forego their normal horseplay. But when they rounded the track, Brett couldn't resist one final jab at the orange clad target. "Don't worry Rex, you're just young and lost your way. Maybe next time we'll all pitch in for some bread crumbs for you. And by the way, the names Brett. With two t's."

Rex's withering glare was answer enough as to who was the victor on this particular afternoon, and as he continued to act out his penance as Wickers' man-servant, the four runners basked in their good fortune of the day. For the moment the future repercussions that Rex would surely inflict on them was deemed to be a small price to pay for the extra spring they suddenly felt in their strides.

Chapter 18

Lying on his back with arms outstretched, he felt the abrasive surface of the outdoor track dig roughly into his shoulder blades. He tuned out Wickers' voice as the sprinters received their instructions and he nearly closed his eyes as he let his thoughts mellow in the gentle spring sunshine. Wickers had uncharacteristically asked the team to meet at the outdoor track, but Brett expected the change from the norm was more a celebration of a pleasant day than for any other calculated reason. He stifled a yawn and regretted staying up for "The Late, Late Show" and with tired eyes watched when Wickers strode toward the starting line.

"Listen up, distance men," he began. "I hope you are all enjoying a bit of God's good graces and are letting the sun thaw your bones." He saw the nods of agreement but as usual did not wait for any actual reply. "As by now many of you know I believe running is a metaphor for life. And in the running that you perform you will experience both pleasure and pain just as you will when you enter the working world. Today's lesson is that life can lead to the unexpected, and that there will be days that you will have to learn to confront and handle the surprises whether you like it or not. In that framework today's workout will begin with a one mile time trial on the track at race pace. For safety purposes you will wear your training shoes, but I still expect all of you to compete at your highest level and battle the adversity you may feel as you circle the track. You will have twenty minutes to become ready to race." Wickers turned around and walked away as a series of muffled groans from the runners filled the air.

"Damn," complained Logan. "At least he could have warned us."

"I think that's the whole point he's trying to make," said Rip. "Like we should be able to compete at the drop of a hat. Right, Brett?"

He didn't immediately respond as he stood up and felt the stiffness in his legs. He respected Wickers, but was angry at both the short notice and nature of that afternoon's workout. "I guess," he finally replied under his breath. "But I'm not so thrilled about it either." He refrained from any more comments and started into a slow jog around the outside lanes of the track. The other runners had become accustomed to his occasional distant moods and let him travel the oval independently. When he neared Wickers he purposely avoided any eye contact in order to conceal the irritation he was currently experiencing. The twenty minutes went by rapidly, but time did little to subdue his displeasure with the coach's plan. When he stood motionless at the starting line with the other runners, he eyed the threesome of Wickers, Rex, and Dog studying the mass of lean athletes with more than a casual interest.

"On your marks, get set, go!" shouted Wickers an instant before the runners shot down the track in a well-trained response to the call. Brett quickly sidled up to Hollywood and traded strides with the customarily fast starting teammate. He sensed the pack beginning to string out, even though the two runners had barely rounded the first turn of the track. He attempted to take the lead from early on and pushed the pace, but cursed the cumbersome feeling of racing in the set of trainers. The tell-tale sounds of heavy breathing emanated from the now trailing blond runner as they passed by the next curve. He knew full well that Hollywood's sharp edged inspirations had arrived far too early for him to take his friend's challenge seriously.

When he flew past the starting line he still avoided the furrowed brow of Wickers as he exalted his charge to a greater effort. "Sixty-two, sixty-three," he called in encouragement to the leading runner.

Brett glanced ahead to the next turn and couldn't help but notice the placid smile on Dog's face when he studied the oncoming runner. Rex in turn chose that particular moment to tend to an untied shoelace that seemingly held some peculiar interest to the assistant coach. Brett re-focused on the event and drove hard around the near turn for the second time of the four lap time trial. He did not feel even a modicum of contact from the other runners and he knew he was destined to be on his own again. Same as it ever was, he thought as a bitter taste rose up into his throat. When he powered past the shot put arena he sensed the eyes of the weight men zero in on him as he unexpectedly drew unwanted attention to himself.

"Two laps to go," he hissed to himself when Wickers called out the second lap split. Like any miler he hated the third lap of the race that a more spiritual teammate had once explained was the lap of lost souls – a so called "limbo" for milers that resided somewhere between heaven and hell. Closer to hell, he thought as he fought to maintain the form that had carried him to a sizeable lead. He spat haphazardly to the side of the track and gained brief satisfaction when he realized he had forced the still seemingly oblivious assistant coach to dance away from the spray. He continued to grind down the backstretch and willed himself to stay upright in the most efficient posture to continue his current pace. He automatically shook out his arms to let the tension drain from his shoulders and he consciously relaxed his facial muscles to avoid tightening up.

"Money time, Brett," Wickers challenged him as he read the splits for the last time. "Three-oh-seven, three-oh-eight."

He felt the world swirl around him and accepted the out of body experience that had now become commonplace during the final laps of a race. Lifting...driving...pumping...his lungs screamed as he strained mightily for the white line that would end his self-induced suffering. Still driving around the final turn, he reached the final barrier and staggered to the outside lane with his hands firmly clasped on his knees. He nearly whimpered from the pain which eased only fractions with each breath he drew in.

"Four-oh-seven," called Wickers from somewhere nearby.

His barely acknowledged the recorded time but lifted his head and looked toward the coach vacantly. "I just wanted to tell you, coach," he said bitterly between rasping breaths, "I hate surprises."

Wickers smiled back at him before turning back toward the rest of the incoming field of runners. "You seemed to manage, okay. Just like I expected."

With his chest still heaving Brett studied the veteran coach from behind and listened to the sound of his voice boom over the track while he shouted out to the fast charging pack.

Chapter 19

While stretching out on the small mat he thought of the myriad of training methods he had used to achieve the elusive heights of peak performance. Mentally clicking off the list he recited them in no particular order -- long slow distance… Lydiard method… heart monitor training… over-mileage… Daniels training… under-mileage… and even the dreaded cross-training. But so far he felt he had been able to avoid sinking into the depths that he would occupy in a matter of moments.

He searched the small room for a familiar face and realized that Marie was more than likely going to be the sole recognizable participant in the group. After studying the smorgasbord of people in the yoga class, he felt distinctly out of place and shifted uncomfortably as he waited on the soft matting. From the plump housewives, to the rapidly aging hippie population, he measured the gathering crowd and felt miles away from the wolf-like competitors he ran against on the track. Only the smattering of college-age students interspersed in the group gave him even the remotest feeling of belonging whatsoever. But after having promised Marie that he would give one of her hobbies a try, he now regretted his momentary weakness in agreeing to accompany her. Nearly reading his thoughts she whispered to him softly. "Just give it a chance…you might even like it."

He wanted to tell her he would rather undergo an enema but with a roll of his eyes he decided to carefully choose his words. "I feel like such a …," he paused searching for the right word.

"Outsider?"

"No…I was thinking more like 'dork'. This just seems so weird -- like I've been beamed to some commune in Tibet. Even the music is creepy," he said commenting on the sitar-filled background ambience.

"It's supposed to help take you to your 'sacred place'. Sort of a sanctuary where you are most at peace. Like the beach or woods or someplace like that."

"I think mine is on the can with the Sunday sports page. Does that count?"

She looked at him with a full-fledged look of disgust on her face. "If you're even partly serious, you are way beyond help." She looked around at the growing numbers of participants and made one last appeal. "You promised you would give this a try. It might even do your hamstring some good and help you with your running. But god-forbid you would do it for any other reason."

"Ok, ok…I'll be a good boy. But you'll owe me one."

"Whatever," she said sounding slightly annoyed. "Now please quiet down so I can hear Yogi Moshi get started."

He knew he had pushed her buttons long enough and decided to hold off on the innate antagonism he felt towards her hobby. While he sat and waited he recognized the paradox of how as they became closer, the more he derived a slight pleasure from testing the limits of her patience. He looked at her and marveled at the dead serious interest she demonstrated towards the gray bearded and frizzy haired man who bowed to the group from the front of the room. The runner estimated his age as over sixty and he watched as the crowd silently acknowledged the white clad instructor with a solemn nod. The yogi projected an unprecedented level of calm and Brett studied him when he settled easily into what his rudimentary knowledge recognized as the "lotus" position. There goes my groin, he thought as he performed a pre-school version of the classic pose. He felt the strain on his inner thighs and listened to the first words from the master's mouth.

"Welcome," he started with a distinct Indian accent, "it is time to shed our armadillo armor and let our skin breathe. Follow me on our beautiful journey to cultivate wisdom and feed understanding. Breathe deep and let the air nourish your soul and free your spirit."

As Brett sucked in the incense tinged air he hoped his digestive system could control his recently consumed bean burrito and not add a foreign odor to the painstakingly achieved mood of the gathering. Still, he could not resist an under the breath comment to his partner. "Oh, no...I think I'm getting a buzz on. I hope I don't keel over from all the purity rushing into my being."

"Shh," hissed Marie in irritation. "You promised."

He decided he had caused her more than enough grief and chose to follow the lead of the sedate instructor. He weakly mimicked the yogi's easily attained postures and was certain he was popping multiple tendons like broken strings on a guitar. Heeding his promise to Marie, he cautiously maneuvered his screaming muscles into a multitude of unnatural contortions that the rest of the group achieved painlessly. He quickly realized that the years of running had hardened his tissues to the necessary demands of his chosen sport at the expense of flexibility. As his breathing quickened he found himself being humbled by the rest of the class in an unexpected lesson in humility that he found hard to swallow.

"Breathe," the yogi encouraged, "and let the harshness of life seep from your pores." He seemed to smile specifically at the runner while he slipped effortlessly into another unfathomable pose.

Brett's competitive edge reared up when he ultimately realized the futility of his efforts. Try to run a mile in four minutes Mr. Yogi Mosh-pit and then tell me about the harshness of life, he thought as he grit his teeth. He instantly knew his ultra-competitive nature was a poor fit for the cooperative tone of the class, and even though the room was filled with relaxed participants, he yearned for a clear-cut winner to rise to the surface.

Marie noticed his grim demeanor and tried to soothe his angst. "Brett, you're doing so well. I'm so proud of you."

With the sitar twanging in the background he thought of all the well intentioned bystanders of races gone by that had blatantly lied in the same way when they told him he was "looking good" as he completed his death march to a distant finish line. He knew she was only trying to positively reinforce his efforts, but he was just as sure this would be his last attempt at the ancient Eastern practice. He wanted nothing more than to bolt from the room to hit the roads and achieve his own inner peace, but couldn't help but notice the glow on Marie's face as she zeroed in on a pose. The slight moistening of her brow rendered insight into the sustained stress of the position that she could hold indefinitely. He was happy that she gained in personal benefits from the ancient art, but he still longed for the hour to come to an end. He studied the mass of beatific faces of the other members in the class and envied the seeming contentment they had been able to attain. It had only taken a matter of minutes before he knew that somehow his wiring differed from the rest of the group and he felt like an imposter as he lamely attempted to perform another unfamiliar sequence of poses. He slowly resigned himself to the fact that he would complete the session in much the same way that he could grind out the final miles of a long run, but unlike his insatiable addiction to running, he knew his experiment into yoga would live a finite life span of only sixty minutes.

"Be still," requested the Yogi to the class when he resumed his starting position. "Feel the beating of your heart and the rhythm of the earth as you become one. Breathe…breathe…breathe," he whispered in the still of the room as he began the mantra that would end the session. Brett lifted his head and peaked around at the participants as they followed his orders implicitly, but was embarrassed when he felt the rumble of his Mexican dinner as it audibly gurgled in an inexorable search for an escape route. His face reddened when he noticed the nearest class members turn in his direction as the spell of meditation was broken up by his twisting bowels. He was grateful when the Yogi finally stood up to signal the end of the session and he arose to sheepishly face Marie and apologize for his disruption.

She smiled in resignation at the obvious failure of the evening before speaking in a subdued voice. "I think you need to find a bathroom before you explode all over the mat. You're probably the only person I know that could flunk out of yoga," she said with a deep sigh.

"Sorry, Marie," he said. "It must have been that armadillo I ate for dinner." He rushed to the men's room and quickly felt the self imposed stress from the class leave his aching shoulders. When he settled comfortably onto his own personal sacred place he realized he had finally found his own natural rhythm to approach the yogi's intended state of transcendence. His only regret was the lack of the Sunday sports page to help him complete the journey towards true emotional bliss.

Chapter 20

With the failed experiment of yoga far behind him, the following Saturday evening lent itself to a carefree run. He had long enjoyed the unstructured runs and reveled in the rejuvenation they afforded him after another draining ninety mile week. As had become their custom, the foursome had planned to meet near the old bike rack that had long stood next to the athletic complex. He continued on with a slow warm-up jog toward the campus and could see his friends waiting patiently at the pre-determined spot. When he heard the muffled voices he knew the usual good natured harassment had already begun. He accepted it was only a matter of time before his adult life would surely get more complicated, but for now it all seemed so pure and easy.

"Brett-meister," called Logan from a distance. "Ready to rock'n'roll?"

"Let's lay some steel, my man," he answered back.

He slid in between the others and smoothly joined the group in stretching their hamstrings on the rusted beam of the rack. He felt the customary pull in his left leg as the runners played the daily game of choosing an agreeable route. Like most runners they each had a few core favorites that they could complete nearly in their sleep, and it seemed somehow that even the most minor deviation from the norm would add an unnecessary degree of stress to the simplest of workouts.

"Let's do the bridge run. That should give us about ten," said Rip ever the statistician. "Medium hard pace?"

"Medium hard – just like Logan," said Hollywood.

"That's not what your sister said," shot back his cohort.

"Let's get going, you guys," said Brett as he ignored their jibes and tried to facilitate the start of the run. He recognized the immaturity of their dialog, but as often as not he craved the spontaneity and adolescent freedom he felt when he was part of it. Thank god Marie's not a psyche major, he thought to himself as they started off at an easy trot. She would think I was a freakin' nut.

It was a perfect day to run; mid-50's and the sun hiding behind a mass of drifting clouds as it sank slowly from the sky. They cut between the cars and made their way through the parking lot until they eventually entered the quiet campus streets. Brett had always enjoyed the looks of the passersby as he settled into the agreed upon pace, and with a satisfaction bordering on arrogance he knew he was more than competent in a sport few could master and even fewer could understand. After looking over his partner's relaxed faces he could only guess at each of his friends' internal motivations for running, but settled on commenting on the most noticeable external characteristic. "A new 'do Hollywood?"

"Streaked," he replied, "makes the babes go wild."

"Right," said Logan. "I'm sure you'll pork a big one tonight."

"Parts is parts," he reminded his friend.

Rip and Brett laughed as the jawing escalated and matched the gradual building of the pace. They never tired of the game where at times the sickest and grossest conversation almost passed for normal. With this group he had found that serious topics were avoided at all costs and that the real concerns of the day were left behind the moment the first stride was taken. Brett could scarcely recall the last time politics or any other topic of real importance had even entered into their conversations. He remembered an older runner at UConn that had once tried to debate Maslow's Hierarchy of Needs with a group of undergraduates over the course of a twelve mile run. Brett sheepishly recalled the applause of the other runners when he roundly discredited the cerebral older runner with his own facetious versions of "Brett's Hierarchy of Needs" that included miles, food, sleep, beer, and sex. The group had heartily seconded his youthful proclamation by a sudden increase in the pace. He doubted that this group would even have a clue about the old theory and he chose to keep quiet as the workout continued. When the trash-talking of the runners had run its course, the conversation naturally flowed to the task at hand.

"Let's pick it up you cornholes," said Rip. "I'm tired of this wussy pace."

They racked it up to six minutes a mile and what most runners could only imagine the group of four attained easily. Years of running had accustomed their systems to a height few distance runners would ever be able to manage. They were almost nonchalant about their current abilities and would gain an appreciation only when their talents one day diminished, but for now the pace seemed as easy as a Sunday stroll in the park. Brett looked at the other runners and as usual saw no discernable trace of effort in their faces. The only deviation he noted was the slightly annoyed expression carried by Hollywood as he ran at the back of the pack. He knew his aptitude toward moodiness and anticipated the possibility that his friend would cast a black cloud over the run. His thoughts were interrupted by the startling bark of a dog that chose to pursue them from a finely manicured front lawn. They had all learned long ago to tolerate the occasional confrontation with aggressive animals and on their previous runs had chosen to steer clear of the unpredictable nature of the outcome.

"Little bastard," said Hollywood with a growl. "I'll teach him to mess with me." They watched as he abruptly turned to run full speed at the braying dog and caught the pet completely off guard. "You want a piece of me? I'll stick your head so far up your ass you'll think it's all you can eat at the Alpo factory!" The dog yelped and quickly hightailed it back to the safety of the porch in a prudent choice of self preservation.

"Lighten up, Hollywood," insisted Rip as their friend rejoined the group. "He was probably harmless."

"I got a scar on my calf that tells me I shouldn't wait to find out."

They all chuckled at his intensity and continued on the run. The evening traffic had become heavy with parkway cruisers out in full force indiscriminately spewing their noxious fumes. The runners were used to the typical battle for the right of way and held their usual uneasy peace. As were most runners Brett was used to the occasional catcall from an occupant of a car who was somehow threatened by his actions. He had never gained an understanding as to the genesis of their derision, but as time passed he had learned to ignore the unwarranted insults. He studied the long string of cars running parallel to their path and gained satisfaction when their pace outran the many vehicles congested in a row. After taking the lead he sliced into a crosswalk that should have ensured a safe passage, but was startled as a shiny black machine attempted to belatedly beat a yellow light. When the car narrowly missed the group it was Hollywood who stood true to that evening's form and was once again the most vocal in his disgust.

"We could've been killed," he shouted at the car as it got held up in traffic. "You think you're playing some kind of game?" They watched as he unexpectedly charged up the road toward the offending vehicle and leapt over the rear fender to land squarely on the trunk. He proceeded to stride onto the roof of the car and continued smoothly toward the gleaming hood. The air was filled with an indignant shout from the driver of the vehicle when he realized what was taking place. When the rebellious runner veered back to join the group the unexpected shot of adrenaline he had supplied immediately kicked the pace to a higher gear. They recognized they had all fought the same impulse before but over the many years of their cumulative running had so far been able to control themselves. With equal parts embarrassment and vindication they wordlessly took to the side streets in order to take stock of their current state.

"Hollywood are you nuts?" asked Brett. "*You're* the one that's going to get us killed."

"Maybe the prick will think twice next time. I'm not in the mood for any bullshit."

"Obviously," said Logan. "But what's up with you tonight?"

Hollywood was silent for a moment until he spewed out an explanation. "My dad's on my ass again. Same old crap," he said emphatically in what the others construed as a means to dissuade any further discussion.

"Sorry to hear that," commiserated Rip, "But still, this isn't a group suicide mission, okay?"

"All right already. I'll try to chill a bit."

The other three shook their heads while they considered the veracity of his outbursts, but realized that the present was not the time to question him about his fragile psyche. The run quieted as they continued the run in the comfortable weather that had greased their strides to a state of maximum efficiency. They maintained the steady cadence wordlessly for a few blocks and it wasn't long before the topic returned to the primary passion in their lives. Rip as usual was the first to return the focus toward the next competition on the horizon. "There's a local 5K next weekend. Since we don't have a meet I think we ought to do it for a good workout."

"Hammer on the locals and impress all the ladies," plotted Logan. "I'm in. How about you Brett?"

"I'll see how I'm feeling. But I may have to get some stuff done."

As usual he was noncommittal about entering the race with the rest of the runners. His father had always taught him to think of races as special events and that when he toed the line he should be fully prepared to lay his guts out over the distance. It was Brett's own belief that if he ever got used to racing at less than maximum effort, the edge he would need in the big race might come up short. The other three knew this was his way and didn't push the subject any further. Brett knew he was due to begin a steady diet of racing in the near future, but he was finding that his post-collegiate status offered only the rarest of opportunities. With a collective silence they approached the halfway mark of the loop and neared the old wooden bridge that connected the two halves of the run. The group slowed tentatively to study the arch of the architectural landmark and considered the glow of cigarettes at its peak.

"Loserville," said Hollywood.

"Don't worry about it," said Rip. "Just keep rolling."

The bridge creaked when the aged boards swayed under their weight but they continued on their smooth stride towards the top. The punks at the crest snickered under their breath and when the runners passed they heard one whisper to his pal about the "faggots in shorts". Hollywood felt a quick burn of cigarette ash on his thigh when a flicked butt found its intended mark. He quickly stopped and turned while the others watched him curiously from a few steps ahead.

"What did you say?" asked Hollywood with a flat tone to his voice. The thugs laughed derisively but didn't reply to his question. Brett automatically felt his own hands clench when he watched the angered runner walk towards the two. "You don't like my shorts?" he asked while he slowly drew them down.

The other runners were silent and watched in amazement as Hollywood proceeded to lay a stream of piss on the smoldering cigarette butt before he raised his aim squarely towards the punk's leg. The shocked facial expression of the urine-covered loser was indelibly burned into Brett's memory just as deeply as Hollywood's self-satisfied grin.

Hollywood sneered before he spoke. "Smoking is bad for your health." He rose up his shorts defiantly before proceeding to casually resume his run down the bridge.

The others watched the hoods look on in astonishment at the dripping pant leg. The three runners then automatically started to follow Hollywood and heard the inevitable cursing echo into the night.

"Skinny faggots – come back here you faggots!" they shouted.

The runners laughed wildly upon leaving the bridge knowing full well there would be no confrontation. As lean as the runners were they knew that both numbers and attitude gave them an advantage that put them firmly in control.

"What the hell was that?" asked Rip as he tried vainly to grasp what had just occurred.

"I used to be a boy scout," explained Hollywood, "and I didn't want the old bridge to go up in flames and start a forest fire."

"You're my new hero," said Logan as they returned to their pace.

Brett let out an unrestrained war whoop when he led the way into the darkening parkway. Hollywood's legend was carved in stone and that night's run became forever known as "The Night Hollywood Earned a Merit Badge".

Chapter 21

With new age music wafting in the background Brett waited patiently while Marie slipped into the bedroom to change into her cycling clothes. He looked over the walls of her apartment and recognized the changes she had made in the décor since the last time he had been inside. He was happy to see the low budget artwork that had previously hung on the walls having been replaced by works she had created with her own hands. While waiting on the couch he admired the sketches of wildlife she had etched on paper and appreciated the nuances of the many creatures. But it was the captured movement of the animals that garnered his attention, and he found her ability to slow down the graceful action to a single frame of time uncanny. Even to his untrained eye he knew it was not a skill easily attained, and he expected her to be both simultaneously pleased and embarrassed by his upcoming rave review.

As he waited for her to get changed he couldn't help but notice a single easel standing in the corner of the room. He suspected that it was a work in progress, but couldn't resist the need to know for sure. He raised the cloth that obscured the secret and felt the air get sucked out of his lungs when he gaped at a partially completed sketch of a runner striding over a weather-beaten track. His pulse pounded as he studied the mixture of primal emotions caught in the face of the runner crossing the shadow of a finishing line. The picture literally begged for the soundtrack of a roaring crowd, but with its absence the silence seemed all the more resounding. Even in its incomplete state he could have examined the work for hours but the rustling from the bedroom altered his attention.

"Be there in a minute," she called as he heard the drawer doors slam shut from a room away.

He quickly lowered the cloth to re-cover the work and felt a sudden urge to flee the premises but found himself frozen to the floor. He had the unmistakable sensation of being trapped in the room and felt like an animal in captivity. Yet, as he stood there he admitted for the first time in his life he had developed a yearning to explore the precarious boundaries of a meaningful relationship. The contrasting pull he had been experiencing was nullified when she re-entered the room and he saw the comforting shine of her face.

"Are you okay?" she asked noting his perplexed look.

"Yeah...sure," he said as he deftly avoided the real reason for his unsettled expression. "I'm just amazed at how good your drawings are. They're perfect."

The red immediately lit up her cheeks. She paused before answering and he found her embarrassment prove all the more endearing. "Thanks. I'm trying to get brave one step at a time. So I figured I'd put them up here first."

"And you should. I have to admit they are a bit better decoration than my old beat up poster."

"But not any more meaningful I'd guess. It's all in the eye of the beholder," she reminded him. "Anyways I'm glad you like them. I've been working on a few other things but they're not quite done."

He nodded mutely while casting a glance toward the easel and decided not to reveal his secretive viewing of her current drawing. He remembered his initial request of a personalized drawing for his wall, and shuddered at the intensity of the statement Marie was making about their relationship. He chewed on a fingernail as he considered his own vulnerability and weighed the likelihood of keeping his own weaknesses buried if their relationship continued to progress. After returning her smile she was seemingly oblivious to his dilemma and he wordlessly picked up her bicycle to carry it out the front door. Together they studied the murky skies and considered the likely possibility of the foul weather that lay ahead. The potential storm did not concern him, but he wondered if she would be game for the possible ride in the rain. With the limited time they had together deep down he hoped she would choose to ride with him even if it meant dodging a few raindrops.

She took her turn looking overhead at the threatening clouds and pondered the alternative of waiting for him to complete another workout. She knew he would run in any element and felt another stab of jealousy at the commitment he demonstrated toward his sport. She resigned herself to her current status on his personal pecking order and decided the chance of a good soaking was well worth some time together. "I'll take what I can get," she whispered under her breath.

"What's that?"

"I said I'm not afraid to get wet."

"Then let's do it," he said happily tugging at his shoelaces.

He started into an easy run and was pleased to have her accompanying him. With full schedules it seemed more and more their time together was literally spent on the run. Marie knew her girlfriends found it odd, but in some way she enjoyed the intimacy the miles together provided them. She had long ago accepted it wasn't the most romantic of dates, but she gained solace in the fact that at least his attention was focused solely on her. In spite of the effort he expended during the runs she had often found him at his most talkative as the miles flew by. She followed his well-honed sense of direction and rolled beside him as he guided her onto the once popular bike path that shadowed the flow of the river. The cracks in the antiquated asphalt kept her on guard and she bounced over the sun-baked terrain with him close by her side. He chose to run on the dirt trail bordering the path because its slightly more forgiving surface ensured less insult to his skeletal system. As they drew in the fresh air they both enjoyed the solitude of the time worn route and the sharp contrast it provided with the nervous energy of the nearby city.

"Am I going too fast?" he asked with genuine concern.

"I'm the one on the bike," she reminded him as she marveled at his ability to carry on a conversation regardless of the pace. "Actually this is a kind of nice way to stay in shape. You know its hard going out with a guy whose butt is so little…it makes mine look bigger than J-Lo's."

"Careful…that's Logan's fantasy you're dissing," he cautioned as he waved an index finger in the air.

"He said *I* was his fantasy!"

"At the time he probably noticed you were breathing. From what I can tell that's his primary criteria."

She shook her head and considered the remark. "Where are the guys today? You don't usually have time to get together on Tuesdays."

"They have a meet in Illinois. Coach Wickers was pretty fired up for it and thinks they're ready to hammer it."

"Do you?"

He thought about the workouts they had recently completed and the aggressiveness demonstrated by the top tier of runners. Admittedly not ego-less himself, he relished in his status as the most skilled runner, but was still objective enough to recognize the other competitors' gradual improvement. "They seem to be getting tougher. And I'm having a harder time dropping them in workouts than at first. I think they are finally realizing how far you can push yourself. Coach says I've gotten them to 'pee standing up'. In his own unique way I think he's trying to say I'm a good influence."

"That's no surprise. But as far as I can tell it seems Wickers has been good for you too. I'm glad your running is going so well, but you know you've never even told me how you started in the first place."

He slowed up to take a drink from an old fountain hidden within the tall weeds. He drank deep from the feeble flow and cringed at the metallic taste of the untreated well water. After wiping the excess from his chin he started to speak in a measured tone. "I think at first I started to run because I was too small to do much in other sports. My dad probably saw the same thing and went out of his way to try to make me keep up with him on his daily 'jogs'. I kept at it and it didn't seem to take too long before he had a hard time keeping up with me. I barely weighed ninety pounds even with a pocketful of nickels, but somehow running always seemed to come easy for me. Pretty soon dad had to ride a bike just for us to be able to stay together. I still remember his old rusted Schwinn rolling beside me like it was yesterday."

"You think of him a lot don't you?"

She was unwittingly tiptoeing on his personal hallowed ground that he had so far been able to keep at arm's length for years on end. But somehow the innocence and purity of her questioning softened one more barrier. "He's there every time I lace up my shoes. When I started high school he even had to fight to get a cross country team together. He recruited ten bony kids to join up and had us work car washes to raise money for our uniforms. The school decided to let him coach because no one else wanted the job."

"How did he know how to train you?"

"By learning on the fly. He had a stack of old running magazines and read anything he could get his hands on. He pestered all the local coaches and even called Bill Bowerman once, God rest his soul."

"Bowerman?"

"He coached at Oregon. Dad said at first Bowerman seemed pissed about being bothered, but later they became friends. One year at Christmas dad sent him an antique horse saddle for his ranch just to say thank you for all of his help."

"Your dad seemed like a great guy," she said as she peddled on.

"He was. I still have flashbacks when I'm running that he's next to me and is ready to hand me a water bottle."

"That's a good memory. Do you mind if I ask you how he died?"

The question hit him harder than the lightening bolts that had been flickering in the darkening skies. The torrent of grief that he had felt at his father's funeral nearly flooded over and he had to take a breath to steady himself. "He had a heart attack when he was riding some trails. He had always been healthy but the doctor said he had developed some blockage over time. I was supposed to have been there with him but I slept in that morning. I always wonder if I had been there if somehow I could have helped." He carefully left out the fact he had been out until bar-time the night before and had not returned home in time for the Saturday morning run. He bit his lip as he felt the flashing memory of the recurrent dream that had often invaded his nights.

"You can't blame yourself," she advised him as she steered around a deep pothole.

I'll blame whoever I want, he thought bitterly to himself.

The run suddenly quieted as they both took stock of the unexpected dredging up of emotion. Brett paradoxically felt himself cooling off during the run when the overwhelming tension of the discussion filtered out of his pores. For a brief moment he wished that he had covered the daily mileage alone with only his usual superficial thoughts to accompany him.

"Are you getting tired yet?' she asked gingerly as if testing the mood of the runner along side her.

"Naw, I'm okay," came his response in a seeming return to the frame of mind that had initiated the beginning stages of the run. "But…I'm not so sure about this weather. Maybe this wasn't such a good idea." He had barely gotten the words out of his mouth when they were both startled by the flicker of nearby lightning. The explosion of thunder was followed almost immediately by the onset of a hard rain. They were both quickly pelted by the sudden onslaught of the downpour they had hoped to avoid. "Head for the pavilion!" he shouted while pointing to an old wooden structure. Marie pedaled hard as she followed his lead, but was still unable to avoid being totally soaked by the driving rain.

"Good job," she complemented him as she ran her fingers through her wet hair. "It'll probably blow over soon." She dismounted from her bike and they both acted like wet puppies and shook the remnants of the storm off of themselves. She looked at him and noticed the increasingly familiar shine in his eye as he studied her soaked clothing. "What's on your mind?" she asked.

"Well…um," he stuttered. "It's just that the wet t-shirt contest you're having makes running seem a long ways away."

She returned his smile and pulled him in close. "Perhaps that's a good thing," she said as he in turn put his arms around her. Time was lost as they shared an impassioned embrace under the safety of the wooden beams. They proceeded to steal a long kiss as the rain continued to pound on the tin roof above their heads. All previous discourse was instantly forgotten as the soggy couple enjoyed the solitude that had been thrust upon them so unexpectedly. The world was their own until they noticed the steam beginning to rise off of the heat of the nearby bike path. They slowly came to the realization that the thunderstorm had abated nearly as quickly as it had appeared.

"Who says running is boring?" he questioned while looking her in the eyes.

"You won't hear that from me anymore," she said brushing back his wet locks. "And to think I could have stayed home all by my lonesome."

"I'm glad you didn't. But we should probably start heading back before we get chilled."

"You might want to wait a minute, cowboy," she said lowering her gaze.

"Whoa," he said as he noticed his dilemma, "I think I'll go over there and stretch for a bit."

With the dark clouds rolling away her thoughts danced as she watched the fresh water drip from the leaves. She tried to savor the moment and ran her fingers on a cracked beam of the pavilion while smiling contentedly. And she calculated that the anticipated shiver of a cool ride home was a small price to pay for the warmth of a romantic moment they had been able to capture so unexpectedly.

Chapter 22

He carefully inked his latest Sunday effort on the wall and gained satisfaction from another hard earned fifteen miles. There were times the numbers on the wall staggered even himself as he continued on the journey to hone his skills day after day. He dared not say a word to anyone to invite ridicule, but he had started to imagine his body hardening to a rawhide level that had previously been unattainable. He attributed his new found monkish lifestyle in succeeding to pare off the last vestiges of body fat that he could afford to lose. Without the outside attractions cluttering up the nights he also recognized his focus did not lag far behind. While still admiring his wall-sized diary he picked up the ringing phone but upon bringing it up to his ear he was greeted by only silence. "Hello? Is anyone there?" he asked a second time. The long pause before a sound was heard immediately put him on alert and he listened to the labored breathing until a familiar voice echoed through the earpiece.

"Brett, honey. Is that you?"

"Mom," he said. "Yes, it's me."

"I didn't know where to reach you. I had to call your old number to find out. Why didn't you let me know?"

"I gave it to you twice already but you were probably — " he said but stopped suddenly. "How are you Mom?"

He heard the unmistakable twinkle of ice cubes in the background as he waited for her answer. "I'm okay. I just wondered where you were," she said as the start of a slur accented her words.

"In Milwaukee. I told you that. I'll be here for a while yet."

"After you're done then you'll be coming home?"

His heart pounded when he closed his eyes and imagined the bleak scene. He could see her lying on the stained sofa in her old flowered bathrobe and smelled the mustiness of her aging body mixed with the unmistakable odor of gin. He knew the collection of scattered magazines and constant squawk of the old T.V. would only add to the overall unpleasantness of the scene. After the dissolution of his parent's marriage, she had resettled into her childhood hometown in eastern Ohio to be closer to her relatives. She had chosen to move into a small townhouse and eventually found work in a small hardware store as a part-time bookkeeper. He had more than once ruminated on how her skill with numbers and college degree in accounting had only manifested themselves into the lowly position.

"Mom, I can't talk now. I'm meeting some friends to study. I'll call you soon," he lied aloud to her as he had so many times in the past.

"You promise?"

"Promise, Mom. Soon."

He hung up as the burning in his gut reached a boil and he felt the intractable guilt of deceiving his own mother. But he knew the pain he would have experienced over another of her rambles was even worse. She had long been a semi-functioning alcoholic whose habitual binges had eventually broken his boyhood home apart. He recalled the countless times he had straightened out the house before his dad had returned from work while his mom "rested" on the couch. But even the cleanliness of the home couldn't cloak the overt disorientation she displayed over the dinnertime hour. He stared at the silent phone and re-lived the tirades of his father as he threatened his mother with divorce unless she straightened out. Somehow even in the shadows of his Milwaukee apartment he could still feel the wind in his hair as he remembered escaping from the turmoil of the home by running himself to exhaustion. The dredging up of old memories resulted in a sudden longing for some fresh air and he stepped out into the sunshine to clear his thoughts.

After collecting himself he drove slowly to Marie's apartment where the emotional gloom of the morning had lifted only slightly. He had planned to spend a day with her at Logan's and Hollywood's annual "Fool's and Vagabond's Bash" enjoying a well deserved break from training. Prior to the unexpected phone call, he had been looking forward to the party, but his previous positive outlook was now radically changed. When he greeted Marie at her apartment she noticed his withdrawn demeanor and how he seemed to hold her longer than usual when he hugged her hello. She had seen him in moods before, but somehow this particular temperament was on an entirely different level. Even after the few months they had spent together she was still trying to figure him out but was admittedly pleased that he had offered a glimpse into his life during the recent weekday run. But somehow she knew there was a sadness at his very core that as of yet she had not been able to decipher.

"Are you okay?" she asked.

"Fine. I just need a few minutes."

They drove quietly to the park and while pulling into a parking spot they noticed the party was already in full swing. The music pounded in the distance and upon exiting the car they were surprised to be instantly greeted by Hollywood's flushed face. "Hurry!" he said pulling them by their arms. "Logan is up and I'm in the lead." He ran them over to the center of the gathering and they were greeted by the soles of the little runner's feet facing the sun. "We're doing upside down beer slams," he explained. "I'm leading at 3.1 seconds."

They watched as Logan steadied his backside against a tree while a plastic cup was nestled against his lips. The official timer readied his stopwatch as Hollywood counted down to the start of the contest. The inverted runner licked at his lips in anticipation of the twelve ounce challenge that was set directly in front of him. At the sound of Hollywood's voice he demonstrated razor-sharp reactions by seemingly inhaling the sudsy brew in a series of gulps and hopping back to his feet. With the back of his hand he wiped the white froth off of his satisfied face and waited for the well-deserved accolades to commence.

"2.7 seconds," said Hollywood as his jaw dropped. "No way."

"I visualized it and made it happen. You just got to believe," Logan bragged as he settled his mirrored sunglasses onto the bridge of his nose. "Brett, your turn."

"I can't you guys. Really, maybe next time," he said as he backed out of the crowd.

Logan accepted the rejection and quickly attempted to round up the next victim while Brett continued his retreat from the nexus of the party. After freeing himself from the crowd he looked at the revelry and remembered the countless times he had been the lead player at parties of a hauntingly similar nature. He had never needed an excuse to partake in the spontaneous activities that seemed to rise up routinely no matter what campus he had resided at. Many of the runners he had known over the years had always welcomed the afterglow of a hard race with an endless supply of foaming pitchers of beer. But as the seasons wore on it became personally almost irrelevant whether the gathering was a celebration of victory, or a numbing of the defeat he had earlier experienced. Eventually as the parties became less of an afterthought and more of a necessity, he remembered his own justification of celebrating a hard ten miler with a cold six-pack of Budweiser. He even recalled the eventual use of a thirty-two ounce magnum of beer as a so called "eye-shutter" on uneventful weekday nights. Marie eventually noticed his departure from the party and followed him all the way back to the park swing he had settled into. She heard the creaking of the metal chain as he slowly eased back and forth on the tips of his toes lost deeply in his own thoughts. She approached him as he lowered his head and sensed the desperation contained in a nearly inaudible sigh.

"Brett, what's wrong?"

He knew he needed to bare his soul from the weight of his own secretive past and the burden that had become increasingly heavy on his shoulders. The shame of his past transgressions rose up and he came to a clear realization that she needed to know the truth about his personal frailties. After looking up he studied the worry lines that framed her tan face and he felt a depth of trust long since forgotten.

"Do you remember how I told you how I bounced around at a few colleges out east?" he asked almost rhetorically. When she nodded he started again. "I told you I had screwed up my grades and I had to transfer a time or two. The truth is I got myself caught up in some things I couldn't control. Things that I'm not too proud of."

She smoothed out a seat on the lush grass before sitting down in front of him. "What kind of things?"

He felt as if he was in a confessional at his old Catholic grade school and looked blankly at her open face. He paused before he spoke but finally opened up the gate that concealed his past. "I drank. A lot. Almost anything I could swallow. It got to the point that I had to make a decision. And I decided to stop. It's been about eight months and I haven't had a drop. But it's hard and some days are harder than others. Today's a hard day," he said as he looked past her into the blue skies.

She didn't immediately know how to react to his disclosure, but knew instinctively that he needed to continue on with his revelation. "Why is that?"

He paused again as he processed the question and cautiously settled upon a benign beginning to the answer. "My mom called. And for a long time I've hardly even talked to her." He looked at Marie once again as he considered his next remark. "Have you ever loved and hated someone at the same time?" he asked abruptly as he stopped the swing dead in its tracks.

She was caught off guard by the question but knew this was a time for straight answers. "No, I guess I've been lucky."

He gave her a look that she knew was his way of giving a silent response to her acknowledgement. "I know she's my mom but things could have been so different. In fact they should have been different," he said as bluntly as he could.

She ached for him and felt the despair that flowed across the few feet that separated them. She rose up and moved closer to him. "Brett, I'm so sorry."

He stretched out his arms and gently held her wrists. "I know it's not your problem but I thought you should know. I think I have the drinking beat, but it's not always so easy. And as hard as dealing with my mom is, so was telling you after all this time."

She felt the heartache in his voice as he lowered his eyes to the ground. She had never before felt such empathy towards an individual and recognized the difficulty he must be experiencing in openly admitting such a primary weakness. She released herself from his grasp and she raised his chin softly before she spoke in a steady voice. "A few months ago I made a decision too. And I decided on you. I don't care about your past as long as we work on the future. Together."

He looked deep into the trusting eyes and saw the strength they contained. He started to mist over from the emotion of the moment and he knew an indisputable bond had been forged. He stood and gave her another long embrace before whispering back in her ear. "Together."

They slowly made their way back to the party hand in hand as the day suddenly took on a new luster. They were bombarded by the raucous sound of the partygoers and heard Gwen Stefani wailing out her chorus to "Just a Girl". They both watched with open mouths as Logan and Hollywood gyrated to the rhythm on the top of a picnic table while smearing suntan oil on their nearly naked bodies. With the crowd clapping nearby Marie stopped him and stared at the two runners. "You have to promise me one thing though."

"What's that?"

"That 'together' means only me and you." He smiled as he watched his two friends continue their dance.

"Marie, come on up," called Logan from the table as he interrupted their heart to heart. "I'll rub a little lotion on you."

Brett automatically laid a protective arm around her shoulder as if to shield her from potential violation. "The hell you will."

Marie smiled and proved she could more than manage the situation herself. "I think I'll leave the oil to Brett if you don't mind. As enticing as it is to be girl number one hundred and eighty nine on your list, I think I'll pass."

"You're such a nasty girl," said Hollywood with admiration as the oil dripped off of his shimmering torso.

"I'm glad Marie has such uncommon common sense among all the fools and vagabonds," said Rip when he stepped into the fray and finally made his party entrance.

When the song ended the two hopped down from their perch glistening in the sun and Logan put his slick hand around Brett's shoulders before speaking. "Grab a brew, studly. It'll do you good to lighten up a bit on the training."

"I…uhh," he replied awkwardly before Marie stepped in.

"We have to study later," she said. "Anyways he needs to think of his running." Brett looked at her gratefully but offered no other explanation.

"It's not like he has the Olympic rings tattooed on his ass," protested Logan. He looked at the funny expression on Brett's face before continuing. "Do you?"

He didn't answer immediately as he weighed the question gingerly. But after taking a deep breath he started into an explanation slowly. "No, not exactly. But…I uhh… sort of qualified for the Olympic trials coming up in August. The 5000 meters." The stunned silence that followed seemed an eternity to him but lasted only a matter of seconds.

"You bitch!" said Logan in a bug-eyed response. "You skinny white bitch! I can't believe you didn't tell us you're in the trials."

"Holy shit," added Hollywood. "For real?"

"Yes," admitted Brett as he saw the pride envelope Marie's face. "About a year ago. I just had one of those days."

"One of those days?" said Rip as he stared dumbfounded at Brett in a mixture of awe and envy. "I'd give my left nut for 'one of those days'. Umm…sorry, Marie."

"I've heard worse. Brett, I thought you had told them?" she added with a quizzical look on her face.

He seemed at a loss for words and stared blankly at the group. He collected himself before he explained his actions and hoped they afforded him the simplest of alibis. "I didn't want to seem like I was bragging. But I was planning on telling you guys at the right time," he confessed while he pawed uncomfortably at a bare patch in the grass.

"When? As you lined up in Baton Rouge?" asked Logan.

"I can't believe it," said Hollywood, "that is so cool. Now I don't feel so bad about getting whipped by you in training. It's like you're supposed to." When he hit the older runner on the arm in a congratulatory gesture the accolades had fast reached an awkward level.

"Enough already," said Brett as he was becoming thoroughly embarrassed. "I'm just like any of you guys."

"Except that you're a few hundred meters ahead of us," said Rip in a rueful voice.

"Don't get all weird on me. You're all a lot closer than you realize. And I think you know you are gaining everyday."

The other runners considered the remark and opened themselves up to the possibilities it hinted at. Their individual desire for success was suddenly magnified until it felt as strong as the sunshine in their eyes. They looked thoughtfully at the senior runner while the contrasting battle between competition and friendship once again simmered in their thoughts. And deep down they silently hoped he was right.

Chapter 23

The weeks flew by in a flurry of classes, tests, and churning strides. Time for much else was limited and even the chance to sleep in occurred increasingly rarely. When the alarm clock ignited the day and blared out the usual talk show blather, Brett opened his sleepy eyes and focused on the bleak surroundings of his apartment. From his floor level vantage point he registered a vague acknowledgement of a collection of dustballs that had accumulated in the corners of the room. He filed away the pressing need for a proper cleaning and sat upright in bed before catching a glimpse of the ever present reminder tacked above his head. With the love-hate relationship he often experienced towards his craft rearing its head once again, he utilized the silent but incessant push the old poster provided.

"I'll see you in a few hours," he said patting the mattress in resignation.

The Sunday long run was a staple in any distance runner's diet and the foursome from Milwaukee were no different. They had all developed a grudging acceptance of its necessity and knew that if they completed it together, somehow the miles became more tolerable. The light of Sunday morning always came way too early for them, but they knew from experience it was best to get the run done before other events cluttered up their day. Get up...get going...and get it out of the way was how the runners had learned to view the latest infringement on their sleeping patterns.

Brett had attempted to make the effort seem more palatable to the runners by explaining to them that by doing long slow distance they were increasing the efficiency of blood flow to their leg muscles. "Making capillaries" he had called it. It seemed armed with that simple fact the difficulty and boredom of the morning runs had become infinitely more productive to the collegiate runners. The group itself had never gone less than twelve miles while Brett himself had run as long as twenty. It was seldom a pleasant experience, but the high caliber athletes all considered it a payment of dues that allowed them admittance into the elite running club to which they belonged. After trial and error they all knew that without the long runs as a base, their true fitness level was as thin as tissue paper.

With the glare of the low lying sun burning in his eyes, Brett quietly made his way towards the agreed upon starting point. That particular morning they had planned to do a thirteen mile loop from Hollywood's apartment due in part to the plentiful water along the route. It was a run they had done many times before, but like all runners they were creatures of habit. It seemed that somehow by passing familiar landmarks the mind numbing miles were easier to complete. As Brett approached the other runners he watched Logan and Hollywood as they laced up their shoes and noticed the fatigue that encircled their eyes.

"Up a little late last night, Logan?" he asked.

"Yeah, three dollar pitchers at Hooligans. We couldn't resist."

"Any luck fishing?" asked Brett knowing the real reason for their excursions.

"Two on the line. At least until Hollywood barfed on their shoes."

Hollywood shook his head as if disagreeing with the statement. "Only a little. Anyways it must have been something I ate. I swear the cheese on the nachos must have been recycled or something."

"Yeah, right...you two will be good for shit," admonished Rip as he fully expected the worst from his friends.

"Just worry about yourself," Hollywood replied in his own defense. "I'm sure a candy-ass like you was nestled all snug in his bed by nine o'clock."

Rip stood up and struck a defiant pose. "Ten-thirty. And I'm sure I'll be glad about that by the ten mile mark or so."

The other two runners stayed distant from the confrontation and looked at each other helplessly. Although they all got along surprisingly well considering the competitive nature of the sport, it wasn't completely out of the ordinary for an occasional sharp edge to arise. Brett had been reminded of that personally when his sternum had been on the receiving end of Logan's bony elbow during a particularly rigorous interval session earlier in the week. He fingered at the fading bruise and took the initiative to further diffuse the conflict by beginning the run at a leisurely pace.

The morning runs were always difficult to get started. It wasn't entirely natural to run as early as they did and they all felt the grind in their joints. The normal stretching routine was ignored and the early miles were used to lubricate the morning stiffness away. In a matter of minutes the awkward shuffle was soon replaced by the more normal flow of smooth motion that had become the custom. Brett also had his doubts about how Hollywood and Logan could handle the morning run, but recognized their current state was entirely of their own doing. Ultimately running was a selfish business and they each had to deal with their own personal obstacles to success. He knew all too well about his longstanding battle with private demons and chose to focus solely only on the drudgery of the task at hand.

The thoughts of the runners drifted in the early miles and the quiet of the run suited the mood of the lethargic runners. Brett himself replayed an argument with Marie the night before which had been triggered by his desire to end their evening and get a good night's rest. She had rightfully complained that as early as he went to bed it was like dating an old man. He couldn't really blame her for being upset, but he was adamant about keeping his eye on the prize that he valued above all else. The trials were only three months off and at this point he couldn't afford any frivolous gaps in his training. The issue was once again left unsettled when he broke away from her and returned to his apartment in a huff. The selfishness he felt was weighed against the knowledge that across the nation the Kid and others were racking up more than their own share of miles. He repeated his sworn vow that no one would gain a spot on the team by outworking him. Not this time. Long ago he had accepted he had been granted some natural ability, but he knew that no one sniffed the rare air of the Olympics on good genes and a smile. Hard work and guts made this a blue collar sport, and he promised this time he wouldn't go down without a fight.

With the run methodically continuing over the quiet terrain he looked over at Rip and admired his undeniable resolve. He had often heard his friend extol the virtues of his father's work ethic in the northern Wisconsin paper mills. His father's propensity for working overtime in support of his family had seemingly rubbed off on his eldest son and Rip never shied away from the daily grind of distance running. Brett had not seen the sturdy runner miss even a single workout, and he seemed to be able to suck in an enormous amount of miles without getting injured. To this point whatever he lacked in fast twitch fibers he more than made up for in his own innate work ethic, will, and desire. In the months they had trained side by side Brett recalled being able to summon finishing speed Rip could only dream about, but in a close fight there was no shortage of guts demonstrated by either runner. He knew first hand that neither would back down from a challenge and he looked forward to the day they would toe it up together in a race of real meaning.

They all felt the miles accumulate uneventfully in the serenity of the morning. The late night seemed to drain the edge from the usual verbal barbs thrown by the hung-over runners and the whole purpose of this particular run seemed only to complete it. Like many of his running friends over the years, Brett had found himself capable of daydreaming about vast array of topics as the miles piled up. But surprisingly on this day he was devoid of any thoughts that might lead him toward even the most transient moment of enlightenment. The solitude of the current run was suddenly interrupted by a groan from Rip after a familiar sound rippled through the air.

"Man, you guys," he complained. "Do you think you could fart a little bit more?"

"It's just the beer escaping. I only wish I had a match," said Hollywood as true to form he remained unapologetic.

"My name is 'Gaseous Maximus'," said Logan in a deep Gladiator voice. "Commander of the runners of the Midwest…loyal servant to Coach Wickers. And with vengeance I vow to crush my competitors in this life and the next."

"Russell Crowe you ain't," said Brett with a giggle.

They slowed to the customary stop at the halfway point in order to drink at the gas station hose. Brett watched Logan and Hollywood suck down far in excess of what he knew their bodies could readily absorb. He had experienced the dehydration effects of alcohol first hand and remembered vividly the state his friends were currently experiencing. He tried to imagine the cotton-mouths of his friends and also knew the taxing effects on their hearts of driving the sludge-like blood through their systems. He decided to hold back on giving them a physiology lesson on the effects of drinking and running when the hypocrisy of such a speech became overly apparent. Yet a simple comment directed toward the slurping runners was too much to pass up. "A little thirsty, boys?"

"Dry as dirt," said Hollywood. "And feeling as raggedy as Logan's Jockeys."

"Can't get your mind off my drawers can ya?" he responded between swallows.

The long runs were a test of manhood and Brett knew ultimately they would all finish. For all of his friends' recreational activities they too were solid competitors not to be sold short when the starting gun went off. He had long ago learned to trust his instincts toward recognizing which of his fellow runners had the baseline capacity to compete far beyond the red-line. Even with the two pairs of bloodshot eyes pleading for a break, he knew Logan and Hollywood would somehow manage to complete the set upon mission.

"Let's finish this son of a bitch," said Logan right on cue.

"The best is yet to come," warned Brett in full knowledge of the terrain that lie ahead.

They again eased into the running and wordlessly plowed through the miles until in the distance they studied an upcoming set of hills. Brett prepared internally for the impending challenge and ratcheted his concentration up one more notch. He had always personified hills as both friend and foe because of their dual ability to increase fitness while at the same time dealing solely in pain. He viewed the long, drawn out incline and recognized it was now truly time to go to work.

"Stay together," Rip urged. They all had learned that there was an undeniable life-force in the pack and by losing contact, the runner would fade aimlessly into the world of self-doubt. They knew that once the imaginary rope that tied them together had been severed there was no way back for the poor soul that was separated from the group. Ever the Green Bay Packer fan Rip continued, "Fatigue makes cowards of us all. Vince Lombardi, 1965."

"Screw all that cheesehead bullshit," said Hollywood. "I'm from Chicago."

They began the finishing drive up the mile long climb and Brett headed the pack by leaning into the hill in the required fashion to best fight the lay of the land. There was no talking when both the rate of breathing and internal focus escalated exponentially as the group attacked the incline. They all understood that the laying of steel was as much in the hard wiring of their minds as it was in their legs. They further knew that in every race a runner faced the conscious decision to stay with the leaders or to accept defeat and drop from the pace. Logan had once called it "hermaphrodite time". When they looked at him quizzically he explained it was "time to show 'em if you got 'em".

"It's nearly over 'Herm'," said Brett in shorthand sensing the runner's struggle to keep up with the pace.

"And I'm nearly dead," deadpanned Logan when the fatigue started to take hold.

There was no longer even a hint of conversation left in the four runners. Each had journeyed to the black hole of pain and grasped at the nidus with clenched fists. To back off now would admit defeat and garner both a loss of respect and ridicule from the others. Even worse it would signify a potential crack in the competitive psyche so essential to any successful distance runner.

Amidst a series of unintelligible grunts and the hoarse rasp of effort they were able to stay together until they reached the top of the hill and eased it into neutral. Mercifully there was nothing left for them to complete but the one mile cool down to the starting point.

"Damn that Budweiser," said Hollywood as the pain of the distance drained from his quivering muscles.

"Building capillaries," reminded Brett.

"Except for the one that burst in my head," he replied as he shook out his arms to relieve the tension of the effort.

They trotted into his driveway and the ability to stop running was a simple pleasure appreciated by all. "Another pound of flesh given up to the great God Nike," said Logan while he walked slowly in a circle. "Man, I love this sport."

Brett smiled as he wiped the sweat from his brow. "And it loves you too."

The runners' small talked as their metabolisms slowly settled into a more normal state. When they started to get chilled they exchanged their goodbyes and talked of the next scheduled workout. And armed only with bone-weary satisfaction they each headed home knowing that another building block of fitness had been firmly hammered into place.

Chapter 24

The well-deserved two hour nap that followed the long run had left him feeling rejuvenated and alert. After a quick shower the early morning workout seemed a distant memory notwithstanding that it had occurred only hours ago. He happily remembered his promise to meet Marie for coffee at the Java Hut even though he suspected the early miles and subsequent sleep had invigorated him more than a dose of caffeine ever could.

He walked briskly to the small café and spied her sitting near the window patiently waiting for him to arrive. As he continued on to the entrance he felt comfort when he saw her smile and wave warmly. In the last few months somehow even a single glimpse of her in a campus crowd had been able to lift his spirits, and for the first time in his dating life the more time he spent with her, the more time he subsequently craved. But he recognized with the trials only a few months off, he couldn't begin to forego his first true love at the time it needed him most. He felt satisfied that his main priority had been fulfilled hours ago, and was now more than pleased to attend to a more pleasurable aspect of his life. After pulling open the glass door he returned her distant greeting but was surprised to see the normally bustling enterprise nearly deserted. He briskly worked his way between the series of tables and slid into the seat she had carefully procured.

"Hi, Marie. It looks to me like we're going to have the place to ourselves."

"It's more intimate this way. Besides everybody's probably sleeping in. It was kind of nuts out last night."

He nodded his head in agreement after remembering the story of his friends' escapades. "I bet Hollywood and Logan are still sacked out. They were a mess this morning during the long run."

"I'm not surprised. I bumped into them last night …literally. I wonder how they could even run this morning," she said as she took a sip of coffee.

"Well, those two are tougher than they look."

"I guess. By the way Logan was filling me in on his nicknames. Can I ask why you guys feel the need to do that for each other? Is it some sort of rule or something?"

He paused as he processed the question and cautiously settled upon a safe beginning to the answer. "It probably is a guy thing. For us I think somehow it just helps to make the running more fun. And by the way I'm sorry I was such a loser last night and turned in so early. I just need to make sure everything stays on track."

She looked at him closely and bobbed her head slowly in acknowledgement. "I understand…sort of. It's just that I have a hard time feeling like I'm always in second place. And I'll probably never understand how running fifteen miles a day can be such a good time. Maybe you can explain that to me if I buy you a cup of coffee," she said as she pushed her chair away from the table and strode toward the front counter.

He sat at the table and saw her calmly waiting in line while the attendant prepared his drink. Why did he run? he asked himself silently. How could he explain to her that it was just something he *had* to do? But was he running to something…or away? For himself…or someone else? He had never been able to answer those questions in the moments when his motivation waned and he battled to take that first step out the door.

He wondered how he would be able to tell her it was probably all of the above without facing the self-scrutiny he had so far been able to clearly avoid.

"Did you figure it out yet?" she asked him as she set the steaming mug in front of him.

"Say what?"

"Don't be such a pain. I asked why you run."

"Hmm, the eternal question asked of the runner," he said trying to lighten the mood. "If you force me to spill my guts, I'll deny I ever told you of the ancient code I've vowed to uphold."

She rolled her eyes at the comment and pressed on. "It sounds so mysterious. And I suppose you'll swear me to secrecy and have Logan put my undies in the freezer if I tell anyone."

"That is a distinct possibility," he said with a laugh. "Since you're going to make me answer no matter what, I'll try to do the best I can. I'll start by saying I think there are as many reasons for running as there are kinds of shoes on the wall."

"I asked about yours."

He was becoming slightly irritated with her persistence but decided that he would answer her questions more directly. "Somehow what began as a hobby eventually became a part of who I am. And running makes me feel something that I can't get any other way. Right now it's gotten to the point that if I miss a day or even a single run, it feels like the whole world is off center."

"Did it ever occur to you that maybe you're the one off center?" she said as she stirred her coffee carefully.

He knew he wasn't going to get off easy with her and decided to work his way through her questions with as much grace as possible. "More than once. But as I got better at it, the attraction deepened until running started to define who I was. It's probably not the healthiest thing to say, but if you want to be a winner, the daily run becomes a necessity. It gets so that all the other events of the day are like trivia happening in between the two runs."

"Like right now?"

He shook his head to emphasize his true meaning. "No, I didn't mean it like that. What I was trying to say was when I first started to run it was just something to do. But after I had some success it became almost addictive. I really enjoyed the challenge of the clock and the head to head competition. But I think mostly it was competing against myself that got me hooked. It was like I wanted to see how far I could push myself and how good I could become. I started to feel like the more I ran, the more I was breaking some new boundary and digging deeper into myself.

'Pre' once said 'I like to make something beautiful when I run'. Sometimes when I'm competing I think of that quote in the hopes of having a perfect race. The same sort of perfection you probably strive for when you sketch," he said knowingly as he paused to take a sip of coffee.

"But I don't make myself hurt when I'm drawing."

"Oh no?" he asked in an increasingly animated voice. "You don't criticize your work and jab at the canvas in frustration? You don't start over when the essence isn't quite right? You don't wake up in the middle of the night thinking of some flaw in your creation that needs to get corrected at that very second?"

She remembered the times she had gotten up in the dark as a sudden inspiration drove her to alter a work. And how through sleepy eyes she would force herself to revise her art before crawling back into bed. She didn't even have a chance to respond before he started again.

"It's just that instead of a pencil I use drops of sweat."

"You do enjoy it though, don't you?"

He thought of the many times he had asked himself the very same question when wrestling with a case of low motivation. But just as he had a few hours ago, he found that he had been able to eventually will himself to head out the door for the next run on his schedule. "Most times. But as I got better the pressure inside seemed to increase every time I raced and if I didn't win, I had somehow failed. Or even if I did win and the clock had ticked two seconds too long, I had still fallen short. Sometimes the stress sucked the air out of me until it seemed I couldn't breathe. It got even rougher when my mom started to get bad and then after losing my dad it only got worse."

"And so you started to drink?" she said softly as the ceiling fan hummed overhead.

He looked at her and sighed as he was forced again to look deeper inside. He swirled his coffee with a spoon and his resulting silence spoke volumes. "I drank," he repeated in a flat voice. "For awhile it seemed to lessen the feeling of failure I had in my head. Drinking was like a cushion that softened the impact I would feel after a bad race. And even after my good runs it helped me forget about how alone I really felt. Soon enough the joy got drained out of everything and although I still ran, I somehow had lost my passion and trained as if I was on automatic pilot. But the day I saw the Prefontaine poster in the running store I felt like I had gotten whacked in the head by a 'two by four'. I realized I was wasting my gifts. And my life. And that maybe it was okay to fail as long as I put my heart on the line."

"The heart is a powerful thing," she said as she touched the back of his hand.

He stroked her fingers gently before he replied. "I didn't really mean what I said before about everything else being trivial. It's since I met you that I realized if I stayed on the tightrope alone, I was destined to fall off again. Now it's like I finally have a partner in my little long distance circus."

"Not like a clown I hope."

"Like my ringleader," he said with a squeeze of her hand.

"Did you ever ask your mom why she drinks?"

He felt his mood harden instantaneously as he measured his words carefully. "No. It's her world."

"Maybe she has some fears too," she suggested. "And just needs someone to help her get off of her own tightrope."

He lifted the mug to his lips and gazed out the window without saying a word. An unexpected dizziness hit him hard when he suddenly battled the combined effects of the caffeine and thoughts spinning in his head.

Chapter 25

After a round of thunderstorms crashed throughout the night Brett awoke feeling fatigued from the draining effects of interrupted sleep patterns. But even worse than the startle of the thunder was the gripping cramps that had overtaken the runner in the dead of the night. He tenderly massaged his arches as they throbbed from the rampant contractions that had hit at the peak of the midnight storms. He had been fighting the usual battle of overtraining, but with Wickers' reassuring hand he still felt modestly in control of his own flesh and blood. Less could be said of his heart and the increasingly intense feelings he had towards Marie. He felt puppet-like as he danced a fine line between committing to her or distancing himself from his unwanted emotions. What am I afraid of? he thought to himself during his walk to the student lounge where he planned to meet up with the other runners.

By late spring it was as if he had been a part of the pack of runners forever, and he looked forward to another casual meeting with his friends. He had never felt as strong of a bond with a group in such a short period of time, but he still experienced an occasional apprehensiveness toward the true nature of the dynamics of the threesome. When he entered the nearly empty student lounge his instincts jumped to red alert when he noticed a gleam in Logan's eye.

"Naked – down the Avenue? Are you crazy, Logan?" said Rip incredulously in response to his friend's suggestion.

"Yeah, a naked mile! It'll be a new tradition," he said as he acknowledged Brett's entrance with a nod of his head. "We'll start from the park, head past the bars and loop back to my house.

It's my twenty-first birthday and I need to do something memorable."

"Like get arrested?" asked Brett when he chimed in with his first remark.

He ignored him and continued. "We'll wear masks of course and no one will know who we are."

"It'll be a blast," said Hollywood nearly backhanding Rip with a wild gesture. "We'll be legends."

Brett shook his head and laughed at the utter tawdriness of the proposed event. But tiring of the grind of school, running, and a bourgeoning relationship he needed nothing more than a carefree stress reliever. He saw them looking at him for his final stamp of approval and he knew that as elder statesmen of the group his words seemed to hold a bit more weight. "What the hell. I'm a mile short this week anyway."

High fives were had all around and the foursome quickly solidified their plans for the evening. The energy resonated throughout the room and they shared in the collective rush of excitement of the planned excursion. After finalizing the conspiracy the smallest of them piped in his final remarks. "Let's meet at the park at ten and be ready to rumble."

"What to wear… what to wear?" Brett said to himself when the impromptu meeting broke up shortly thereafter. He knew the right mask to be a very important touch and he needed to make a statement that would stand the test of time. A satisfied smile fell over his face when the definitive answer suddenly came to him.

Following a routine day of classes and a light workout the campus clock chimed ten o'clock as he trotted toward the park. With the usual evening fog drifting in from the lake, he felt the cool dampness nearly engulf his body. He squinted through the mist and barely made out the sculpted stone lions that stood guard over the park entrance. On this particular night the sculptures served the additional purpose of serving as an agreed upon starting point for the excursion. He stood silently and was struck by a stark feeling of betrayal, but reconsidered his wavering confidence knowing it would be taboo to break the morning pact. As the minutes ticked by he shivered in relief when he picked up on the peripheral movement that signaled the arrival of two more participants for the evening run.

"Brett, over here," called Hollywood as he motioned towards the lone park bench.

After reaching the bench he heard Rip's voice whispering from the dark shadows that covered the grounds. "Logan called me and said he was going to have a surprise for us. That worries me. I'm even afraid of what he's thinking even on his good days."

Logan spoke up right on cue after he almost magically surfaced in the darkness. "So I scare you do I? I never knew I could have that effect on people."

Brett could have sworn with the distant street lights burning in the distance that the little runner seemed almost aglow. But realizing his friends' far from angelic intentions for the upcoming event he waited for the anxious dialog to play its way out.

"Jeez, don't sneak up on me like that," said Rip. "I'm not so sure about this as it is."

"Don't flip out big-man," said Logan as he set down a small bag on the bench. "We're making history." The crumpled lunch bag only added mystery to the event and peaked the curiosity of the runners.

"What's in the bag?" said Hollywood motioning towards the suddenly intriguing package.

"Just something a little special for the occasion. I'll show you after we get our masks on."

Rip was the first to display his wares. "I had to go to my aunt's house to get this one and told her it was for a costume party." After turning his back to the other three he slowly returned to face them fully displaying a well-worn Buzz Lightyear mask. "Dang thing's hard to breathe through too."

Hollywood was up next. "I had to go to Goodwill to find mine. Retro is in and I found this stupid old happy face." He slipped on the yellow moon faced smile as his long hair cascaded over the plastic eyeholes.

"Somewhat ironic but I like it," said Brett with a laugh. "It's my turn now. As you all know I'm a little older and I felt the need to portray a more dignified image than you cretins." To emphasize his point he pulled the latex mask over his head and attempted to recreate a presidential legend. "My fellow American's, we are gathered today for this momentous occasion. I am proud to be part of this great affirmation of our right to the freedom of expression."

"Tricky Dick! How perfect," said Logan in admiration. "Where did you find that?"

"Back east we used to play a game called the 'Drinkin' Nixon's'. It was kind of like truth or dare, but if you were caught lying you had to put on the mask and do a shot."

"Drinkin' Nixon's," repeated Logan. "You sir, are a true patriot. But I also chose my mask in order to make a point. What could be a better choice than the largest of all beasts – the ancient dinosaur." He proudly slid a purple Barney mask over his face to the amusement of all.

Brett smiled and slowly shook his head. "I'll never view children's TV the same again. Now what about this big surprise you had for us?"

They all paced nervously in anticipation and waited while Logan retrieved his mystery package. Still hiding behind the park bench they braced as a cool lake breeze blew in and watched him rifle through the small bag. "Glow in the dark spray paint," he said excitedly as he waved the can in the air. "Could there be a better way to accent our units?"

"This is getting too weird," said Brett. He had been more than ready for a diversion to help sidestep the stresses that had been building inside, but with the final touches taking place he was suddenly unsure of the true merit of the excursion. He recognized the suspended adolescence of the adventure and looked to the heavens in hope that his father was somehow too occupied to view what he would surely classify as "locker room humor".

Logan seemed oblivious to his dilemma and laughed hysterically as he liberally sprayed the three organs with the pink paint. "That didn't take very much. I only hope there's enough left for me."

"Don't flatter yourself," said Hollywood as Logan inflicted himself with his own handiwork.

Fully engaged in the moment, Brett could only shake his head at the baseness of the production. His musing was interrupted by Logan soon after he finished his amateur artwork. "Say hello to my lil' friend," he said swaggering towards them as if he was a Tony Montano reincarnate.

"I think we can reach the house in five minutes," said Rip doing his best to ignore his friend. "Just don't get busted. If we get separated, just find your way back the best you can."

They lined up in the familiar starting crouch with Logan taking charge as the starter. He raised a single finger in the air to imitate a starting gun and prepared the runners for their unencumbered run. "Ready…set…go – nads!" he called.

They began their sprint from the park and crossed onto the edge of the avenue. Their nervous wails echoed in the cool air as they fast approached the first intersection. Cars honked when the runners entered the lit area, and they in turn waved as the pace picked up in accordance with the flood of adrenaline. They quickly found their stride and reached the cruising speed normally reserved for the collection of gear heads that routinely patrolled the campus streets.

"I think we're a hit," said Brett while he raised his fingers in the air to make the familiar Nixon victory sign. "I am not a crook!"

Rip laughed from under his Buzz Lightyear mask and joined in. "Infinity and beyond!"

They continued to stride past the crowds waiting to get into the college watering holes and laughter erupted from the students as they pointed to the streaking runners. Brett spied Marie's shocked face in the collection of students and could only hope she wouldn't recognize him as he completed the most juvenile of runs. He was relieved when he remembered the anonymity the mask afforded him and surged even faster when the rush of the run coursed through his veins. He surged past his friends and felt invigorated far beyond his expectations when the pace of the excursion hit its highest level yet.

"Have a nice day," shouted Hollywood through the smiley mask.

Logan noticed two girls peeking through their hands and he belted out his own version of Barney's well-known lyrics. "I love you...you love me," he called in his best sing-song.

The group spied a police car approaching and the mood of the expedition suddenly turned serious. With the sudden cry of the siren and the squealing u-turn of the squad car the runners quickly abandoned the set upon course.

"Cut between the houses and follow me," yelled Rip when he instinctively made a hard left.

They followed his lead and the trailing threesome ran the back alley as if they were entering the gun lap of a race. Brett instantly got up on his toes and pounded down the narrow passageway narrowly avoiding a crash into a set of dented garbage cans. The shrill squeal of a stray cat matched the pitch of the siren that still wailed threateningly in the distance. Their strides eased when they approached the safe haven of the final destination and they all reached for the crest of the battered alley fence.

"I'll lose my scholarship for sure if we get caught," moaned Hollywood as he struggled to get over the barrier.

"Shut up and keep moving," said Rip as he leapfrogged gracefully over the rusted metal fence.

Brett and Logan in turn scrambled over the carelessly strewn trash bags and stumbled in the dirt of the neglected backyard. Their sweat picked up an accumulation of filth from the ground before they quickly returned to their feet. They hopped up the steps of the rear entry way to the apartment and tried to control the breathing of another hard effort.

"Jesus, that was close," said Logan brushing the remnants of the yard off of his backside.

"But not a bad time at that," said Rip as he looked at his stopwatch. "4:48."

"Just for once can't you give it a rest?" asked Hollywood. "If we would've gotten nabbed, I could never have explained this one to my dad."

"I'm more worried about getting this stuff off," said Brett as he looked at his glowing unit. "It's evidence."

They all considered the dilemma they had gotten themselves into and considered the repercussions. After gingerly examining his own situation Logan blurted out his own solution. "I've got an idea. How about a little paint thinner?"

"Not on me you sick bastard." said Hollywood.

"It'll probably wear off in a few weeks," offered Rip. "Just stay out of the locker room so coach can't see your little pink wanker."

Brett looked over at his friends and decided the moment needed one final summarization. "I now declare the running of the first naked mile to be officially over. Unfortunately there was no winner but there are four losers. I nominate it to be an annual event at least until one of us gets arrested."

"I second the motion," said Hollywood as he raised his hand in a mock ceremonial fashion.

"A birthday celebration for the ages," said Logan with a truly contented look on his face.

As each runner tended to their own business Brett couldn't help but reflect on the crassness of the last hour of his life. But as the streetlights flooded through the windows, he realized how the frivolous nature of even a single mile could achieve the desired effect of loosening the noose of self-induced pressure.

Chapter 26

He backed through the glass door of the laundromat and dragged the heavy sack of clothes over the doorstep. While slowly making his way toward the rows of overworked machines he shook his head in disgust and surveyed the bleak surroundings of the Quickie Wash. He could scarcely believe that his night life had decayed to the extent of doing dirty laundry on a Saturday evening. "The loneliness of a long distance loser," he said to himself mockingly. He downplayed his plight by rationalizing that because he had an early morning run scheduled and Marie was out with friends he had more than enough built in excuses. With grudging acceptance he knew that at the very least the quiet night would allow him the necessary rest to help fill in another blank spot on his wall.

Through the dirty plate glass window he watched with envy as the crowds strolled by on their way to a night out on the town. He observed the couples holding hands and felt the sting of uncertainty when he thought about Marie. Their trust seemed implicit, but he knew firsthand the motives of the hormonally charged male patrons that prowled the neighborhood joints. He thought of snapping the rubber band on his wrist, but ultimately the faith he had in her quieted the unsettling thoughts.

After filling the machines with his faded clothing he rationed out the rest of his detergent, and when they quickly whirred into action he sat and listened to the low drone. Oddly enough he had always appreciated the hypnotic rumble that resonated throughout the laundromat and the sedating effect it had on him. It was when he was alone that he was most at ease and because of that he knew he had chosen the right sport. He soaked in the silence and let his mind drift through the events of the previous days. After his recent heart to heart with Marie, he had felt a subtle shift in his personal bedrock that had formed his foundation for so long. The crack in his privacy she had unwittingly created still resonated even within the calm of the evening. Without warning the sudden crash of an overturned chair from the back of the establishment quickly shattered the sedate nature of the setting. His internal alarm sounded when he spotted the eyes of an unknown intruder peering at him from over the rows of the white machines. He studied the unkempt hair and corkscrew beard of a disheveled vagrant and his alarm bell rang even louder. When the man stood up and slowly shuffled down the aisle the runner braced for an expected confrontation. Through half closed lids the man licked his cracked lips before he sputtered out his intentions. "Mister, can you spare a quarta'?"

The runner was shocked into silence when he was immediately assaulted by the overpowering stench of old sweat and liquor emanating from the homeless man. He swallowed his disgust and contemplated the likely liquid outcome of any donation before he decided on a different course. "What do you want it for?"

It was now the drifter's turn for silence and he seemed genuinely surprised at the question. He scratched at his scraggly beard while considering his response. "Jus' a cup of coffee," he slurred.

Normally he would have waived the bum off but the solitude of the evening seemed to soften his stance. "That I can help you with. And maybe something to eat too."

He could feel the wary eyes watching him as he pumped a series of quarters into the vending machines. After handing the coffee and a Snickers bar to the drifter, he took notice of the puzzled look on the man's face when he snatched up the food. When hunger overtook the man he devoured the candy bar before proceeding to lick the remnants off of his greasy fingers. He then sat down and from a safe distance sized up the runner. Decidedly non-threatened by the slight frame he knew the likelihood of a physical confrontation was minimal and he smiled through broken teeth. "Why you do dat?"

"I'm not sure," he replied. "I guess you just looked hungry."

"I gets enough. You jus' got to know where to look. Anyways... is that yours?" he questioned as he pointed to a crumpled sock under Brett's chair.

"No," he answered with a shake of his head. He leaned over and picked up the single sock before waving it towards the vagrant. The man quickly snatched at it and brushed the runner's hand before stuffing it into the oversized jacket already bulging with his most cherished belongings. The man saw him watching and cast a suspicious eye as if he was unsure of Brett's ultimate intentions. They studied each other in silence and the runner became suddenly aware of his own meager wardrobe. His typical uniform of aging jeans and a race t-shirt of years gone by matched up well with his nubby-less Nikes. When the silence continued he began to feel increasingly uncomfortable in the small space and was starting to regret his act of spontaneous generosity. As the foggy eyes of the man measured him the quiet was finally broken.

"You a college boy ain't cha'?"

"Yes."

"You goin' to be rich someday?" he said in more of a statement than a question.

"Doubtful," Brett replied with a smile.

The man sipped at the paper cup before responding again. "Yeah, you are. You gonna get a big house. Take care of your momma. I know it."

Brett didn't reply as he was becoming increasingly repulsed by the grime on the man's face and the colony of flakes salting his hair. Even though he knew it to be nonsensical, he wondered if a man of this sort even *had* a mother. Further, if he did, was it even possible there could be any kind of a relationship whatsoever? He couldn't help but wonder how the man had gotten to this point and yet he sensed the drifter was almost content with his lot. With seemingly little in common the runner still succumbed to a strange need and began his own line of questioning. "Where do you stay?"

"Lotsa places. Mostly by the river. I got a spot," said the drifter in a secretive manner.

"Sometimes I go there too," he replied. He saw the concern in the man's eyes and clarified his remark. "On the trails." The man visibly exhaled when the threat to his well-hidden home lessened. He wondered what the man could possess that could possibly be of interest to anyone until he thought of his own five dollar poster. "One man's treasure," he remarked to himself.

"What you say?"

"Ahh…nothing."

When the man finally stood up he blinked at the runner as he edged in closer. The smell of alcohol wafted from the man's sour breath and hit Brett harshly in the face. He felt the aroma awaken a buried portion of his past as the battle between revulsion and attraction reared an angry head. He still hadn't had a drink in months, but the craving still came in waves at the most unexpected of times. After a hard test…a successful workout…a lonely night in the library …and now after an encounter with an alcoholic panhandler. He suddenly wished the man would disappear into the cracks from which he had surfaced so that he could re-discover the balance he had so painstakingly achieved.

"Any more quarta's?" the man asked as he jarred Brett from his flashback.

"No," he replied firmly as he stared into the lost eyes that confronted him. The man dropped his gaze and began the slow shuffle towards the door in search of his next contributor. Brett watched him through the smeared window until he disappeared into the darkness, but upon remembering the touch of the drifter's hand he felt a sudden need to be cleansed. He quickly made his way to the public sink where he vigorously scrubbed off all traces of the man that had infected his world. While licking his dry lips he looked in the tiny mirror over the basin and studied the unsettled reflection it captured. Unable to escape the feeling of being soiled, he looked down and noticed the barely perceptible tremors in his hands. He squeezed his eyes shut and clenched down on the rim of the chipped porcelain until they began to slowly subside. He stayed that way until the washer buzzer echoed in the air and jolted him back to the starkness of the reality at hand.

Chapter 27

With the sun beginning a slow descent through the cloudless sky the runners caught the final rays of the day. As they stretched out on Hollywood's patchwork front lawn they reminisced about the recently completed track season. Their spirits were high and they happily reflected on the outdoor track championship that had been delivered to the university's doorstep. Thoroughly enjoying the respite from the stress of training, the collegiate athletes felt the burden of competition lifted from their shoulders.

"We sure as hell made Wickers' year," stated Hollywood. "'Coach of the Year' and hardware for the trophy case. I never thought I'd see the old boy get so emotional."

"You got to admit it was pretty cool," interjected Rip. "He may have his moods but at least you know he cares. Brett, you should've been there for his victory speech on the way back to Milwaukee."

Brett looked on in silence and watched the runners become increasingly animated. He thought back to his own collection of bus rides home from distant competitions and suddenly missed the shared camaraderie and spontaneity of team victories.

"Yeah," said Logan, "we were all just screwing around when he stood up to face us with this big 'ol cup of coffee in his hand. At first I thought he was going to get on us for the noise until I saw him smile at us. Then he takes off his baseball hat and I'll be damned if I almost said something about the size of his head. It was bigger than a Halloween punkin' and almost the same color. He even has this liver spot on his skull that's shaped sort of like a dog turd."

"What did he say?" said Brett as his interest was sufficiently peaked.

"I doubt I can do it justice," Logan responded as the other runners started to giggle.

"Go ahead," urged Hollywood, "I want to hear it again."

Logan smiled as he stood up and dramatically cleared his throat in an attempt to lower his voice an octave or two. "Gentlemen," he quoted the old coach, "I can't begin to tell you how much this championship means to a saggy old bastard like myself. Success ain't easy …nor should it be. But the fight you showed today tickled my innards more than Mary Lou did in the closet back at good 'ol St. Alphonsus. Today I was proud to watch all of you bark with the big dogs until they turned tail and cowered in the woods.

"First off," he continued in his imitation of the coach, "my weight men. You threw the implements better than those steroid-packed cro-magnums you competed against. Remember how I told you there was a way to make me *and* your girlfriends happy at the same time?"

"Technique, technique, technique," answered Rip and Hollywood in unison.

"Correct." he replied enthusiastically. "And you sprinters. You may have caused me to down a case of Pepto-Bismol during the season, but today I think the track still has scorch marks on it from the vapors you left behind. Those cocky sum-bitches from Illinois were so far behind they had to sniff like coon dogs to find their way to the finish line.

"And I can't forget the distance boys," Logan continued in a deep voice. "None of you weigh more than one of my thighs but you put a tear in my eye with your performances. First you, Hollywood. You may be as purty as a 'fancy boy' but you showed me so much 'spit' on the track today I'd give you odds against my mean old granpappy even after he had a snoot full of bourbon.

"And you Rip," he continued as Hollywood giggled in the background, "after watching you run I'd weigh your marbles against a Pygmy I saw once in a *National Geographic*. He had some sort of gonad-al elephantitis and had to use a gold-darn wheelbarrow to carry his-self around in. But I expect he had nothing on you."

"Anything about you, Logan?" Brett asked the storyteller with a laugh.

"I'll take it from here," volunteered Hollywood. He puffed out his cheeks and forced the blood to rush into his face as he forged on to recapture Wickers' victory speech. "Christopher," he started as he used the small runner's first name, "I couldn't be prouder of you after your victory in the mile than if you were my very own son. But as I've told you before it ain't the victory I value, but the fight you put into the tryin'. Deservedly so today you won on both counts. And as undoubtedly your legend at this university will live on forever, so will the memory of you in my heart."

"You're going to make me cry," sniffed Brett. "I wish I could have been there."

"I have to admit the old man does get it going sometimes," said Logan. "But the best was at the end when he put his cup in the air to toast us and spilled some coffee on his crotch."

"Let me finish," pleaded Rip as he took his turn standing up. After taking a deep breath and inflating his gut he raised an imaginary coffee cup to the sky in a mock toast before pantomiming a sudden spill onto his vitals. Using a gravelly voice he completed the coach's speech. "Damn, I just hope the 'beans' ain't too cooked to perform tonight 'cause I got me one hell of a big present for the Missus!"

"We laughed so hard I almost tossed my Big Mac," admitted Hollywood with a shake of his head.

"You guys deserved it," said Brett as he imagined the pandemonium on the victorious bus ride home. "I only wish I could have been there." When their laughter faded into the breeze they returned to the task at hand and focused on the impending run that would put the final stamp on the season.

"Everybody ready?" asked Logan after he hopped up from the ground and brushed the dirt off of his shorts. "Us peons better help get Mr. Olympic Trials a few miles in before it gets dark."

Brett shook his head in silence at a total loss for words. After having admitted his trials qualifying status at the lakeside party,

161

they still hadn't allowed him the ability to live it down. Somehow though it had strengthened the bond of the runners because they now all shared the responsibility of assisting one of their own.

"Rex is still flipping about the trials," said Hollywood with a satisfied smile. "He's not the big dog anymore and he can't handle it. Of course thanks to you he took it out on us all season."

"Sorry guys," apologized Brett. "Next time I'll slow down so I don't cause any trouble."

"It was worth every minute seeing that guy knocked down a peg," said Rip. "But I wouldn't worry about Rex. I got a feeling what goes round comes round. Anyways, what do you guys think about doing the river trails today?"

"Perfect," said Hollywood. "It'll be nice and cool in there."

The trails were a special treat to the runners with the soft contours a welcome relief from the pounding of the roads. The forgiving ground and meandering route always helped the miles melt by quickly. They started off with a slow stride and by the time they approached the woods they had all turned off their competitive instincts in anticipation of an easy run.

"Watch out for the potholes," said Rip. "None of us needs an ankle sprain today." Even though not specifically directed toward anyone, the true target of the statement seemed more than obvious. Luckily, Brett had been surprisingly injury-free since he had begun running under the watchful eye of Coach Wickers. He had experienced the usual aches in nearly every muscle group in his lower torso, but had been able to escape any dramatic alteration of his training schedule. Only the bothersome tug in his hamstring demanded a daily accounting for and served as a daily reminder of the sins of his youth.

"Don't worry about me - I'm as nimble as a Fin," said Brett recollecting his own imaginary trail runs with the legendary Finlander Lasse Viren.

They ran for miles through the undulating terrain and the narrow path forced them to form a single line to accommodate its width. As the twigs cracked underfoot, the leaves that had found their way to the earthen floor added their own distinctive crackle to the sounds of the run. The runners silently absorbed the unmistakable fragrances of the surrounding greenery and soaked in the damp thickness of the humid air. Only the knotted roots that dotted the dirt path held out any semblance of a threat to the serenity that had fallen onto the pack. When Brett noticed the many trails that wound through the woods he wanted to tell them to take the path less traveled, but felt his fractured rendering of Robert Frost would fall upon deaf ears. It was natural to let Logan lead the way as the runner seemed to have a natural compass built into his small frame. Brett followed his lead and the odor of the stagnant river brought back the memory of his brush with the laundromat drifter. He couldn't help but wonder if the group would literally run into his secret hideaway in the banks. To this point he had chosen to keep the news of his encounter quiet from the other runners when he decided privacy was important no matter what status in life one held. His philosophical musing was interrupted by a loud groan from Hollywood at the rear of the line.

They were ready to question him when he suddenly veered off the trail and started a stiff-legged walk into the woods. "Damn, I think I'm paying for the bag of Chips Ahoy I ate while watching 'Jerry Springer' this morning. I feel like one of those hillbillies on his show," he said rushing into the woods.

With a knowing laugh Rip called out to his rapidly disappearing friend. "Careful of the poison oak or you'll be standing for a week." They had all been in a similar predicament themselves and waited patiently while swatting at the armies of bugs swarming their moist skin. When Hollywood crashed through the bramble moments later he sported an unusually concerned look on his face.

"Are you gonna be okay?" asked Logan as he openly worried about his friend's well being.

"I think a spider bit my ass," replied Hollywood.

"Maybe that'll teach you a lesson," said Brett.

"It's great that you have such a balanced diet," said Rip. "I hope at least you had some milk with them."

"Mountain Dew. But at least I got a good sugar buzz out of it," Hollywood explained as he shoed away a horsefly that had honed in on his scent.

Brett thought of his own barren refrigerator that currently only protected flour tortillas and a super-sized jar of Skippy. Anything to fuel the fire he had often rationalized knowing full well he could get away with a few missteps in his diet due to his astronomical caloric demands. He thought back to breakfast and sheepishly calculated nearly a thousand calories devoured between the bowls of Cap'n Crunch and a handful of Marie's home-baked cookies. As usual running was the great equalizer for his enormous appetite or "food hole" as she had once so eloquently labeled it. He remembered laughing at the phrase, but it did little to slow him from clearing the load of spaghetti from her plate.

When they began again he formulated a related question that had of late been increasingly on his mind. He was currently composing a paper on performance enhancing substances for long distance runners, and he was curious what a straw poll of friends would divulge. With the outbreak of banned and accused athletes emerging from all corners of the globe, the question of doping was on the forefront of many competitors' minds. Brett himself had been careful of ingesting any supplement aside from an assortment of low budget Walgreen's vitamins. Once after downing a handful of the tablets he bragged to Marie that he surely had the "most expensive piss in town". Willfully ignoring his own hesitancy toward any other supplement, the quiet of the run emboldened him to break taboo and ask a rare thoughtful question.

"What do you guys think about doping to get better?"

Just as Brett had expected Rip was the first to break the awkward pause. "Hell, no. It ain't right and what's worse it wouldn't feel right even if it helped. And I don't understand how those guys can even look in the mirror much less step onto a victory stand. They oughta be ashamed of themselves. So…I just wouldn't do it."

"Tell us what you really think," interjected Logan as he picked up on the conversation. "Personally I never really considered it. Man, running is supposed to be fun and if you have to do 'roids to feel good what's the point? Anyways, I plan on whipping everybody au natural."

Brett smiled and added his own thoughts. "Big talk from a little man. But I agree with you. Sometimes I think of running as the last pure sport left. Nothing but an eight ounce pair of shoes on your feet and an open road ahead. Call me weird, but sometimes when I'm running I feel stripped down to the bare essentials of existence. And if I doped, I would be contaminating my own groundwater."

"You're right. You are freakin' weird," agreed Logan. "Not to mention I don't even know what the hell you just said."

"Never mind," Brett replied with a smile. "Hollywood, how about you?"

He was slow in responding and Brett noted the discomfort in his face. "I never really thought about it."

The lack of conviction in his voice led Brett to believe Hollywood might be a bit more ethically challenged than the rest. He couldn't help but wonder if the "silver spoon" upbringing of his friend had led to a deep seated feeling of entitlement that might embrace the "end justifies the means" adage. Still…as far as he knew the edgy runner was as clean as the rest of them. When the topic had run its course Brett was almost sorry he had darkened the mood of the run.

"A couple more miles?" he asked the leader in an attempt to change the topic.

"About two more," said Logan, "that is if you can handle the bugs." He swatted fiercely through the air and his emotions were accented by another cry from the rear of the group.

"Ptoey," spit Rip suddenly as he fought off the effects of a swallowed mosquito.

"A little protein?" asked Brett. "You thinking about starting the Atkin's diet?"

"I'd rather swallow a 'skeeter' any day than have a spider up my butt," said Hollywood unsympathetically as he brushed a low hanging branch out of the way.

Amid the flying insects they soon continued the run in the quiet of the woods. They knew the reserves of adrenaline needed for the hard workouts were a byproduct of simple aerobic efforts like today. The talking dwindled as the shimmer of the leaves and ripple of the aspen mellowed their thoughts. With the muffled footsteps of the trails coming to an end, Brett summarized the miles. "A nice run for the head," he said, "and chicken soup for the legs."

"There you go again," complained Logan.

"I'll try to keep it a little simpler in the future my little ectomorph," he promised.

"You calling me an insect? Cut out the smart crap and just talk normal."

"Okay, okay…I just mean it was a good run for all of us."

"Easy for you to say," Hollywood said as he scratched at the puncture mark left by the spider.

Brett smiled as they slowed to a walk when the run was completed. He welcomed the wave of contentment that washed over him and he relished the completion of the most important task of the day. But as he watched Hollywood inspect the spreading redness of the bite, he realized that even the easy runs held no guarantee of going unblemished.

Chapter 28

Marie settled onto the splintered stands of the stadium and squinted in the summer sun as she watched Brett start into his methodical preparation for the task at hand. Her eyes followed him as he jogged through his warm-up and she shook her head in disgust at the stories he had told her only moments earlier. Frightened dogs...dented cars...and poor dripping boys were not something she found particularly humorous. She knew she could never understand the juvenile nature of their experiences and wondered if he would ever grow up as long as he stayed with the group of runners he had grown so attached to. Yet, she had difficulty rectifying that it was his curious mixture of maturity and childlike spirit that had attracted her in the first place. She re-focused on him after his preparation was complete and he began his attack on the track with a startling ferocity.

She had seen him perform the ritual many times before. After he completed the first few circuits, she watched him recover between laps with his chest heaving and hands on his knees. She saw the suffering he readily inflicted on himself and wondered why anyone would put themselves through such agony. Then after a brief rest between quarter miles, his raspy breathing returned close to normal and off he would go again. When he finished each lap she watched him pounce on his stopwatch as if time was a silent and mortal enemy before he called out the lap times for her to record. He stared unblinkingly at the glowing numbers and would then either nod in acceptance or mutter a vulgarity under his breath. "56.2, 57.1, 57.3, 56.9," she said aloud as she read off his first set of times. The numbers meant little to her, but by the harshness in his voice she knew that to him they were as vital as sustenance to a starving man. She studied him on his slow walk between laps and could see his face slowly aging from the intensity of the effort. She found the sickly, pale look completely unappealing, yet couldn't look away from the event as it unfolded. "56.1, 57.2, 58.1, 57.0," she repeated to herself after his second set of quarters. After emitting a deep sigh, she admitted to herself she had no understanding how he could drive himself to such an extreme effort. She had drive too she thought. The midnight studies…the cramming for tests … she knew all about having drive. But she had a purpose. A career to have. A contribution to society. But just to run? To run harder? To run faster? To make yourself hurt? It didn't make sense to her and deep down knew that maybe it never would.

She could not understand the power running had over his soul. Once he sheepishly tried to explain to her that when he ran it felt like the air was cleaner and the sun shone a bit brighter. He tried to tell her about the flowing of his thoughts and feelings that intensified as the miles accumulated. As he had talked she wondered if she was ever a part of those explosions of thought. But she was afraid to ask the question.

After completing the final set he jogged over to her and she caringly offered him his water bottle. "56.8, 57.9, 58.2, and 55.9," she read off to him as he approached. Noting the fatigue in his eyes, she was surprised he could still even manage a semblance of a smile. Somehow he felt good about his current state even with the pain he had just initiated on his own being.

"Thanks," he said as he gulped down the water in a feeble attempt to quench his thirst.

She watched the excess liquid drip from the corners of his mouth and became aware of the blotchy pigmentation that checkered his face. "Are you ok?"

"Hell, yeah," he replied with a tired smile. "Never been better." He tossed her the bottle and once again forced his legs to a shaky start. "Just wait ten minutes for me to cool down. I'll be back before you know it."

Wait ten more minutes today and for the next run tomorrow, she thought angrily. But she knew she would sit passively in the stands just as she had done so many times before. She watched him from a distance and realized it was as if he emitted some addictive chemical that would keep her coming back for more. When he finished his cooldown laps he sat down next to her and toweled off his lean body with a faded race t-shirt of years gone by. He absently picked at a loose spike from the bottom of his flats and tossed it to her before speaking. "Here…a souvenir for your charm bracelet."

"Thanks, every girl's dream," she said while examining the small object nestled in the palm of her hand. "I hope you know I could find a lot better things to do than to watch you leave your blood on this old track."

"Ahh, poetry in motion. Pure poetry in motion."

"Bad poetry, maybe. I can't even begin to guess what you're thinking about when you're out there running so hard," she said to him seriously.

He paused before answering and looked at the track with a pensive expression. "I don't know if I really think," he started. "Somehow I just focus on the pain of the run and go deeper into it. Like it's some black tunnel that I have to claw through. I don't hear or see anything when I'm in it, but just keep pushing until I hit the white line. Then it's almost as if the tunnel ends and the light reappears."

As he toweled his face some more she spoke. "You're getting pretty deep for a physiology major."

He ignored her and continued. "Sometimes I feel as if I want to punish myself to see what I can handle. To see if I can make it one more lap… one more straightaway…one more step…one second faster. It's a challenge that never ends, but it's the only way I know that I can use the Gift. Sometimes I even wonder what the 'Kid' is doing in his own training. I pretend he's half a step ahead of me and it makes me fight harder lap after lap. Like he's a carrot and I'm the damn rabbit chasing him." He paused when he almost told her that even in practice he didn't always catch him. "I doubt he realizes some half-assed runner two thousand miles away is racing him every day. Still… even after a hard workout like today I feel so damn alive it's like everything is going to be okay. I know it's only running, but it makes me feel like I have a place in the world. Like I matter."

She looked at the resolve in his eyes and the contentment that nearly resonated from his being. "You'd matter to me – even if you didn't run," she finally said.

He grasped her hand and looked her straight in the eye. "I've known that since our first date...and that's why I love you," he said in a soft voice. He turned away quickly as if he had inadvertently revealed more than he had intended. The power of the words blindsided her and it was all she could do to muster a short squeeze of his hand. He seemed to need to escape as he stammered: "I have to get the rest of my stuff."

She watched him trot over to get his gear and wished she would have told him how she felt, but knew the time for that had passed. She stared at the solitary track spike resting in her palm and knew someday she would let him in on the depths of her own feelings. But that time wasn't now.

"Time," she said to herself. "With him it's always about time."

Chapter 29

With the decreased load of classes in the summer he had been able to step up the training to a full scale assault on peak fitness. His time in Milwaukee had been his best since his father's passing and he wished only that it would continue. With the balance of school, friends, and the increasing depth of his feelings for Marie, his life was finally on firmer footing. He also knew his conditioning was at an all-time high and his confidence did not lag far behind. In an attempt to better measure them both, he had decided to enter a local 5K event in order to continue sharpening for the demands of the upcoming Olympic Trials. The well thought out plan included mimicking his competitive race routine even down to the wearing of his post-race "500 mile club" t-shirt that his father had awarded him in high school. When he approached the park he took a deep breath to calm his increasingly agitated nervous system and began to forge the necessary racing mind-set.

He walked hesitantly toward the check-in area to claim his bib number and immediately felt out of his comfort zone. He rarely raced the local events because of his preference for the controlled world of the track and its inherent rhythm that was uninterrupted by hills, turns, and changes in terrain. From early on he thrived on the long flat grind of the track and pictured himself sinking his teeth into the oval's flesh and not letting go until the final straightaway was conquered. Conversely, he viewed road races as an unpredictable creature with far too many variables to manage. But with only three weeks to go before the trials, he recognized he was seriously short of the race work that was crucial in sharpening his skills. Aside from the scattered regional races and regular time trials, only the upcoming Milwaukee Invite was still penciled in on his competitive docket. He gained comfort in knowing that he was reaching his peak when earlier in the week he had ripped off a solo 3:58.8 mile witnessed only by a solitary walker circling the outside of the track. The excitement of that achievement was tempered by the realization that an empty pocket book eliminated the ability to travel to any high caliber national meets. He knew from experience there was no substitute for racing and that the intensity it demanded was always well beyond even the hardest of workouts. He felt the usual quivering in his gut when he realized the time was becoming scant for him to get hardened to the physical and emotional stress he would soon be experiencing at an unprecedented level.

He had purposely chosen the Lakefront 5K because it had a reputation for being a fast course and he had heard that all of the local hotshots were anticipated to race. After studying the masses he recognized a few of them to be "Badgerland Striders" members and still others from their visits to the store. He knew that he would be an unknown at today's race just like he would at the trials, and he had chosen to register under a pseudonym to help maintain his current underdog status. In a further attempt to stay under the radar he found a quiet place in a nearby park to begin his own idiosyncratic warm-up routine for the evening event. He felt the beat of his heart as his internal clock counted down to the beginning of the race.

"Five minutes until the start," called the race director through the bullhorn. "All runners please report to the starting line."

The pack slowly accumulated and the usual pre-race jitters were evident in the mass of runners. He was unaccustomed to racing with athletes of average ilk, and although he found the circus-like atmosphere of the event strange, it was also somehow refreshing. He studied the wide variety of body-types and knew that only a handful could relate to his abilities, and a more casual runner would view him as some sort of aerobically endowed genetic freak. As he walked toward the starting line he tucked away the random thoughts and focused his nervous energy by raising the needed powers of concentration to an alert pitch. He willfully lifted his excitement to the top of the bell curve, but knew anything beyond that was just over revving the engine and would waste valuable emotional fuel. When the runners began to line up he eased to the front and was greeted with the usual good luck wishes from the other nearby competitors. He had long ago refrained from offering or accepting the pleasantries when he realized it was only a hollow gesture that was void of any genuine meaning. When he stepped to the starting line the faces became a blurred opposition that he wanted to crush the breath out of one step at a time. He remembered his father preaching about the "controlled aggression" of the distance runner and he purposely hid his fierce determination behind a blank expression. Under his father's tutelage he had learned that racing was a passive activity only to the casual runner, and that by contrast those who chose to become champions needed to be able to parcel out their anger and fire one step at a time. His father had believed that even if in the race, the flame somehow began to diminish, the strong willed runner could find a way to summon the necessary adrenaline to help restore the heat. Brett had learned the time for goodwill was after the race when the pool of runners re-lived the experience of the common ground they had just covered. With those thoughts in tow he was now ready to go to war.

"Runner's on your mark…get set…go!" shouted the starter with the blast of a gun. He settled in the rear of the front pack and drafted behind the wall led by a well tanned runner. He had set a goal pace of 4:30 per mile and thought fourteen minutes would be achievable on the relatively flat course. When the initial jolt to his system faded, he allowed his breathing to regulate slowly, and the noise of the well-wishers was soon all but blocked out. He recognized his nearness to the desired zone when he felt the steady pound of his heartbeat and the subsequent melting away of his racing-induced anxiety. The pack formed through simple attrition and quickly settled into half a dozen runners able to stride at the required pace set by the leader. He intentionally stayed out of trouble at the rear of the group and carefully watched the tangle of flailing arms and legs. The amoeba-like movement of the pack transformed itself into a single line and he studied the leader from ten yards back. The runner in first place seemed unafraid to carry the race and it wasn't long before Brett felt the irresistible need to regain contact with the pacesetter. He maneuvered around the other runners to quickly make up lost ground and shook the remainder of the leading group from his internal rear view mirror. He was content to perch himself on the runner's tan shoulder and they both strode boldly down the open road fully engaged in the moment. When the morning sun split the clouds the second place runner suddenly recognized the smooth stride of the frontrunner.

"Mornin' Rex," he said calmly as he approached the leader's right flank. "The name's Brett…with two t's. Remember?"

Rex appeared visibly startled as he glanced toward the relaxed runner at his side. Brett had to battle the surge of adrenaline that hit him and he braced for the impending challenge he had wished for since the day they had met. When the aftershock of the chance meeting simmered the two opponents settled down to the business at hand with Rex feeling the need for a pushing of the pace and a resulting half-step lead.

"4:28…4:29," shouted the volunteer at the mile marker. Right on schedule, Brett thought. He used a pointed index finger to wipe the salty sweat from his brow and studied the outward appearance of his nemesis. His breathing was still comfortable so he knew fitness was not an issue, but the years had taught him the mind was often another story altogether. After rounding a sharp turn, Brett surged hard and quickly opened up a threatening five meter gap. He waited for Rex's response and just as he had expected he soon heard the return of his competitor's breath. He recognized round one as a draw and began to feel the pain of the effort himself, but was able to block it out before throwing his second roundhouse. The surge seemed to stagger the faltering runner and the new leader no longer felt the bond of competition in his soul. He committed a cardinal sin of running by peeking behind and catching a look at Rex's suddenly struggling gait. But when an instant later the second place runner glanced back to the trailing pack Brett knew the competitive rope had been cut. His experience told him he had broken the other runner's spirit and unless he faded himself he was likely to be the victor on this day. When he passed the two mile mark in 9:05 he knew any celebration of victory was premature and braced himself for the remainder of the effort. He resigned himself to the steady descent into pain and settled into a runner's own lonely version of slow death. Rarely had he run a race he could describe as pleasurable, and as he continued to pound away at the pre-ordained pace was acutely aware this race would be no different.

To the untrained observer his stride still looked effortless and he knew they had no concept of the true emotional battle being fought even by an elite runner like himself. It was unnatural to run this hard and he had to focus intently on the task at hand. He grit his teeth as the effort intensified and he felt the familiar black tunnel start to set in. But just as he had planned before the race, it was now time to visualize another runner on his hit list.

"I'm still here," he rasped in an imaginary conversation with the Kid, "and I'm not …going…away."

When he bared his teeth his breath came in short gasps. He continued his attack on the ghostly crimson singlet and got on his toes before beginning his drive to the finish line. He sank deeper into the darkness and drove down the final straightaway as he came abreast of the shadow of the Kid.

"Stevie, no!" shouted a woman as she grabbed a small child that had run under the flags of the finishing chute. The interruption snapped the runner out of his trance and he narrowly avoided crashing into the confused child. He slowed to cruising speed and before smoothly striding through the victory ribbon he eyed the overhead clock as it read 13:58.

He immediately bent over with his hands on his knees and gasped for the air that he so desperately needed. The sharp stabs of his breathing startled the volunteers at the finish line, but he waved them off knowing his suffering would end shortly. When he was finally able to straighten up he felt the satisfaction of humbling Rex, but his mind was drawn back to the still unfinished battle with the Kid. It's not over yet, he vowed to his distant rival…not by a long shot.

Chapter 30

He opened the door after an insistent knock interrupted his studies and stepped aside when an unexpected visitor barged into his apartment. "Did you see the paper today? Some guy kicked Rex's ass in the Lakefront 5K and ran a 13:58!" said Logan excitedly as he plopped into Brett's bean bag chair. "I didn't recognize the name but it was something weird."

"Not a bad time. Maybe I should have entered," he replied halfheartedly while closing up his book.

"Damn straight. It would do you some good to quit sniffing the track all day and come mingle with the unwashed."

"Maybe someday, Logan. I guess I'm just a creature of habit."

He watched as his friend's eyes wandered over the humble décor of the apartment and when the rattle of a secondhand air conditioner blew cool air into the room he waited for his friend's appraisal of his belongings. "Hey, is that your workbench?" he finally asked with a wave towards the mattress on the floor. "I bet you and Marie burn off some calories on that puppy."

He looked at the old mattress settled snugly into the corner of the room and could still recall the dumpster that he had reclaimed it from. He remembered how he justified that by using the old bedding it would help him to "stay hungry" in his continuing quest to toughen his resolve. When he thought about his friend's question it dawned on him that Marie had yet to complain about the bed's meager support on those rare nights she had chosen to stay over. "It's not like that with her," he answered as truthfully as he could. "Somehow it's different...like it's okay to wait or something."

"Wait? Hell, if I'm on a date I can hardly wait until the pizza's wiped off my face before the dangle is letting me know he's hungry too."

"Logan, you're such a barbarian. With guys like you around it's a wonder the campus isn't filled with lesbians."

The oversexed runner writhed as he rolled on the floor. "Oh man...two chicks together. That is so hot."

"You're utterly hopeless," he said as he fought unsuccessfully to contain a smile.

"Actually, I'm quite the opposite. I see myself as extremely hopeful. But how about you? Are you getting nervous at all about the trials?"

He ran his fingers through his shaggy, uncombed hair and weighed the legitimate question asked by his friend. Reaching a physical and mental peak was an inexact science, but he was confident he had done all he could to arrive in the competitive crosshairs at just the right time. "I wouldn't say I'm really nervous yet, but for the first time in awhile I feel I've done the work and nothing can get in the way. My legs are good and after next week's invite I'll start to taper. And as bizarre as this may sound, meeting all you guys has finally given me a feeling of having solid ground under my feet. And for that I'll always be grateful."

"Hey, you did the work. We just took turns trying to keep up with your bony white ass."

He smiled at the remark and knew it was time to come clean with his friend. He had never found it easy to admit even the tiniest personal flaw, but as he stood over his friend he prepared himself for an unvarnished confession. He looked at the "Pre" poster for strength and recognized that he had been able to stay true to the quote that had first motivated him nearly a year ago. "And by doing so you kept my head on straight. It didn't always used to be that way."

Logan looked at him with a knowing smile on his face before he shrugged in a nonchalant manner. "We kind of guessed that."

"You what?"

His friend looked at him and carefully measured the surprised expression looming from above. "Relax, buddy. It's just that you're sort of secretive about your past. For awhile we thought you were in the mob out east and came here in a witness protection program or something. Then we realized it was probably just some personal stuff." As his voice softened he continued. "And we all noticed how you seemed a bit nervous at our parties and never even had a beer."

The remark caught him by surprise and he struggled for a response. "It was that obvious?" he asked looking away as if to hide his embarrassment. "I should have told you a long time ago, but I found out the hard way that drinking just doesn't work for me."

It was his friend's turn to measure his words and he looked thoughtfully at the older runner. "There's nothing wrong with that. In fact we think you're more of a stud because you've kept things under control."

Brett rubbed at his temples somehow hoping that he could massage away an impending headache. "You know I never judge you guys," he said as he looked toward his friend. He thought back to the carefree looks on his friend's faces after they indulged in another barstool game of "quarters" and spoke with a trace of regret. "In fact I sometimes envy the fact that you can handle it better than me."

Logan settled deeper into the chair before responding. "We're just screwing around. My personal motto is, 'Run fast, die young, and leave a skinny corpse'. But actually you're not missing all that much. Hell, hanging out with Hollywood isn't always the joy it seems. Anyway, I know firsthand how things can get out of control."

"What do you mean by that?"

He fixed a stare at the ceiling as if searching for a written word that would help him get started.

"Do you remember how I told you my dad owned a bar?" he asked. When Brett nodded silently in acknowledgement he continued. "Well, for awhile he pretty much worked all the time to help get it started. The pub was near the power plant and dad would tend the bar for most of the day so that all three shifts could stop in for a 'quick one' after work. Pretty soon he got so used to the regulars buying him shots that he became less of an owner and more one of the boys. I was just a kid but I remember mom getting worried about him. She says he nearly lost the bar but that he quit cold turkey when my sister was born. I'm not sure what happened but I think there was some kind of accident that happened with her that my folks will never talk about. And he's been clean ever since…except that he still smokes like a freakin' fiend."

Brett smiled at his last remark before responding. "I give your dad credit because I bet it wasn't easy. In fact I'm sure it wasn't."

"If it's something worthwhile, it never is," reflected Logan as he paraphrased his coach. "Anyway, just keep your mojo clean and let me do all the dirty work. I know it might be better for us to be choir boys, but I just have too damn much fun. But when it comes to the track I don't think the nights out ever get in the way. If they do, I hope you'll rap me upside the head. Or at least have Marie me a little 'spanky' on my bottom," he said in a return to his more typical persona.

"You have such a fertile mind. Just watch where you plant your seeds," Brett warned.

"I've always seen myself as a kind of aerobic 'Johnny Appleseed'," he bragged as he elevated his legs on the wall and studied the data it contained. "Man, look at this book you've written. What will your landlord say when he sees it?"

"He probably can't even read. Anyways what's he going to do? Take me to court and claim my dented toaster oven?" I'm just using this old wall to remind me of the prize. But claiming it is another thing."

"How fast do you think you can run? From what it says here you're more than ready to kick a little ass."

Brett felt the tension freeze up his shoulders at the mere thought of the ultimate competition on the horizon. With an instantaneous quickening of his pulse as a consequence of the brief jolt of adrenaline, he blew out a puff of air to help stabilize the rush. "I'm not sure," he said in a halting voice. "I guess I'll just have to see." He kept secret his goal time of 13:25 that he had scribbled on a dozen post-it notes hidden in a variety of places including the medicine cabinet and the inside of his refrigerator. Decidedly uncomfortable in disclosing his lofty goals aloud, he shifted topics by tugging at his suddenly sagging pants. "I do know one thing for sure and that is I'm getting skinny as shit. Marie says I look like some starving rap star as low as my pants are hanging these days. The other day I swear some guy started hitting on me almost as if I was trying to show him something."

"Be careful how you dress or you may even have Hollywood knocking on your door soon. He spends so much time checking out what other guys are wearing I worry about him switching teams."

"I wouldn't concern yourself with that," said Brett as he moved toward the front window to check on the street action below. "He'll never find anyone he thinks is as good looking as he is."

"Yeah, I guess you're right," admitted Logan. "He's my partner in slime. Did I tell you last week we went online and got some Victoria's Secret closeouts? I look so damn good in this little red teddy I got *myself* hot. I'm saving it for Halloween."

He tried to ignore the bad visual that his friend had just supplied, but admired the boldness of the plan. "Just don't let Wickers see you or he'll revoke your scholarship on the basis of 'gender confusion'."

"Nah, Wick and I have an understanding. He's afraid to ask and I ain't stupid enough to tell. Actually I think he's secretly sweet on me."

"I bet that's news to his wife," Brett suggested as he stepped over the books that were scattered haphazardly throughout the room.

"They're always the last to know," Logan sighed. "Anyways, I wanted to let you know we'll all be at the trials going ballistic. But you got to do me a favor. If you meet any chickie sprinters with bone crushing thighs looking for a cheap date, you gotta hook me up. I heard --,"

"Logan, it's time for you to go," he said as he pulled his friend up from the chair. "I need to study."

"But I just want to expand my horizons."

"I know what you want to expand. Now please. I have a test tomorrow," Brett pleaded as he led him to the door.

"I'm going, I'm going," said the runner as he made his way cautiously down the front steps. "You don't have to get so pushy."

Brett paused as he weighed the necessity of disclosing one final piece of information to his retreating friend. Eventually unable to resist his own impulses he shouted down the steps. "And by the way, the name of the winner in yesterday's race was 'Lance Isadick'," he said as he closed the door firmly behind him.

"Yeah, that's it!" Lance Isa…well I'll be a son of a bitch," said Logan incredulously as he turned and looked back toward the smiling face of his friend peering out from the second-story window.

Chapter 31

Brett stopped in the door entryway and watched Tony as he balanced on a ladder and dusted the old trophies that lined the shelves. He had never seen him pay even the slightest attention to them before and was surprised to see his diligence in cleaning them. When the store owner suddenly stopped his work, he watched the old man dip his head for a moment as if reciting a silent prayer. The entering runner closed the door gently behind him in a respectful attempt not to infringe on the owner's apparent soul searching. Just as Rip had forewarned him all those months ago, he had grown fond of the older man and his gruff yet charismatic demeanor. He could nary remember a workday that had gone by without him having used a salty colloquialism that would help the hours sail by effortlessly.

"Tony, are you okay?" he asked as the door squeaked shut behind him.

"Brett! I didn't hear you come in. You shouldn't sneak up on an old fart like that," he said in an irritated voice. "And to answer your question I'm just fan-damn-tastic."

"Do you need any help?"

He turned his attention back to the vast array of awards and exhaled audibly before he responded. "I think I can manage to knock the cobwebs off of these relics myself, thank you."

He looked at the store owner and yearned for a glimpse of the experience that he knew was locked tightly inside the aging shell of a man. After a pause he chose a carefully worded compliment that he hoped would begin to pry the past wide open. "Rip says you were quite a runner in your day. He said you were close to getting on the Olympic team. I've been meaning to ask you about it for some time now."

Tony paused before he spoke. "Rip ought to mind his own business." The terse statement hung in the air as he slowly limped down the ladder. "I'd tell you the same thing but I know you're as stubborn as my ten year old case of jock itch. But I'm guessing it's that very same mule-headedness that comes in handy on the track, doesn't it? I've watched you run more than once and I see you doing things that I can only dream about now. But there was a day...," he said before he paused again.

"Tell me, Tony. Please."

He began slowly as he fingered a pair of racing shoes on the wall. "I was damn good in my day. Back then we darn near had to cobble our own shoes. Just a piece of rubber glued on leather as hard as jerky. But oh how I loved to run," he said with an unfocused gaze. "I was young and ambitious and filled up to my eyeballs with piss and vinegar. Hardly anyone I knew then cared a lick about running, but it was about the only thing I found out that I was good at. One time my momma even wanted me to go see a head doctor after she saw me sweating all over town. She said I must be running from something even though I told her I was running *to* something. I wanted to be just like the great Abebe Bikila and to this day I can still remember reading every story about him that I could get my hands on. You ever hear of him?"

"Two time Olympic champion in the marathon. I like the history," replied Brett as he eyed up the store owner. He could tell he had greased the skids and an avalanche of long buried words was ready to pour out of the old man's mouth. "Did you ever get a chance to meet him?"

"Hell no. But I wanted to be just like him. So I ran. More miles than there are hairs on Coach Wickers' back. And I got good enough for the '68 trials in the marathon. That's where it all went to hell."

"What happened?"

The old man narrowed his eyes as if focusing on a distant memory. The stillness of the room magnified until words echoed in the air. "I didn't know my own ass from Lyndon Johnson's.

But I still ran with the lead pack from the get go. It was filled with some of the toughest hombres you'd ever want to meet. None of these sponsored billboards hiding behind sunglasses like you see today. Just road warriors pounding away at the miles until one by one a carcass was dropped and left for the buzzards. Those were different days back then and the men I knew ran from the gut. There wasn't some coach leading them by the nose and worryin' if you ran too many miles that week or that your 'lactate acid' level was too high. Most of us had full-time jobs and trained our asses off two or three times a day never expecting anything but the good feeling we got from leaving our own sweat and blood on the roads. It was just a collection of men that were driven to succeed in a sport that barely anyone cared about but us…a sport that back then was as pure as the snowfall and meant all the world to me." He took a deep breath as if to re-settle his thoughts and started in again. "Anyways, I was ready to run that day and feeling pretty chippy through ten miles with even enough nerve to claim the lead for a stretch. I still remember running like a dipstick and even passing up water a time or two just to prove how tough I was."

"Been there, done that," interrupted Brett as he shook his head knowingly.

He glared at the young runner before continuing on. "Do you want to hear this goddam story or not? Anyways, eventually the pack fell apart when the miles took their toll and all the pretenders were dropped. For me it was at about fifteen miles plus when I knew the race wasn't going to be like playing 'paddy cake'. We were in the middle of nowhere and the only sounds in the air were of our own hoofbeats and breath. Even though it was getting harder, I was cocky enough to still be thinking I'd be wearing the colors at the games in Mexico. By then the pack had melted down to me and two others running down the road like a trio of wild dogs. At about twenty miles I started sucking a little faster on the thin air of the mountains – they ran the damn race in Alamosa for god sake! Anyway, when I started breathing harder Kenny Moore and old George Young just turned towards me and *smiled.* I damn near crapped my shorts and that's when I did it."

"Did what?"

"I stopped. Like a little boy afraid of getting a whipping from his daddy. And I just stopped. I told myself I was dehydrated but I knew. And I still know. I was afraid. And I've regretted that day for the rest of my life. What I wouldn't do for a second chance at those two bastards."

"But all these awards?"

"I blew out my achilles at a marathon in Minnesota. After that the best I could do was win the 'Yellow Piss 5K' and other ten cent races."

"I'm sorry Tony. I never knew."

"Life can be cruel," the old man said as he looked at the trophies again. "But I believe we are all given one chance to make our own fate. And I'll have you know up until right now I had never told anyone about Alamosa. You're the first."

"Why me?"

The old man measured him before speaking in an even tone. "Because fate might look you squarely in the eye. And when your time comes I want you to smile back."

He stared at the old man as he abruptly turned away and once again made his way toward the ladder. He knew consoling him was out of the question and that no words could salve a thirty-year wound. When an awkward silence overtook the room he watched as the gray haired man moved the ladder to the next set of trophies and limped back up to continue his work.

Chapter 32

T he sun had barely begun to warm the day when Brett walked to the head coach's office with an overriding feeling of anxiety. His erratic answering machine held a message from the coach asking him to come by for a "sit down" as soon as possible. Wickers had never called him before and he remembered the coach's stern warning that had been issued the first time they had met. With an elevated pulse he made his way to the office before he gently rapped on the door and hoped for the best.

"Coach? I can come back later if you're busy."

Wickers looked up at him as he sat at his desk. "Come on in, Brett. I'm just sitting here trying to figure out how to get the sprinters to worry more about how they do than how they look. Next year's crop has heads that are softer than the foam in the high jump pit."

He smiled while he considered the comment. The speed freaks were truly a different breed than the distance runners, and he had little advice for the coach's quandary. "I stopped trying to figure them out years ago when they all took to wearing full lycra bodysuits. But I wouldn't mind having their jets in the last two hundred meters."

"I ain't much for their fashion myself," he said pushing his ever present hat back further on his forehead. "But from what I've seen your speed isn't too shabby itself. And although I've had some good distance runners before I have to admit I've never had one quite like you. For the two decades I've been here I've yet to see talent like yours matched with the cajones you show. Pardon my French."

Paul Maurer

"Thanks coach," he said surprised by the unexpected compliment. "I'm just trying to do my best."

"That's easy to see. From what I know you've been churning out some pretty impressive workouts lately. As good as I've ever seen. And I hope you don't mind if I get straight to the point and separate the wheat from the chafe. Given your recent results I can only assume you ain't been drinking?"

With the coach's propensity for being painfully direct he shouldn't have been surprised by the abruptness of the question. But he still allowed a few seconds to elapse before he responded to his inquiry. "No, I haven't. It hasn't always been easy, but so far I've been able to manage it. And I want to let you know I appreciate all you've done for me and hope I haven't let you down."

"Let me down? You haven't switched to smoking wacky weed have you? That's dang near the dumbest thing I've heard in awhile," he answered. "The boys think you're some kind of an apostle in spikes. Hell, if you farted, they'd probably try to bottle it and use it as cologne. That's why I called you in."

"You want me to fart?"

"Smart ass," he said with a smile as he leaned forward in his chair. "What I meant was I have a proposition for you. I have a spot on the team open next year and I'd like you to join on. We can use someone like you."

"But you know I'm out of eligibility. Otherwise you know I'd love to."

Wickers tugged at his cap in exasperation. "Not to run numnuts – to help me coach."

"To coach? But what about Rex? I'm not sure we'd get along so well."

"Rex is in the crapper…literally. I caught him filling his gear bag with rolls of toilet paper from the storage area. Imagine trying to rip off the very hand that feeds you. Even worse than that it proved to me what I had been starting to believe – that his character is fading as fast as my momma's memory. And that's something I just can't live with."

"That's too bad," Brett responded as he struggled for the right words. "But for whatever reason we weren't real close."

"Hell, I've seen gators going after dead chickens closer than you two," the coach snorted as he started to pick up steam. "But I've also seen the way the guys take to you. When you speak they listen and by trying to stay in your slipstream they all got tougher by the week. There's something about being coached by someone who's been through the wars and knows what it feels like. Shoot, the closest I got to a distance runner when I competed was almost splitting one open with a discus. I know that you're graduating soon, but I believe coaching will help both your mind and legs."

"I don't know what to say," the runner replied as he soaked in the unexpected flattery. "I never really thought about it. I assumed I'd just get a job somewhere and keep running."

Wickers chuckled aloud before he replied. "Sounds like you had it all figured out. I think you're a natural to be a coach. I've noticed the intuition you have about running and that's something you just can't teach. A great coach has to have a feel and I see that in you. The job doesn't pay much but I think in the end it would be a good deal for both of us."

"As long as it keeps me in Ramon noodles I'm not worried about the money. I honestly didn't know exactly what I would do next, and I'm honored that you'd even consider me. I'd love to take the job but only under one condition."

"What's that?"

"That I get to use the whirlpool. Alone."

"Logan," said Wickers with a shake of his head. "If you decide to coach, that little son-of-bitch is your problem for his senior year. That by itself might get you a raise."

As Wickers started to rise he looked Brett dead in the eyes and started again. The thick face suddenly oozed seriousness and he moved forward to perch himself on the edge of the desk. With his already imposing stature looming even larger he started to speak in an unusually warm tone. "But before next season starts there's still a few things on the horizon for you isn't there?"

"Just a few," Brett agreed as he waited for him to continue.

"If I was you, I think I would be feeling pretty good about your current fitness level. I know there aren't that many races around the midwest in summer, but you were fortunate to find those two in July."

"You're right, Coach. The first 5K in Iowa was as tough a race as I remember. It was at this track literally dropped into a cornfield somewhere outside of Des Moines. But it was blowing like a hurricane and I ran a crappy time."

"13:52 if I remember right."

"13:51.6 to be exact. I earned that last point four by my lean at the finish. At least I had a guy with me until the last half-mile until I was able to drop him."

"And the other race was in Illinois, right?"

"At DePaul University. Hollywood knew about it and drove me there. It was an open meet sponsored by the 'Chicago Runners' club and a few of the guys there weren't too bad. I think I must have a black cloud following me because it poured buckets during the last half of the race and I barely broke fourteen minutes. I had a lot left for the gun lap, but I was pretty happy how good I felt competing."

Wickers smiled at the implication. "We both know there is no replacing the racing intensity that you need. But with the time trials you've had and your recent success in the road race you may be ready."

He looked at the stern and knowing look on Wickers' face and smiled in embarrassment. "Uhh...you heard about that?"

"Sure, a little bug told me."

"Like a dung beetle about five foot six inches tall?"

"Give or take an inch. Logan is not the most reliable person to keep a secret. If I could get his legs to move as fast as his gums flap, he'd be a shoe-in for the gold in Beijing. Still, when he graduates I'm going to miss that little guy. But don't go telling him that or he'll be hard as hell to coach next year."

"Your secret is safe with me."

The seriousness returned to the venerable coach's face and he resumed the conversation in an even tone. "You know I'm not much on predictions, but if an old coach's opinion is worth doodly squat I think you have a chance to do some major damage at the trials. You're on pace to peak at the right time and you just need to sharpen up to a razor's edge. No one there will be expecting you to do anything because you've been out of the loop for awhile. In fact I believe the first time a few folks lay eyes on you they'll think you're some kind of a ghost from Christmas past. But if you keep your head screwed on tight, I don't think you'll have anything to worry about. We both know it's going to be hot as hell so forget about the time. Any one of the first three spots are golden so that's all that you really aim for. I truly believe you will be able to hang around until 'money time' and by then all bets are off. And if you focus like I think you can, there's not a runner in the 5000 you should fear. Not a one."

"What about the Kid?"

"The punk? I've seen him run a dozen times and he loves to gradually break the field with a long drive. Usually nobody stays with him and I've yet to see how he reacts to a bug on his ass. Hang tight with him and see if he's worth all the hype. Funny things happen when a race heats up. Just think of him as the bacon sizzling in your fire."

"Usually I burn the bacon."

"That's just about what I was hoping you'd say," he replied as he narrowed his eyes and pierced the runner with an intensity he had never shown before.

Brett returned the look and suddenly felt his confidence soar as he contemplated the words of advice. He stood up to face his advisor and took a breath before carefully parceling out his words. "Coach, I have to tell you this. I haven't felt like I've had a real coach since my dad died. I mean they'd all try, but it was like I was treated differently than the other runners. I'd get away with stuff until I messed up enough and then they had to kick me out. I just want to say thanks for helping me. And for drawing the line."

"You're welcome," he answered. "You'll learn when you start coaching that sometimes a kick in the butt works better than a pat on the fanny. But I had a feeling the first time we met that the world had smacked your ass long enough and that maybe you were finally ready to grow up. I know some of the guys think I treat them like dog-meat, but I'd do damn near anything for them if they'd compete from their heart. As you have."

Brett looked at him and the cumulative admiration he had gained for the man nearly spilled over. "I like listening to you talk. You just have a way."

"There is power in words. But the power on the track comes from somewhere deep within yourself. So remember when you line up at the trials in Baton Rouge that regardless of what the press says there may be more than one hero on the track that day. The way I see it is that when you boil it all down a race is just a collection of meat and tendons controlled by beating hearts. And yours is in the right place."

"Thanks for the advice. And the second chance."

"No charge."

"And don't forget to pack your ice skates for the trials," Brett said to remind him of an old promise.

The runner left the room quietly and felt the strength of Wickers' words harden his resolve. Still, as he walked down the abandoned hallway he found himself shivering as he visualized himself at the starting line in Louisiana. A few years ago it may have been a wave of uncertainty as the internal pressure raged to a boil. But today it was the old feeling of anticipation and excitement that he remembered from the early years. He knew it had been a long time since he felt this way and he welcomed home the sensation like a long lost friend.

Chapter 33

The sun pounded hard on the track as the athletes waited for the completion of the national anthem that signaled the start of the annual Milwaukee Invitational. The competitors stood motionless and watched the flag droop passively on an unusually windless day. The lack of the normal cool lake breeze was bemoaned by every distance runner in attendance because of the effect it might have on their performance. When Brett shifted his feet nervously during the final notes of the traditional song, his own thoughts were zeroed in on Tony's recent heartfelt reflections of his dashed Olympic dreams. He remembered when their conversation had ended the store owner had avoided him the rest of the day and uncharacteristically cloistered himself in the back office. Brett had proceeded to do much the same and he had gone on with his work displaying a diligence far beyond the norm. Tony had ultimately chosen to leave the premises in silence hours before his usual quitting time. Brett found himself lost in reflection as he walked to a predetermined spot under the bleachers in a calculated attempt to avoid the draining effects of the summer sun. Rip was already waiting for him and they proceeded to kill time by engaging in idle talk of the day's competitions. Their words helped battle the boredom of the daylong event until both runners' ears perked up when they heard a static filled blast from the overhead speaker.

"Last call for the steeplechase…first call for the one hundred meter dash," boomed the announcer from high in the antiquated press box.

"Hollywood and Logan are doing the steeple," said Rip as he peeked between the rows. "I bet Logan wears a Speedo in honor of the water jump."

Brett nodded his head in agreement and replied in an offhand manner. "Knowing him he'll probably wear a thong."

They both looked up when Coach Wickers rushed by the stands with a scowl on his face. He had held the annual invitational for as long as anyone could remember with the initial plan of using the meet as both a tool to publicize his program and to help keep his runners focused during the off season. But as word of it spread, he now accepted other collegians and a sprinkling of open competitors still reaching for greater heights. When the quality of the meet progressed he had even received certification from the USA Track and Field Federation that they had sanctioned the invitational.

"Hot enough to fry an egg on my ass," they heard him say under his breath.

"But wide enough for an omelet," said Logan as he jogged by on their way to the starting line.

The two runners rested in the shade of the bleachers and they watched the beginning of the rarely contested event. They enjoyed the mutual give and take racing tactics of their two friends and studied them intently as they circled the over-heated track. They knew first hand the pride of the two competitors and watched with mounting interest when the battle on the track intensified to full throttle. The bystanders pounded on the bleachers as the two runners fought down the backstretch, and they whooped noisily when Logan edged ahead at the finish line by a matter of inches. Winning "by a schwantz" he would explain to them later.

"I thought I recognized a few voices under here," said Marie as she waved to them through the bleachers. "I finally get to see both of you run."

Brett squinted up at her and shaded his eyes from the sun. "Hope it's worth your while. It's not the greatest day to race but we'll do our best."

"I'm sure you'll do wonderful," she said sipping a cold drink and smiling at them both. "And I'll meet you back here when you're done."

He nodded absently when the mention of the upcoming race transported him to an inner sanctum that disallowed any extraneous thoughts. "I'll see you after the race. It's about time to start getting loosened up."

After she headed to her seat he caught a glimpse of Rip dousing his face and neck liberally with handfuls of water. He knew his training partner was serious about the competition, and that he was intent on hanging with Brett as long as possible. Brett in turn hoped to be pushed out of his comfort zone and viewed the race as his last all out effort before the trials. They both knew the moment they stepped on the track their friendship would temporarily be on hold until the finish line was crossed. Each runner chose to warm up on his own and after completing their final striders, the runners were called to the start. He looked around to acknowledge his friend's presence, but accepted the fact that Rip was already far too lost in his own thoughts to seek out any well wishes. When the group of a dozen runners lined up Brett took a deep breath and readied himself for the 5000 meters that lay ahead.

At the gun he strode to the front in an attempt to stay out of the typical jostling and restlessness of the pack. Leading the race so early went against his grain, but he wanted to be safe from any accidental falls and hoped to be able to tuck in later if he could find a taker for the lead. After towing the pack through the mile he decided to ease out into the second lane and let another runner take his turn carrying the race. Over his left shoulder he saw Rip stride into the lead apparently unafraid to take his place in dragging the long string of runners. Brett felt a burn in his throat and after licking at his dry lips he wished he wished he had taken in more fluids before the race. He returned to the first lane and attempted to catch his breath when he slowly angled in behind Rip. In an intuitive gentlemen's agreement they started to alternate laps in order to share the burden of setting the pace for the field. With Rip leading after two miles he unexpectedly had to work hard to cover an increase in pace that his friend had suddenly pressed upon the pack. The older runner could feel a subtle twitching of his calves and hamstrings, but he entertained no doubt that he could maintain his stride for the duration of the race. With only two laps to go he was caught off guard when his teammate made an even stronger surge in the pace. He suddenly realized Rip was intent on a using a sustained drive in the overriding hope of draining the kick from his legs. He actually thinks he can beat me, he thought wildly. At the bell lap he closed in on Rip's outside shoulder and felt a rush of adrenaline course through his body. He decided to bide his time and wait until he hit the far turn before making his move and blasting past his opponent with ease. He relished the power and arrogance of pure speed and consciously ignored the increasing scream from the fibers of his legs. When he strode powerfully down the final homestretch, he turned back to check his position and suddenly felt a knife-like stab in the back of his left hamstring.

"Dammit!" he yelled aloud as he slowed to reach the finish line. His finishing sprint degraded quickly and he gingerly stepped past the finish line with Rip rushing by a split second later. He sucked in the hot air with a deep wheeze and protectively grabbed at the back of the injured leg with his hand. Seconds later he felt the meaty arm of Wickers cover his still heaving shoulders.

"Good job," he said through sun-burned cheeks. "But it looked like you eased up at the end and Rip almost got you."

Brett chose not to say a word as he straightened up and watched the coach move on to congratulate Rip. He suddenly felt like he was in a vacuum and the noise of the small crowd was instantly blocked from his mind. His total focus was on his throbbing hamstring and the seriousness of the race-induced injury. From somewhere far away he heard Wickers' voice as it boomed over the track.

"Rip," called the coach to his exhausted charge, "are you aware of what you just did? You beat the qualifying standard and you'll be joining Brett in Baton Rouge for the Olympic Trials. You just ran a 13:47 5000 meters!"

Rip looked at him blankly but soon let go an unbridled howl to the heavens. With an apparent second wind he danced down the track in an uncharacteristic display of emotion. A bewildered smile covered his face and he sought out his friend. "Did you hear that, Brett?"

He answered him with a bear hug but was too focused on the fire in his leg to do the celebration any justice. As Rip was pummeled by Hollywood and Logan, he limped cautiously back to the spot under the bleachers that housed the rest of his gear. His mind raced with the certainty that the years of hard work would be wasted and the opportunity lost. Only two weeks to go and now this! He thought of the pain he had endured in practice and the sacrifices made. At that instant he missed his father terribly and at the same time hated his mother for her weakness. Why waste your life running when all you get is a ripped hamstring and another broken dream, he thought angrily? The Gift is bullshit! his mind screamed.

"Great race," he heard Marie say from above as she met him at their pre-determined site.

He felt ready to explode when the frustration of the years boiled over. Scarcely able to control himself he looked at her with pure anger and spat out a reply. "What the fuck do you know? What do you know about anything?"

He couldn't have hurt her more deeply even if he had carved out her heart with a knife. She stared at him with a dazed look as his unexpected onslaught assaulted her sensibilities. He felt the venom still coursing through his veins when he noticed the moisture gathering in the corners of her eyes. She in turn looked at the man who for the second time in her life had caused her to be speechless at the track. With an open mouth she tried to blink back the tears before she turned and ran along the length of the bleachers.

He watched her as his anger slowly burned out. Why did I say that, he thought? What did she ever do to hurt me? He closed his eyes and tried to sort out his overflowing emotions.

When he opened them again she was gone.

Chapter 34

The night had fallen and a cool lake wind whipped through the air. The runner had walked the campus grounds for hours, but he still felt the heaviness of the day's events weigh on his shoulders. He wished he could erase his action at the track but knew the situation would be anything but that simple. After his outburst Marie carried the pained look of a broken heart and had walked away without so much as a glance back. At that moment he couldn't come up with the words to fix the situation any more than he could reverse the scar tissue in his burning hamstring. More than ever he needed time to think and had declined an earlier invitation to go out and celebrate Rip's accomplishment. He promised to meet up with them later at Hollywood's house, but he knew deep down that he never would. As happy as he was for Rip, he couldn't bring himself to celebrate his friend's good fortune at a time his own emotions were so decidedly fractured.

He wandered down the avenue and noticed the blinking of the Hooligans sign in the distance. He weighed the possibility that Marie would be there with her friends and he would have a chance to apologize to her in person. He hadn't been at the pub since their first date and the irony of seeing her there again to start things anew seemed almost poetic.

He opened the old wooden door and was assaulted by the smell of hanging smoke in the air. The bar looked darker and smaller than he remembered, but he still recognized the world weary look of the walrus mustachioed bartender. He nodded to the barkeeper but quickly looked beyond him and surveyed the scattered patrons of the establishment. It was far too early for much of a crowd, and he quickly realized that his dream of running into Marie was a fantasy at best. He exhaled forlornly and felt the specter of the day's futility cover him like a heavy shroud. Staring blankly around the bar, his shoulders slumped as he finally succumbed to the cumulative fatigue of the day. In resignation he sat down on a stool and looked out vacuously at the street.

"What can I get you?" asked the bartender from across the premises.

He hesitated because he had focused solely on talking to Marie and hadn't considered the possibility of staying if she wasn't there. But not having eaten since lunch he suddenly realized the emptiness in his barren stomach. "I'll have a cheeseburger with fries."

"And to drink?"

He licked his cracked lips and thought about the question. He owed it to himself to have one drink to relax he rationalized. Just one he thought.

"A Bud," he answered.

The beer came quickly as he waited on a stool by the window. He closed his eyes before taking a sip of the cold drink and felt the smooth liquid flow down his throat. With the feeling of pleasure far overriding his guilt, it took only a matter of seconds before he greedily gulped down the remaining contents of the mug. With the wave of a raised index finger he caught the eye of the bartender and signaled his impassioned needs. The second beer went down a bit slower, but the long ignored desire was unleashed and raged unimpeded to the surface. He took a deep breath and felt the familiar warmth travel through his body while the day's pain started to lose its sharp edge. When the cheeseburger was delivered the barkeeper assumed a refill was in order and replaced the empty glass with yet another frosty mug. He found draining the long forbidden amber liquid nearly as automatic as he did lacing up a pair of shoes for another run. He felt bolder when the alcohol flowed through his system and heard himself call out for a pitcher of beer that was soon carefully set in front of him. The insatiable craving that had been neglected for so long rose from the depths and suddenly clamored for his undivided attention. He drained mug after mug and felt the swirling confusion of his own thoughts surround him as he mindlessly played with the icy glass. The mixture of alcohol-induced exhilaration was laced with self-contempt and he felt fatigue engulf him as he poured himself another round. He allowed the foam to settle and gazed out the window as an old jogger in baggy sweats approached his vantage point. The shuffle was accentuated with an exaggerated arm swing of an aging runner trying to fight off the inevitable decline of the years. As he studied the ashen face, he was startled when the feeble old man seemed to nod in acknowledgement at him through the glass barrier.

"That's pathetic," he slurred in a tone laced with bitterness. "If I ever get like, that please shoot me."

When he raised the mug to his lips the glare of car lights caused him to see his own reflection in the window, and he was startled to see the tired eyed look of just another aimless drifter staring back at him. With shaking hands he set the half-filled mug down and felt the salty burn of tears well up in his eyes.

He pushed away from the table and rose to his feet in an unsteady lurch. He rushed to the heavy door and after pushing it open felt the cool night air slap him in the face. Instinctively he began to run towards the lake in an attempt to distance himself from the demons that were close behind. He ignored his aching leg and he ran harder and harder with a wearying desperation dogging his every step. With his heart pounding, the contents of his stomach rose up and he found himself retching on his hands and knees. He wiped his mouth with the back of his hand and tried to control his breathing as he had done so many times before.

"Who's pathetic now?" he said to himself as the sickness slowly subsided.

With the night wind blowing back his hair he could hear his father's old pre-race talks whisper in his ear. "It's not about how many times you fall," he heard him saying. "It's how many times you stand up."

The runner stood up.

Chapter 35

He awoke in the clothes he had worn the night before. The dried spittle on his shirt was a stained reminder of its ending, and he angrily stripped off the dirty shirt before throwing it into the corner. After a restless sleep the only thing on his mind was how he could fix things with Marie. He stood up and looked out the front window at an overcast morning that appropriately matched his mood. He thought back to the chain of events of the previous day and vainly tried to figure out why he had attacked the only person in the world that he could truly depend on. Upon viewing the gloom outside, he decided as difficult as it might be he would face his mistakes head on. But even after a lengthy shower he couldn't wash away the tainted feeling that seemed to cling to his soul. The walk to Marie's apartment was arduous and he was admittedly more nervous than before any race. He had never felt towards anyone like he did to her, and the day at the track when he told her that he loved her it seemed like the most natural thing in the world. Her ensuing silence had embarrassed him, but somehow he felt infinitely lighter with the words having been said. When he finally reached her place he took a deep breath before he rapped softly on her door and listened intently for the sound of footsteps. He felt unsettled when her quick opening of the door resulted in an awkward silence that was left for him to break.

"I'm sorry," he heard himself lamely saying. His carefully prepared lines had escaped him the moment he saw her face. "I don't know why I said what I did. It's just that when I hurt my leg—"

She cut him off before he had a chance to finish. "You hurt your leg?" She continued on but he noted the decided flatness in her tone. "I didn't know that. Is it bad?"

He was surprised she even cared enough to ask about his running because as far as he could see it had only caused her pain. He sheepishly continued the conversation and felt a glimmer of hope the meeting would end on a positive note.

"Dog?"

"Our trainer. I'm due there in a bit." He shifted uncomfortably on the front porch and looked anywhere but into her eyes. As the seconds passed he was acutely aware that as of yet there had been no invitation for him to enter.

"I hope it's not too bad. I know how much the trials mean to you," she said as a trace of sympathy trickled into her voice.

Damn it! he thought to himself. He hadn't come here to talk about his running. Tell her how you feel!

With red rimming her eyes she started again before he even had a chance. "Brett... I don't really know what to say right now. What happened yesterday has me hurt and confused. Somehow I'm not sure I know you like I thought I did. And I think I need a little time. I'll call you," she said vaguely as she lowered her eyes.

He didn't immediately respond because the suddenly curt demeanor had caught him off guard. A mumbled "okay" came out more as an escape of air from the pit of his stomach than an acknowledgement of her statement. When she closed the door he stared at it numbly before he turned and walked aimlessly adrift in his own thoughts. The nameless faces that passed him by only added to the overwhelming feeling of isolation that surrounded him. With every step of his aching leg he was further reminded of both the chasm he had created with Marie and the jeopardy of the nearing Olympic trials. He continued moving through the streets as if on automatic pilot and his subconscious guided him to his ultimate destination of the athletic facility. On the walk through the barren corridors of the complex his limp seemed magnified and his altered footstrike echoed in the empty hallway. He eventually made out the glow of the light burning in the training room and he rapped softly on the door before entering.

"Brett," Dog called to him amiably. "I've been waiting for you. I understand you ran into a bit of bad luck yesterday. Coach said you were pretty shook up after the race, but you left before I could even check things out. Come on in and we'll take a look."

The grizzled veteran had seemingly been the trainer forever and the runner's faith in him was limitless. He looked appreciatively at the old man and was grateful for his commitment where even on a Sunday morning the wrinkled medic was the first one at the deserted complex. The hands at the end of the Popeye-like forearms jutted out from his white t-shirt and were nearly itching for the chance to examine the runner's injured leg. He closely followed Dog's instructions and carefully climbed onto the table to settle in for the ordeal. He laid back and tried to relax but soon grimaced as the trainer stretched and twisted his throbbing leg out of necessity before rendering a final verdict. He closed his eyes hard in an attempt to control the pain and only hoped the diagnosis would be something he could stomach.

"You'll live," said Dog with conviction when he went to the sink to wash his hands. "It's a good pull but nothing we can't patch up in time. With a little bit of ultrasound and deep tissue work we'll get you healed up. I'll have to keep you in the pool for a few days but you'll be running again by next week." Anticipating the runner's questions he continued: "The rest may even do you good. It'll force a proper taper that you endorphin junkies hate so much, but the pool work will keep the meat from piling up on your bones. I'll tell you more than one record has been set by a runner fresh from the mend. An old Englishmen named Bedford and our own Joanie Benoit come to mind. You just got to have faith."

"Faith in what?" he asked with a trace of bitterness.

"In God's plan. I ain't the most religious man, but I believe there's gotta be a reason we end up where we do. And maybe there's a reason this happened too. It just may be that you got to figure out why. So right now I want you to lift your fuzzy chin way up and decide that you're gonna make it. Either that or you'll die trying."

He wanted desperately to believe the old man and he felt the emotional turmoil of the last twenty-four hours rise unexpectedly. He swallowed hard and stared at the ceiling in a conscious effort to collect himself. Sitting up on his elbows, he needed reassuring that he had heard the trainer correctly. "You really think I'll be okay?"

"As sure as my prostate is large," he replied with his blue eyes twinkling in the fluorescent light.

"If you're right, I'm going to owe you one."

"Thank me after the trials. Because if you think you have pain when you race, just wait until I get my knuckles in you. I'll be giving you a big damn bullet to bite," he warned.

Brett smiled sadly at the old trainer before he replied. "Pain is the least of my worries, Dog. Trust me on that."

Chapter 36

The dim light of the trainer's office gave a false sense of serenity to the injured runner, and as he lay face down on the worn table he wondered how many other athletes had preceded him. But he remained quiet as he followed Dog's sage advice and tried to relax while the skilled hands kneaded and stroked his injured leg. Just as he had been forewarned, the daily treatment was one more insult the runner would have to absorb in order to reach his ultimate goal. The hour long massage had proved to be the most excruciating ordeal he had yet to experience and only because of the trainer's reassurance did he allow it to continue. "This table must be about a hundred years old," he commented through gritted teeth.

"Give or take a few years," Dog replied as he masterfully applied a pointed elbow to a resisting trigger point. "This old bench has held a lot of dreams and nightmares. And filled an old man with a noggin' full of memories."

"You ought to write a book someday."

"My old pappy used to say 'what's said in the boat stays in the boat'. And that's the way it'll be here too. But I figure my table may have just a little magic left in it for one more go 'round."

"For anyone in particular?"

"You know damn well who I'm talking about. I've had a thousand athletes lay down here and they didn't amount to much more than a fart in a windstorm. Most of them had a chance for greatness, but settled on running with the pack. What those boys never realized was that winning has a steep price but the cost of cowardice lasts a lifetime. But unless I'm wrong about you I got a feeling that's something you already knew."

Brett let the remarks sink in as Dog's work intensified. He wanted to continue the discussion but the pain of the treatment overpowered his ability to speak. He concentrated on his own breathing and gripped the table in a fight to control his composure. He nearly whimpered until he finally felt a subtle lessening of the pressure. "Jeez, that's the closest I've ever felt to being violated," he said with a grimace.

"Relax, Gomer. Your skinny little cheeks would be safe even in prison. I'm only trying to get at the origin of your hamstring. Just breathe deep and let it go."

"You gotta be kidding me, Dog. I feel like a fish being gutted."

"And you're flopping around like one too."

The runner's sweat soaked then table as he fought against the deep tissue work, and he was relieved when he felt the coolness of the ultrasound gel hitting his leg. "Finally... my pain threshold just hit a new max. Where did you learn to do that?"

"New York," said Dog as he applied the wand of the ultrasound. "I was a student trainer at Columbia University way back when. Coach Wickers threw the weights there. And not very well if I remember correctly. He even smashed the Chancellor's windshield with the discus once, but we lied and told him some band of pot smoking hippies did it. As tough as he was he still hid in his closet for two days 'cause he was so afraid of getting turned in. He did end up getting off scot-free though."

"I'll have to ask him about that someday."

"He'll probably deny it because he's got an image to keep up. Anyway, I once had to work on his throwing shoulder under the watchful eye of old Ted Corbitt. Ever hear of him?" he asked as he fiddled with the machine's dials.

Brett felt the deep wave of ultrasound and shifted uncomfortably before he answered the question. "I don't think so. Should I?"

"Yup," replied Dog, "Teddy was a running legend. He used to run thirty miles before breakfast just as an eye opener. I'm bettin' he left more sweat on the streets of New York than an army full of hookers. But he was also a physical therapist twenty years ahead of his time. Ted was quiet as a church mouse, but he had the hands of a maestro. So I watched him and for a lifetime have tried to measure up. Wickers and I have been a team ever since."

"A match made in heaven."

"He pounds the snot out of you and I get to clean you up," said Dog shaking his head. "But he flat out told me you're the best he's ever had. And that you just fell into his lap like 'pigeon shit from the sky'."

"How flattering," said the runner with a smile.

"He told me the opportunity to coach someone like you happens once in a lifetime and I for one agree with him. I watched you at the invite and saw the same burn in your eyes I used to see in Corbitt's. That a gift from God that's what it is. Now you just got to find a way to spread that burn over 5000 meters in Baton Rouge. There are a lot of us old coots here hoping we'll get a whiff of a champion before we go. And I believe you may be the one or I wouldn't be wasting my time on your bum."

"I appreciate all of your help," said Brett as he felt Dog adding additional gel to his leg. The room quieted as the trainer tended to his work and after a few minutes the runner began to feel increasingly melancholy as the fatigue of the cumulative events began to take a firmer hold. He realized how far he had traveled, but recognized the distance he still had to go and he spoke up in a wistful tone. Feeling safe with the trainer, he added one last comment: "But sometimes Dog, I wonder if it's all really worth it. I mean the early morning runs…battling the heat and cold…always worrying about who's better than you."

Dog continued with the ultrasound and a deadened silence filled the room. Brett heard a slight wheeze in the old man's breath a moment before he spoke. "I'm not sure if you are asking for my advice or just looking for a shoulder to lean on."

"Both I guess," Brett responded in a resigned voice. "Running is just so hard sometimes."

"No harder than life I'd guess," Dog said in a controlled voice. "I'll tell you a little story that you can do with what you wish. It seems almost like another life, but way back when I had no idea what I wanted to do with myself. I thought about joining up in the Army or Navy, but I didn't feel like getting shot at or falling off the ship. So I bounced around until I realized that holding athletes together with a pocketful of tape was going to be my lot in life. And once I accepted what my role in this old world was, it all boiled down to the only thing I really had control over. That little something was that I'd work to make myself the best damn trainer I could ever hope to be." He exhaled slowly before he chose to continue. "That might not seem like much to anyone else breathing on this earth, but it means everything to me. So much that when I turn in at night I'm able to turn out the lights and sleep like a baby. Full of sweet dreams and all." He lifted off the ultrasound wand and toweled off the cool gel before asking one last unexpected question. "How do you sleep, Brett?"

He was caught off guard by the trainer and searched for the right words before he realized it was a rhetorical question. He struggled with the uncomfortable images the question conjured up and he nearly closed his eyes in thought. "I want to run…and I want to win," he said in a voice that barely rose above a whisper.

"Then run, boy," Dog urged with conviction in his voice. "Run toward the dreams with a vision in your heart and strength in your step. If you do that, no matter where you end up you're bound to sleep soundly and wake up with a smile on your face. And I guarantee you'll never look back and wonder if it was all really worth it."

He almost felt tears well up as his emotions rose to the surface one more time. "I'll do my best, Dog. I only hope I won't let you and Coach Wickers down."

"I doubt that will happen," he said in a confident voice as he tossed the soiled towel into a bin. "As far as I'm concerned you were born to run as much as any boy I've ever seen." He proceeded to wash his hands off and added one final comment to the conversation. "I heard the old man has so much faith in you that he offered you a job next year. If that's true, I won't even mind sharing my old tub with you," he said lightly as he motioned toward the gleaming metal structure.

"Really?"

The smirk he attempted to hide remained only partially hidden behind his white stubble. "Not at all. It's just that I have a problem with a little leak now and again. The old bladder's got a few holes in it I guess."

"Oh man, Dog. How am I supposed to relax in the whirlpool now with that as a visual?"

"I'll tell you what son," he said as a smile crossed his face. "If a little piss is the worst thing that happens to you, you'll die a happy man."

"Are you truly happy, Dog?"

"Like a calf sucking on her momma's teat."

He smiled as he watched the wizened veteran gently wheel the rickety therapy cart back to its resting place. After bracing himself he climbed down from the table and gingerly tested the aftermath of the latest treatment. And armed with no more than a fading pain and a fistful of trust he walked quietly from the old trainer's place of work.

Chapter 37

The rapidly mending runner lay on the grass that surrounded the concourse of the campus and was more than content to let the sunshine soak into his skin. The heat of the muggy August day was seemingly tailor made to gently melt away his cares. But even in his semi-conscious state, he still felt the sudden onset of shade through his closed lids. He opened his sleepy eyes and was startled to see Marie's face looming from above.

"You look about as lazy as they come," she said in a subdued voice. "Maybe I'll switch majors so that I can live the good life."

"Just bronzing my Adonis like body. And thinking."

She sat down on the grass next to him and absently picked at the blades. A moment passed before she spoke again. "Sorry I haven't called yet. I've picked up the phone a few times but didn't quite know what to say."

"And now?"

"I'm still working on it. But I just bumped into Rip and he told me you're going to be okay," she said as she deftly switched subjects. "I'm happy for you. I'm sure you'll do great."

"Thanks, Marie. It seems my injury wasn't as bad as I had thought. I guess I overreacted some. But no matter how bad I was hurt you didn't deserve what I said. And I'll regret it as long as I live," he said as he looked her in the eye. "I'm sorry Marie."

She ran her fingertips softly over her lips as if she was sizing up the situation. He nearly spoke again before she finally responded to his apology. "I know you are. And you're right I didn't deserve it," she said matter-of-factly. "But more than that it scared me. And it still does. It made me realize that somewhere inside of you is an anger that you've managed to keep hidden from me. And the raw pain I saw in your eyes surfaced only because of some running injury. But now that a week has gone by I bet you've been able to tuck everything away to a secret place. A place I don't want to see again."

"It won't happen again. I promise."

She shook her head slowly as she considered his statement. He watched her eyes as she narrowed them in concentration. "Brett …don't you see you can't even make a promise like that? What happens after the next bad race or injury? How can I be with you if I'm worried about some time bomb going off in my face? That wasn't some pain inside you that can be covered up with a thousand miles and expect to stay buried. I saw a neglected wound that needs to be taken care of before it destroys you. And maybe even us."

He could scarcely control the wave of aggression that rose up as he felt himself being challenged. He nearly stuttered as he felt himself blurt out a response. "So how am I supposed to fix everything? Go back in time and start all over again? God knows that I wish I could but I can't. All I have left is a broken down mother and memories of a dad I miss more everyday. Marie, there's a part of me that knows you're right, but I have to deal with things my own way. I don't have a family to help me fix everything like you do."

"You have a family. It's just not the one you want," she countered. "Your father passed away, but your mother didn't. You need to try and fix it with her so you can fix yourself. And I can live with being in second place to your running for awhile but not forever. But for us to work through this it has to start from inside you. You can't see it now, but you're going to be alive a lot longer than you'll be able to race on the track. When you're done running someday you'll just be a man named Brett. And you'll need to be able to live in his skin. I wish you would think about that."

Her thoughts multiplied the intensity of the heat he felt from the sun. He could scarcely imagine a world without running and was disoriented that she could suggest otherwise. To him his identity as a runner was the most treasured attribute he had been able to cultivate over the twenty-six years of his life. But somehow at this very moment she had been able to force him into an introspection that was anything but comfortable. He proceeded to look at her and struggled for the right words.

"Marie, you once asked me why I run. I'm not sure of a lot of things in my life right now, but I do know this: I have to run. It's not something I can even control. And I may never be able to make you understand, but it's who I am. And I have no choice. I am a runner." He looked at her and felt more exposed and vulnerable than he had ever been before. And yet he knew she would understand the pain that engulfed his soul. "I'm trying to make it right, Marie," he continued. "I'm really trying. You just don't know how hard it is."

She softly laid her hand on his cheek and stroked his browned skin. "I've seen you run and I believe you can do just about anything you set out to do. This is just one more time you'll have to fight through the darkness all the way to the finish line." She took a deep breath and removed her hand. "I have to go to art class now. Not all of us can spend time lying around all day."

"You know I'm still waiting for something to hang on my wall," he said as he recalled their first date.

"Soon. Maybe someday soon."

"Will you be there in Baton Rouge?"

"One way or another," she replied. "Bye, Brett."

After she firmly secured a bulging backpack to her shoulder, she strode through the concourse. He watched the spring in her step as she made her way through the small population of summer semester students. And he knew even in their current estranged state he loved her now more than ever.

Chapter 38

He picked up the phone for the third time and stared at the numbers as if lost in a daze. On a gut level he knew Marie was right, and that for his own well-being, he needed to make the call he had been avoiding for years. He had found it more than ironic that at the very time he needed to be at peak physical strength, he was spending time on cleaning up his own emotional baggage. But somehow just as he had always found the resolve to toe up the line at a hundred races, he steadied himself and finally pressed the buttons.

"Hello?" came the voice from the other end.

He paused briefly as he considered a quick retreat of hanging up the phone, but abhorring the cowardice of such a move he ignored the impulse. He breathed slowly but didn't utter a single word.

"Hello?" the voice echoed again in his ear.

"Mom," he said in resignation, "It's Brett."

"Brett?" his mother said in a questioning tone. "I'm so surprised to hear your voice. I don't get many calls from you anymore."

He didn't answer immediately but instead spent a moment measuring the steadiness of her own voice. He had purposely called early enough to reach his mother before she had started into her daily routine. He had lived through it more years then he cared to remember and he could recite the steps verbatim. After she ingested a pot of coffee and a fistful of cigarettes, he knew of the sequence that lay ahead in her day. On a work day she would resist the temptation until she had fulfilled the requirements of her employer, but on an off day such as this, her addiction called for attention that could only be satisfied in the usual fashion. His surprise call had been purposely planned to occur early enough to interrupt the routine well before his words fell on deaf ears. Her steady voice told him he had planned right.

"How's Milwaukee?" she asked.

He was pleased she remembered his whereabouts so that he wouldn't have to go through the frustration of explaining again. "I'm doing good. I'll be graduating soon and I might be helping out Coach Wickers next year. We're working out the details. But I really feel like I fit in here."

"I'm glad," she said with a layer of melancholy in her voice.

The wistfulness of the voice told him that her emotions were most decidedly mixed. She had often lamented about her inescapable loneliness, but he knew he didn't possess a simple potion that could cure her ailment. He had long since strived for independence that limited his responsibilities toward a mother that he had drifted well away from. He had always been able to justify his separate existence because of both her ailment and the mandatory selfishness inherent in running. The end result of such rationale was contact that transpired only through the intermittent placing of an obligatory phone call.

"Mom, I'm happy here. Between school and running everything is coming together pretty well. Did you get the last picture I sent you?"

"Yes I did. And your girlfriend is so pretty. You look so nice together. But I can't believe how thin you are. You look almost like a carbon copy of your father when we first met —" She stopped suddenly as the pain of memories rose up into her throat.

Brett was caught off guard by the remark but he vowed to forge ahead. "Mom, it's okay to remember because sometimes that's all we have left," he said softly as if to urge her on. "I miss dad more than anything but I have to move on. To a different life. One where I won't try to block everything anymore. It's taken me awhile but I've come to the realization that keeping the hurt inside just doesn't work." He waited for a few seconds and decided to let the honest thoughts continue to flow. "I'm trying to figure things out and I called because we both need to talk about the past. And even though years have passed I never told you the real reason I flunked out of Connecticut. Mostly it was because I couldn't handle what that was going on in my life at that time. I know it was partly the running and the feeling of always having to win. Somehow it seemed that after dad died, the pressure of winning wore me down. But as hard as running became, more than anything I missed having a real family. Eventually I got so balled up inside I started to drink to help me deal with the stress I felt. I realize now I drank partly to forget the past, but also because I was afraid of the future. And it took me a long time, but I made a decision to stop screwing up my life. It's not always easy but I'm trying not to hide anymore. And I hope that maybe someday we can even be a family again." He heard the breathing over the line and continued. "Mom, do you understand what I'm trying to say?" He sensed the trembling at the other end of the phone and realized he had poured out more thoughts than he had intended. But he pressed on in his need to know. 'Mom?"

"Brett, I —" she said before quieting to a whisper. "I don't think I even have the right words to say to you. But I know you deserve so much more than I've been able to give you."

"I never wanted much."

"I didn't mean things. I meant a normal home. And I want you to know I wasn't always the way I am now," she said in a faltering voice. "When you were born it was the most exciting day of my life. I just held you in those little clothes and listened to your breathing for hours. I still remember dressing you up and holding you tight. But I —" she said before stopping again.

"Mom, you have to talk to me."

"After awhile I just didn't seem to know what to do. I would sit and watch the other mothers in the park and they just *knew*. Things that I didn't. And the harder I tried, the darker I felt inside. Eventually I got so covered with guilt that I felt like I was pretending to be something I could never be. Like a good mother …or even a good wife."

Brett remembered the walks in the park and his mother watching him play from a distance. Alone. Always alone. He could still remember the hidden sadness he sensed in her even though he was just a child. What's wrong, Momma? he could still hear his tiny voice ask. But with the silent response of a sad smile he would run off again to join his playmates.

His voice came out haltingly. "But there were good times too."

"Maybe. But after awhile it got harder to pretend. I remember feeling like I could barely get out of bed to take care of myself. And somehow being a mother and wife was more than I could bear. I felt so guilty and knew I was failing you and your father that I— " she said as she stopped for the third time.

"Started to drink," he said completing her sentence.

Her next words came out in a pained whisper that Brett found barely audible. "I only wanted to be a good mother. But I didn't know how. I'm so sorry Brett."

He bit his tongue and considered the variety of responses he could make back to her. Yet his heart spoke before he tempered the words that he suddenly blurted out. "No matter what happened you're still my mom. And I refuse to keep being bitter about the past anymore and trying to run away from it. Until recently I had forgotten that dad used to tell me 'run with my heart'. As much as he was talking about running, I think he was telling me about life. To live open to the world and do it with a passion. And today I'm willing to start over again if you think we can."

"Will you come see me?" she asked in a voice drenched with hope.

He flashed again to her disheveled home and the unshakeable image of his mother passed out on the couch. He squeezed his eyes shut to blacken out the memory. "If you can stop. But I can't see you the other way. I just can't."

He sensed the trembling again and heard the quickened breathing. He had been disappointed so many times before that he steeled himself to the expected response. Yet as the seconds ticked away, he detected a subtle shift in her emotional stability.

"Brett," she started slowly with her voice carrying an uncharacteristic hint of resolve. "I stayed up all night and looked at the picture you sent. And I didn't have a drink. Not one. It's been a long time since I couldn't bring myself to have something. Longer than I care to remember. But when I saw the two of you together it made me realize how much I'm missing. And how much I've missed." She paused as the words seemingly hung in the air. When she started to speak again he heard the waver return to her voice. "Brett, I feel so sick. And so alone," she said as her voice broke completely.

He listened to the muffled sobs of a broken woman and found himself standing when he replied. "Mom, you need help. I'll find someone for you. And maybe I can help too. It's the only way," he said hearing his own voice crack.

The phone was quiet while he waited for her to collect herself. He wavered when he heard the fragile voice in his ear. "Brett, I want more than anything to get better. I have to get better. And maybe be the mother you deserve," she said in a struggling voice. "You know I love you."

He felt off balance again when the words reverberated in his brain. He hadn't been able to open up his heart to her since he was a child and he struggled to reply. "I love you too," he finally whispered.

The four small words echoed between the two. He imagined a steady hand reaching out to his mother just as Marie had said. He only hoped it was strong enough to lead her off the tightrope she had been on for as long as he could remember.

Chapter 39

Dog seemed to be a soothsayer as once again his prognosis was right on target. The runner's healing had progressed well even though the trainer had complained the deep tissue work made Brett "scream like a sissy". Dog maintained that the runner had needed the work for years and that perhaps he would even come out all the better for it. He was running easy again and felt more and more like a wild colt locked in a stall. Wickers had told him "the chicken done pinched out the egg" which in coach-speak meant all the necessary work had been done and that any additional hard running was superfluous. But his mind and legs were impatiently waiting for the chance to let loose the stored energies on the track. After having just gotten off the phone with a travel agent, his lone credit card ensured the final details of his journey to Baton Rouge.

On the drive to the store he was admittedly uninspired to attend the going away party Tony was holding for the two runners. The support the store owner showed was appreciated, but he still felt empty knowing Marie wouldn't be there for the festivities. Their chance meeting on the concourse had helped clear the air, but Brett knew the hurt he had caused her was still too fresh for any quick resolution. Although he accepted her feelings it still troubled him that she would not be at the evening's celebration.

"The man, the myth," called Hollywood when the subdued runner entered the store. He greeted the trials qualifier by placing a birthday party hat on his head and carefully placed the elastic string under his chin. He stood back to admire his latest work and scratched at his own chin while offering comment, "Now you're styling, my young Jedi."

Brett himself couldn't pass by on the early results of his friend's latest makeover. "But I bet the force would be with me if I grew a goatee."

"I'm trying to look a little more worldly," he explained. "But for now all it does is itch like hell."

"I'm sure you'll live," Brett said confidently as he noticed activity from the backroom.

"It's about time," said Logan as he strode in with Rip from the rear of the store. "We thought with all your pent up juju you were getting in a quick twenty."

He shook their hands before responding to their question. "That's not too likely. I don't want studly here kicking my ass around the track at the trials."

"You never can tell," said Rip playfully as he punched him on the arm. The two competitors had not talked much the last week and Brett looked forward to catching up with him on their trip. He knew Rip was thrilled beyond words at the unexpected qualifying time he had obtained at the Milwaukee Invite. Although he was more than likely to end up as a trials footnote, the accomplishment was for the time being still alive and vibrant.

"You been feeling okay?" asked Tony as he snuck up from behind.

"Actually, yeah. I can even touch my toes for a change. I'll probably never be a gymnast, but my leg feels pretty good." They too had scarcely talked since their last in-store encounter, but Brett felt magnetically drawn to him after his revelations.

"We're all rooting for you two. I doubt either of you realize it but it's like that 'Enema' guy says–" Tony started before being interrupted.

"You mean Eminem?" suggested Hollywood as he scratched at his growth.

"Yeah, you know who the hell I mean. He says 'You only get one shot. One opportunity'. I hate most of the crap you guys play but that dimestore hood got it right. You both better not assume you'll be getting to the trials again because it just might not happen. Leave it all on the track. Every piece of you."

Brett considered Tony's words and heard the rhythm of Eminem's nasal voice in his head. He looked at his old friend and thought of the dark secret the man had buried deep inside all those years ago. He silently promised to avoid the youthful error that Tony had learned to regret for over thirty years.

Rip studied the store owner curiously as the passion in the old man's voice had surprised him. "Don't worry, Tony. I expect to scatter my DNA all over the track. I know Brett will do the same."

The older runner nodded before agreeing. "Guaranteed."

"That's all I wanted to hear," said Tony. "Now enough of the talking and let's get on with the show. Ozone get over here and have a seat. We all pitched in and got a little going away present for you," he announced as he set a small package on Brett's lap.

"I'll only open it if you tell me Logan didn't pick it out."

The little runner feigned surprise at his friend's admonishment before he protested in reply. "My reputation is totally undeserved and I resent the implication."

Brett carefully opened the box and lifted the sheer lycra singlet into the air. He fingered the bold lettering that stated "Team Fate" over the front of the garment. He continued on and touched the graphic under the lettering which he immediately recognized as the insignia worn by Prefontaine in his last race. "Unbelievable," he said succinctly as he draped it across his lap.

"We figured you couldn't go to the trials in that ratty piece of shit you normally race in," said Tony. "The announcers would think you were some kind of farmboy or something."

"It's perfect," said Brett. "I mean that."

Tony then carried over a larger package and set it firmly in his hands. "And this was dropped off by a friend of yours."

He didn't even notice them drifting back into the storeroom. He picked up the envelope taped to its surface and gently broke the seal. After sliding out the card he smiled at the hand drawn picture of a soaring eagle caught in mid-flight. He slowly opened it and read the inscription softly. "You have the Gift. It's time to use it. Marie."

He tore back the manila paper protecting the package and his memory was jarred as he gaped at the finished portrait of a runner completing the race of a lifetime. He studied the tortured features of the runner and the rapture of pleasure and pain captured by her hand. His body shivered as he held the picture frame aloft, and he studied both the beauty and passion it contained. After swallowing hard he realized she had come to an understanding of the love he held for his sport. He couldn't help but pick up the card and read it again. He knew she was right…and he had been waiting all his life.

Chapter 40

He had lay in bed for hours and his eyes traced the outline of the streetlights that rimmed his drawn shades. After shifting his glance, he studied the shadows hiding the running log that now covered the wall of his apartment. In just over eight months of occupancy he had been able to fill in nearly every inch of its available space. The sheer mass of the miles jumbled his thoughts and only served to further increase his festering restlessness. Even closing his eyes brought no relief as his mind contemplated the fast approaching race and forced his heart to pound even more. In his current state he knew that sleep would be a long time in coming, and he felt the call of the streets when he sat upright in bed. Just as it had so many times before, he calculated that an easy run might calm him and settle down his ever increasing anxiety.

He laced up his shoes quickly and stepped out into the cool evening air. The stars glimmered overhead and he took a deep breath of the thick mist that had drifted in from the lake. He took off at a slow jog to test his rapidly improving hamstring and was happy to sense only the slimmest trace of tension in his leg. With five more days before his first race, he could only pray that his fading injury would continue to heal.

He stepped lightly and made his way automatically towards the lake. He jogged past the base of the steep hill and remembered where the team's sweat had marked the earth at the battle of the "Meat". Even far removed from that workout, he felt a surge of adrenaline when his subconscious anticipated the stress of another hard effort. He smiled at the knowledge that tonight's run would not demand the focus of that past workout.

The Gift – A Runner's Story

He eased in closer to the lake and gently trotted up the long climb where he had first met the trio of runners that had embraced him fully. No matter what the future brought he knew that both the joy and suffering they had shared had permanently bonded them together. He could hardly believe that a lifetime full of memories could have taken place in under a year.

He ran slowly and approached the stoplights glowing in the night mist and remembered the warm day in March when he had first met Marie. In his mind's eye he still pictured the slow turn of her face as she greeted him with her intoxicating smile. His step automatically quickened as he allowed himself to drift back to the simplicity of their first meeting. And even in the dark he neatly avoided the maples that continued to guard the parkway.

The campus was as quiet as a cemetery and he covered the concourse without encountering even the trace of a single soul. As the jog continued he heard his footsteps echo off of the pavement and the great buildings that loomed high overhead. In a matter of hours the grounds would be teeming with energy, but at that very instant he felt ownership of the silent arena. He squinted into the distance and spied the low lighting over the athletic complex where he had been granted the ability to hone his skill. Sentiment arose toward the brick structure that had housed so many of the people he felt a deep gratitude towards. He could only hope he would be able to find a way to properly thank them when he stepped up to the starting line in less than a week.

His jog continued onward toward the track where workout after workout he had displayed both his weaknesses and strength for all to see. He peered through the fence and had little trouble making out the quarter mile oval as it seemingly floated through the mist. His eyes traced the four corners of the track and he could still sense the secure grip of his spikes churning on the tartan. When he reached the final hundred meters of the loop he absently touched his leg as if experiencing his injury anew. He forced his eyes to remain open as he recounted his limp past the finish line and the subsequent panic in his thoughts.

He followed the apparition of the injured runner under the stands and re-lived the desperation of the moment. He could still see the smiling face from above that had enraged him and had

222

unexpectedly received his fury over the frustration of the years. With a heavy heart he remembered the feeling of emptiness that had overwhelmed him when her small frame disappeared from view. And he reflected on the sadness that had followed him ever since.

He pushed himself away from the cold fence and jogged away with a sudden weariness in his stride. He let the street lights be his guide on the way back to his meager apartment and the sweat trickled in his eyes when he approached his old front porch. He looked to the heavens as the sting of the salt blurred his vision of the flickering stars. While sitting on the cracked wooden steps, he gazed overhead and realized he had never before felt the power of the universe as clearly. And the frailty of an individual with an enormous task in front of him.

Chapter 41

The take-off to Baton Rouge had gone uneventfully and the two trials participants settled into the seats of the 747 and daydreamed about the adventure ahead. Brett looked out the tiny windows and when the plane pierced the clouds on the ascent from the Milwaukee airport he felt a stirring sense of freedom. He and Rip had been seated separately which afforded him even more time to attempt to tie together the threads of the last few weeks. He regretted having left without having a chance for a proper goodbye to Marie after her own departure on an annual family summer vacation. The brief message she relayed on his answering machine left him feeling unsettled and had only served to re-kindle his desire to see her again. Yet, it seemed somehow appropriate that he would have to face the upcoming monumental challenge once again on his own.

His eyes burned and he felt the fatigue setting in from the aftereffects of the broken sleep of the night before. He knew the recent soul-searching with his mother had managed to dredge up a basketful of memories long since tucked away. After he had completed the midnight run he eventually found himself dreaming fitfully again. Once again he had slipped into a dream of a run from years gone by, and he felt himself floating effortlessly over the landscape. With a solitary eagle watching him from its perch, he was startled when it suddenly took flight and cast a shadow on him before it flew out of sight. The dream continued and he joyfully recognized his father fast approaching him on the wheels of his trusty Schwinn. Even while looking out the airplane window at the billowing clouds, he could still recall shifting uncomfortably in his sleep when his subconscious anticipated the worst. Just as his father had so many times before, he started to lose control of the bike when it careened wildly toward the cliffs. The runner felt himself once again reaching toward the bicycle in a desperate attempt to help his father avoid the impending fall into oblivion. But for the first time since the dream started to penetrate his nights, he watched his father proceed to perform a graceful roll that enabled him to end up in a seated position on the worn dirt pathway. The runner gazed out the window and blinked back his emotion when he recalled the embarrassed smile on his father's face that was punctuated by a short statement. "Silly old man," he said. "I only came out to drop off some water to you." A lurch of turbulence exploded the current daydreaming like scattershot and he looked longingly across the cobalt sky as it stretched out into nothingness. "I miss you, Dad," he mouthed to himself as he eased the seat back to its fullest extent. "And thanks for always being there for me." He closed his eyes and after settling into the courtesy pillow it took only minutes before a deep and restful sleep overtook him.

He met up with Rip in the terminal and after throwing the worn university duffle bags over their shoulders they set out to hail the nearest cabbie. The airport traffic was brisk and as a line of cars passed by the terminal doors they waited patiently at the curb. When a battle-scarred yellow vehicle screeched to a stop at their feet, the driver had barely gotten out when Brett barked out the destination. "The Hyatt on Golden Avenue," he instructed the cabbie as they slid into the back seat.

"Yes sir, boss," replied the bored driver through thickened lids. "You got it."

"You're acting like a big-city boy," said Rip as he settled into the cracked leather seats. "But I'm glad at least one of us knows what he's doing." With unspoken gratitude both runners appreciated the ability to travel together recognizing that it made the uncertainty of the next week seem far less threatening. Even the normally mundane task of checking into the hotel took on a new light when they gained entrance to their elegant room courtesy of the United States Olympic Committee.

"Man, if Logan could see this place he'd go nuts," said Rip as he checked out the suite. His eyes widened further when he ogled the expansive king-sized beds lining the wall.

"He and Hollywood would trash it like they were rock stars. But too bad we're here on business," Brett reminded his friend. "Hey, how 'bout checking out the Expo center? I heard it's huge."

Rip was scarcely able to conceal his unabashed excitement for the idea and his voice bubbled over with enthusiasm. "Let's do it." They both chose to forego even the simple rite of unpacking their clothes in their chase to explore all aspects of the experience. Brett himself felt like Alice emerging from the rabbit hole and couldn't wait to sample the city's offerings.

They walked the short distance to the running Mecca and like wide-eyed tourists their heads swiveled as they soaked in the aura of the downtown. Brett couldn't help but notice the bustling activity within the open-aired bars as a mixture of visitors and locals prepped for the week-long event. After the failure of his own latest barroom exploits, he found the desire for even the simplest revelry to be at least temporarily extinguished.

"Come on in, men," drawled a sidewalk barker trying his best to entice the runners to enter. "Live nudes! Crawdads! All you can eat!"

Brett tried to sneak a peek through the darkened windows and offered up a thought of his own. "I just hope no one gets them mixed up."

"Keep your mind on running, you sick puppy. Hey, there's the Expo," Rip said while pointing to the flashing lights in the distance. "This oughta be fun."

When they entered the Olympic Exposition the two runners stopped dead in their tracks as their senses were bombarded by the gypsy-like atmosphere of the trade show. Row upon row of tables were set up to display the wares of the many vendors who had gathered together to hawk their products. The two runners gawked at the flashing lights and feverish activity of the crowd as it skittered between booths like a swarm of kids in a candy store. After their nervous systems became accustomed to the jolt of activity, the runners crept in slowly and began their tour of the running paraphernalia.

"This is crazy," commented a wide eyed Rip when the surge of the crowd led them toward the first booth.

"This is worse than shopping with Marie when there's a sale on. And God knows how much I hate that. But I guess it doesn't hurt to look."

A salesperson eyed them up as they approached the first of the brochure laden tables. "Gentlemen, slip off your shoes and try out our famous 'Heel Healer'. Guaranteed to stretch your arch and keep your plantar fascia as soft as Pamela Lee's implants," he promised with a wink to the young runners.

"It looks like it could be a sex toy," said Rip under his breath as he examined the long knobby covered tube.

"You surprise me sometimes, country-boy," replied Brett with a smile. "You'll have to tell me about your dark side later."

Rip ignored his baiting and dropped the tool on the table before they continued to meander down the aisles. They fought the jostling crowds for the assortment of freebies offered by the gregarious sales reps and Brett felt as if he was caught up in another pack of aggressive runners. But as he quickly filled his complementary *Running Times* bag, he became another participant in the aerobic Christmas that had arrived months ahead of schedule. Packets of Blister Free, Super-goo, Thin Skin, Mondo Sunscreen, and Itch Away filled his bulging plastic bag. Literature of watches, shoes, shorts, heart monitors, and climate-ready gear lent itself to be future reading material waiting to be studied in the solitude of the hotel. Handfuls of bee pollen, vitamins, fluid replacements, energy bars, fat burners, and a wide variety of instant carbohydrates added bulk to the menagerie of goods overflowing from his bag.

"Hell, if we put all this stuff into a pot of boiling water we'd probably have the ultimate running stew," commented Rip.

His culinary musings were interrupted by another smiling sales rep shilling his goods. "NATUROID products are the ultimate performance enhancer," he bragged while handing Brett a page of product testimonials from an extended list of users. "We have a long list of runners setting new PR's every week."

"What's in it?" Brett asked.

"A variety of natural ingredients specially formulated in our high quality labs overseas. Our product will naturally enhance your normal level of testosterone and allow rapid recovery from training. We do more so you can too!"

"But what's in it?" he asked again impatiently.

"Sea kelp, tortoise shell, and our own ingenious additive of ground bull testicles from the pampas of Argentina."

"Mmm, sounds tasty. But at least it's all 'natural'," he said accentuating the final word.

"Naturally!" said the smug salesperson with an exaggerated showing of his chemically whitened teeth.

"Thanks, but no." The runner knew the last thing he needed was an unexpected positive urinalysis courtesy of another fly by night nutritional supplier.

They wandered again as they were drawn further into the buzz of the overflow crowd. Brett began feeling vaguely uncomfortable with the commercialism, but he nevertheless continued to gather the free loot until he broke the silence with a call to his partner. "Hey! There's Don Kardong signing autographs."

"Don who?"

"Kardong. He's a former Olympian and a pretty funny writer. I think he still works for *Runner's World*."

"What's so funny about running?" Rip asked seriously.

"Never mind," said Brett realizing the futility of an explanation. "But I'd be willing to bet he could even find something to write about you guys."

"Right," he grunted with a dismissive wave. "I'm sure it would hit the top of the New York Times Bestseller list with a bullet."

"You never know." He handed Rip his bag and motioned towards the men's room. "Wait here for a sec and I'll be right back."

When he entered the crowded bathroom he waited patiently for his turn in the three deep lines. He finally entered the urinal and looked to his left to absently acknowledge the next patron. He felt his heart skip a beat when he recognized the familiar face he had memorized from his vast collection of magazines. Frank freakin' Shorter, he gulped to himself. A sudden onset of stage fright resulted in a complete inability to commence even the feeblest of flows. Panic set in when he heard the breathing of the legend, and he felt the pound of his own heart exceed the limits of his well-trained aerobic threshold. He sighed when the former Olympic champion finally retreated and he could return to the task at hand. But inexplicably he was still unable to complete his set upon mission, and he quickly decided to flee his failure as gracefully as possible. He rushed excitedly toward Rip and couldn't wait to fill him in on the once in a lifetime experience.

"You won't believe this. I took a leak next to Frank Shorter! But I freaked so bad I could only dribble on my sock."

Rip looked down at his friend's footwear in disgust before responding slowly. "I'm sure watching you piss yourself was a precious moment for him too. But at least you've got free socks in your bag to change into," he said analytically as he handed him his tote bag.

Brett shook his head at the wonderment of the experience and knew Rip would never appreciate his unexpected brush with fame. He was still floating from the encounter when they re-entered the crowds and proceeded to hit the last remaining booths together. After purchasing duel Suzy Favor Hamilton posters for Logan and Hollywood, the two trials participants slid onto an empty bench to finally rest their legs. Rip quickly hopped back to his feet in order to fulfill one final item on his agenda.

"My turn. I'm gonna go see if I can find a legend to take a leak with."

Brett ignored the barb and gathered the plastic bags onto his lap for safe keeping. He observed the churning activity of the Expo and studied the legions of running aficionados filling the hall. As he looked over the mass of runners he categorized them into three simple subsections – "never tried", "didn't make it", and "been there". After locating Shorter's smiling face in the crowd he knew which category he fully intended to run himself into within a few short days.

Chapter 42

He toed the line anxiously and waited for the other runners to settle into their starting positions. The twelve runners in the qualifying heat were spread evenly along the curved line and Brett heard the nervous breathing of the fellow competitors that flanked him on both sides. He knew there was no particular advantage of his placement in the third lane, and his primary goal for the first two hundred meters was to stay out of trouble. His father had long ago regaled him with instructional tales of the crushing falls of past American greats like Jim Ryan and Mary Decker that had dashed their own Olympic dreams. "Run like a big dog, but just stay on your damn feet!" his father had counseled him moments before a major high school race. But just as soothing as the words themselves had been, it was the memory of a confident wink that he supplied to the nervous runner that settled him down for another successful performance.

"Runners take your marks," commanded the starter with the runners staring grimly ahead.

The sound of the gun shattered the silence and the group strode frantically toward the inside lane. As he expected, the jostling was heavier than usual due to the stakes having been raised to a level of unprecedented heights for most of the group. Although Brett was running in the second heat, he had no idea how Rip had done in the previous race due to his conscious decision to avoid any distractions. He had promised himself long ago that for the next thirteen plus minutes his thoughts would be unencumbered by extraneous baggage and be focused solely on his own self interests.

The pack dawdled through the first lap and he firmly resisted the temptation to take the lead. He was content to bide his time in the fourth position and knew full well the first three finishers were guaranteed a spot in the finals. Just as Wickers had suggested, he willed himself to concentrate on the ultimate prize of securing an Olympic berth. He knew with the Kid having run in the first heat there might be an absence of a willful leader in the race that followed.

"Seventy-one, seventy two," the timer called as they completed the first lap. The crowd clapped in the hopes that their urging could spur the runners to a more competitive performance. Damn, thought Brett as he looked at the runners ahead, run for god-sake! Almost as if on cue an Adidas-clad runner surged to the front and quickly opened up a five meter gap. He welcomed the sudden change in pace and although he had faith in his milers kick, preferred the safety of stretching out the group of runners until the pretenders were dropped and only the fittest remained. He barely heard the shouts of the crowd as he delved deeper into the zone that he could scarcely understand much less explain. He had once tried to make Marie understand the power of the sensation by describing it as the implosion of all of his brain waves until they were reduced to the size of a microscopic computer chip. Her response of an unintelligible grunt informed him that his analogy had fallen firmly on uncomprehending ears.

"Two-sixteen, two-seventeen," the timer shouted when the runners completed the second lap. Brett's trance continued as he maintained his position, and he felt a surge of confidence when he recognized his hamstring would hold up for the duration. He pounded away through the laps and the race became one of attrition when the line of competing runners stretched out to an eventual fifty meter length. He had no trouble remaining in contact with the leader as the laps narrowed down and he felt his confidence still rising. In a matter of steps he passed the third place runner and realized he was far from his personal red line. He floated effortlessly and wanted to smash his rivals and dominate the last few laps of the race, but instead tucked away his ego and held firm in his position.

"One lap to go," shouted the race announcer as the bell clanged in the background. Four hundred meters, Brett thought, sixty seconds to the finals.

With a quick glance back he knew he was in no danger of losing his coveted position, and he contentedly let the trailing runners battle for the provisional qualifying positions. After crossing the finish line he completed the perfunctory congratulations to the runners ahead of him and then walked briskly down the track.

"Good job, son," said a finish line worker assigned to ensure his physical status. "One more race to go."

"You got that right," he replied in a voice laced with unintended aggression. "And those assholes better all be ready."

The worker watched him curiously as he continued down the track. And for the first time since the opening lap the runner noticed the hordes of fans that had lined the oval in their search for a vicarious taste of victory.

Chapter 43

The runners worked hard to maintain their focus in the midst of the weeklong whirlwind of activity. While sporadically attending the track and field events at the stadium, they also carefully balanced their need for rest in the last stages of preparation. Brett had even found solace by remaining in the suite and watching a weeklong cable station's retrospective of "Gilligan's Island" reruns. He had consciously chosen to avoid the hotel's day spa after he found himself measuring up his chances against every hardbody that entered the shared jacuzzi. After one particularly crowded session in the bubbling waters left him feeling more tense than ever, he made the decision to cloister himself safely inside the comfortable room. The latest exploits of the "castaways" was interrupted when Rip entered the room after his completion of a mid-day walk.

"Are you still lying around? That couch is going to have a permanent dent in it from your ass."

"A little R and R. It does a body good."

"Hey," said Rip as he quickly changed subjects. "I meant to tell you I got a call from Logan on my cell. They had a bit of car trouble, but they got down here in one piece. But I'd be willing to bet Coach and Tony regretted agreeing to drive down with those two."

"I heard they were in Hollywood's Delta 88. Logan probably sat on a phone book just to see over the steering wheel. And poor Tony couldn't even straighten up after the ride so they took him to some chiropractor to knock his bones loose."

"It's too bad they missed us in the preliminaries. I still feel lucky that I squeaked into the finals as a 'provisional' while you made it look so easy," Rip said as he stretched his achilles. "I had to work like hell to stay at the back of the lead pack and caught a break when the Stanford guy cramped up at the end. I barely even saw the Kid after the first lap. How did he look?"

"I didn't watch. I had to focus on my own race. But I heard it looked like he was in a jog at the park. I got to talking to a guy from Colorado that said even though he wasn't acting like an ass it's like he still was. He's always got that look that makes me want to belt him."

"Save it for the track," Rip cautioned. "But you looked good too."

"I felt okay. I ran even splits and kind of melted into the pack until I picked it up at the end. I didn't really mind the temperature and I think Wickers' heat workouts really helped. And even though no one knows me, after the race I even got interviewed by some 'Weldon' dude from a running website. I hope I didn't come across like a moron."

"I doubt that. I'm sure you were the running intellectual we've all come to know and love. But at least someone wanted to talk to you. Everyone thinks I'm just some sheepherder from Wisconsin who trains by chasing the animals across the fields. Even so… it rocks just being here," said Rip as he completed his stretching routine. "This whole experience has been nothing short of amazing."

"That's for sure. Getting this far makes it worth every damn mile."

"And in only a matter of hours we get to do it again for real," Rip said thoughtfully.

Brett glanced at his friend as his internal juices were immediately activated by the thought of the upcoming finals. "I've probably run the race a thousand times in my head. And I was kind of hoping you won't be offended if I go off to warm up alone before the race."

"Are you kidding me? When I get on the track you're just another bug on my windshield that I hope to splatter. No offense here either."

"This ain't the Milwaukee Invite my young friend. And I'm not about to mess up again."

"I know that was a rough day for you," Rip acknowledged. "I ran into Marie before we left and she said you guys were trying to work things out. Are you okay about her not being here?"

A multitude of feelings tumbled haphazardly while he measured up the question. He knew he could be honest with his friend and felt comfort in being able to speak so freely. "I guess I have to be. In some ways it allows me to focus on the race, but deep down it's still kind of hard. I've been through a lot of garbage in my life and she's not afraid to help sort through the trash. She even motivated me to call my mom last week and I caught her on a good day. We talked for awhile and she promised to get some help but was afraid to come down for the race. The stress and all. I know she's screwed up, but she's all the family I have left. Who knows? Maybe things will get better with her. But to answer your question truthfully, I do wish Marie was coming. I don't think I would have made it here without her. I'd probably be another loser at Hooligan's just looking out the window."

"I bet they'll both be watching on TV," said Rip. "And speaking of TV, Logan and Hollywood said if they could get on camera it would be their fifteen minutes of fame."

"Shame is more like it."

Rip settled into a nearby easy chair and took a deep pull from his omnipresent bottled water before he focused his gaze on the outstretched runner. "You know I owe you a lot, Brett. I guarantee I wouldn't be here if it wasn't for you letting me ride on your coattails."

"I think you're being a bit too complimentary, but thanks anyway. But the reality is that nobody but yourself got you into the position you're in. And now for 5000 meters tonight you're going to have to do the driving yourself."

When the room quieted Rip suddenly turned pensive and spoke in an uncharacteristic whisper. "Brett, can I ask you a question."

"I'm full of answers. It's just they're usually wrong."

He watched his friend ignore his joke and chew on his bottom lip before he forged ahead with his query. Taking a breath he finally spoke. "Do you ever get scared out there?"

He looked at his friend and recognized the need for a thoughtful answer. After taking a sip of his own water he started slowly. "During the race, no. When my legs start to move it feels like I'm in the only place in the world I can control. It's like a dream that for once I have the ability to end on my own terms. And although I may not always win, but while I'm running at least I *think* I'll win."

"How about before?" Rip asked through narrowed eyes.

Brett studied the anxiety in his friend's face and realized the sensitive emotional state the younger runner was in. He felt uncomfortable being *anyone's* emotional role model but still answered the question as honestly as he could. "That's a whole different ballgame. There was a time it was as if I had ants in my brain all crawling in different directions. Sometimes the thoughts and anxieties nearly kept me from even getting to the track. And probably among other things led me to drink. But except for one mis-step, that's better now. And I doubt you even know it, but you've helped me too."

"Me?" he said as his eyes opened wide in surprise. "I feel like such a 'grinder' out there compared to a thoroughbred like you. My dad has worked for thirty years in a factory and it's like I'm him on the track. A regular blue collar runner."

"There's nothing wrong with that. I once read about another grinder named Pfitzinger that won the marathon trials years ago. It can be done."

"But this is different. I'll never have your leg speed over the last few laps," Rip worried aloud as he sat up attentively.

He settled into his role as the more experienced runner and formulated an appropriate response. "And maybe there will be a day you won't need it. Boxing trainers say 'if you kill the body, the head will die'. That means just keep pounding away until your opponent collapses. I learned first hand at the invite that you would have made one hell of a boxer. I've watched you train and race and I've seen dozens of runners with more ability, but only a scattered few with your desire. And that by itself has been a kick in my butt to remember the way it used to be when I first started. The sheer satisfaction I used to have from simply running my hardest and doing my best. I mean it when I say you would have

236

made 'Pre' proud. He once said, 'I run to see who has the most guts'. I think that's the way you run too."

"Thanks, Brett," said Rip as he contemplated the words. "That means a lot to me."

"No problem. Just watch the low blows when we get on the track."

The two runners quieted and let their thoughts drift independently until it was time to leave for the stadium. They both daydreamed and reflected silently on the thousands of miles and countless hours logged for this one chance. Miles and hours that would be boiled down to less than fourteen minutes on a steaming oval track.

Chapter 44

He walked out into the fading sunlight of the stadium and felt a blast of warm Louisiana air hit him in the face. After having loosened up in the quiet of an indoor facility, he moved slowly and set his gear onto the partitioned area within the infield of the track. The stadium enclosing the oval was just as he had envisioned it in the imaginary races he had run on the days he had gazed out Tony's front window. He looked over the far reaches of the gleaming structure and marveled at the number of track and field fans that filled the state-of-the-art stadium. The bowl-like layout seated over thirty-thousand fans and except for a scattering of open areas, the event was well attended. He stood alone in the infield and suddenly felt like Logan's beloved "Maximus" awaiting his turn at entertaining the masses. After almost bowing before them he chose to meticulously re-tighten his spikes before he slowly paused and raised his eyes to the heavens in a moment of silent prayer. When he closed them he felt the last vestiges of sunlight bathe his face and an unnatural calm settled over his body. With quiet confidence he started into a slow jog and squinted towards the stands in the faint hopes of recognizing even a single familiar face. He was surprised that after covering only half a lap he recognized a small but vocal fan club that shouted a raucous cheer from the far reaches of the stadium.

"Check it out," yelled Logan as he pointed at the familiar pink paint that decorated his bony chest. Brett smiled when he saw his name emblazoned across his friend's puny pecs and Rip's name adorning Hollywood. He broke into a full laugh when he noticed the aging bodies of Tony and Coach Wickers with the single word "Rules" scrawled on their sagging midsections.

"They can be quite persuasive after feeding me a few beers," called Wickers. "But I'm a man of my word."

"Give 'em hell," said Tony as he wiped the sweat from his brow. "Leave it on the track. No regrets."

"You have my promise," said Brett as his preparation turned increasingly serious. "I'll see you all later."

He began to circle the track and heard an increasing ripple of activity churn through the crowd. In searching the grounds he understood the reaction when he saw the Kid waved to an adoring and enthusiastic public. Finally eyeing his opponent up close he felt a pounding in his temples as his body braced itself for the upcoming fight. The bile rose in his stomach when he watched his adversary round the track, and even though he knew he should focus on his own warm-up, his eyes were riveted on the race favorite. The Kid had adorned himself in a pair of gaudy gold spikes and as he strode past Brett he winked confidently. That son of a bitch thinks I'm just another loser, he thought.

He slowly regained control of his emotions and returned to his preparation for the thirteen laps that would define a lifetime. A lifetime of sweat and sacrifice that had so far only resulted in unfulfilled dreams and a logbook of painful memories. But with his newfound resolve nearly overflowing from his pores, he readied himself and absently touched at the sweat soaked insignia that decorated his chest.

"Last call 5000 meters," the speaker blared. "All runners please report to the starter's tent."

The track had taken on a surreal quality as the overhead lights cloaked it in a supernatural glow. The burnt orange of the track's surface was broken up by the white lane markers and was dotted by shadows from the far-reaching stands. The hum of the crowd added to the effect and the trial's rookie felt a slight confusion overtake his mindset. The ominous nature of the scene caused him to consider whether or not the ghost of Prefontaine himself was not lurking in the recesses of the teeming stadium. Only a cursory tug on his battered rubberband snapped him back to his senses. He felt his self-induced pressure fade like steam escaping from a valve when he viewed the four letters Logan had imprinted on the band in a moment of whimsy. "WWPD?" boldly stated the block letters. "What Would Pre Do?" Logan had long ago asked Brett when he had groaned at the thought of a difficult workout. "Whine like a pussy like you are?" A smile covered his face as he scanned the filled stadium and soaked in the excited buzz of the crowd. He had never run before a crowd of this magnitude and to help settle his nerves he chose to focus on the white lines circling the track. He filed away his memories of the restless crowd for a future day and concentrated completely on the impending demands of the upcoming challenge. He knew the 5000 meter event had long been considered one of the most difficult races in the history of the games. As far back as Paavo Nurmi, the competitors of the event were expected to combine the speed of a sprinter, with the sheer endurance required of a world class marathoner. Brett had long been keen on the history and recognized the long standing difficulty of running the event at an elite level. He stowed away the weight of the past and after one last firm tug on his laces, trotted towards the starter's tent for a final check-in. When he located Rip he toward walked towards him and offered his hand only to receive a firm handshake in return.

"Good luck, Rip," he said in a voice steeped in honesty. "It's time for you to punch in."

"And time to open the gift," he answered back knowing full well Brett's underlying motivation.

They both nodded and locked gazes as the intensity of the moment deepened even further. But it was at that instant the line between friends and adversary was drawn and their separate quests had officially begun. Last man standing wins, thought Brett. He waited impatiently and fidgeted when one by one the cast of runners were introduced. The uniforms of the field became blurred when the first of the competitors approached the pre-determined spots on the arched white line. When Rip's name was finally called he couldn't help but wonder of the emotional state of his friend. But the momentary lapse of his concentration was short-lived when the call of his own name caused him to instantly spiral deeper into the necessary focus.

"Representing the Team Fate Track Club...number one hundred and one...Brett Rodgers," the announcer called. He jogged out to his lane and offered a half wave to the appreciative crowd. He scarcely heard the polite applause of the audience and began to study the other runners as they completed their own pre-race rituals. His painstaking preparation for the race had even included filling a notebook with the tendencies and talents of each of the final's competitors. "Knowledge is power" his father had said and with the acquired background of the other runners he felt infinitely more in control. He instinctively raked his spikes against the track and once again felt like an impatient racehorse pawing at the ground in wait of the opening of the gate.

Immediately after the introductions were completed he performed a few routine striders in order to help lessen the building internal stress. When he finally lined up in the fourth lane he noticed Rip on the outside and silently wished him the best. He couldn't see the Kid and had purposely ignored his introduction, but knew shortly after the gun he would become unavoidable. He had game planned to try and run with him knowing that if he was successful in doing so, a place on the coveted team would likely be guaranteed. He became acutely aware of the silence in the stadium, and as he toed his spot he watched the starter raise the gun in the air only seconds before the countdown began.

"Runners on your marks," he called as the tension of the runners reached its peak.

At the sound of the gun Brett felt the burst in his legs and thought of how Dog's forced rest had seemed to bring an extra spring to his already powerful gait. He was thrilled his sore hamstring had fast become a faded memory of one more setback he had been able to overcome. After he rounded the first corner he looked ahead in an attempt to locate the Kid, but was not surprised to see a familiar Wisconsin runner quickly take the lead. From both his studies and personal encounter he knew the collegian to be a front runner, but in an event of this magnitude he considered the tactic to be questionable at best. He calculated the inherent risk of the move and his experience told him that a slow and painful death would be the likely end result of such a rash decision.

As the laps progressed a few of the pretenders were invariably weeded out and they slowly drifted away from the pack. Brett had finally been able to catch a glimpse of the Kid's jersey hidden deep behind a crowd of other runners that shadowed the race favorite's every step. He watched the swarm of combatants from a safe distance and quickly doubted his pre-race plan to be one of complete originality. He still had not been able to locate Rip, but he was admittedly unconcerned of his friend's well-being at the moment. When the mile passed the leader in 4:16, Brett knew it to be too fast for the conditions, but the bold Badger runner had made a statement and had to be prepared to live with it. He methodically spent the next eight-hundred meters working his way through the pack and felt the unmistakable energy of the crowd flow when he was finally able to tuck himself behind the Kid. The Kid in turn appeared unconcerned with his second place position as he also knew of the leader's unabashed racing habits.

The jockeying of the pack continued for the next few laps, but he steadfastly maintained his contact with the Kid. He was pleased to still be in his comfort zone, but when the two mile split passed in 8:40 the game changed and any runner still in touch felt a distinct change in the intensity. The Kid was getting serious and Brett surmised the west coast runner didn't like anyone stealing his media thunder. He emotionally geared up for an increase in pace and wiped the dripping sweat from his eyes. Through the stinging haze he continued on with his increasingly painful fight to hang close to the fast charging runner. Brett's intuition led him to believe the Kid seemed doubly annoyed at being trailed so closely and his apparent inability to cut into the lead of the frontrunner. The overwhelming race favorite visibly pushed harder as he drove down the track in a blatant attempt at driving for the lead. The ticking of the clock had lost all meaning and Brett began to feel a measurable weariness set in. After struggling to cover the latest move of the talented runner, he tried to ignore the subtle crack he felt in his own resolve. Amidst the crowd noise he heard the echo of "no regrets" reverberate from somewhere deep within the crowd. With less than two laps to go the runner wheezed past the line a body length behind the Kid, but was fast losing the confidence that he could maintain his current standing. He thought of his father and wished for a sudden pearl of wisdom, but knew it was his own soul that the power needed to rise from and he dug even deeper. The Kid was charging hard and Brett knew this was the time every runner trains for; the chance to become either a champion or just another pedestrian runner settling for the consolation prize. He squinted in the low sunlight and from two meters behind focused desperately on the back of the Kid's singlet. His quivering calves rebelled as he strode harder around the turn to enter the final lap. To the surprise of both himself and his opponent he unexpectedly regained the necessary contact with his primary foe. Their collective drive had resulted in drawing them both closer to the lead runner who was still showing no outward sign of collapse. As the gun sounded for the final lap, Brett begged for the agony to end, but knew it was only just beginning. Through a blur of pain he willed himself to stay with the Kid for fifty meter increments and after completing the distance vowed the next fifty would be the last. His breath came in tortured gasps, but he took solace in hearing his more storied rival doing the same. At that late stage of the race the easy victory was well beyond the crowd favorite and he too was thinking only of survival. They matched strides on the backstretch and both ran purely on muscle memory fueled by the rawest of instinct. He felt one final charge from his opponent and nearly stumbled when his exhausted legs screamed as he tried to cover it. The track blurred, but through the fatigue he dimly realized that he had focused so hard on the Kid that he hadn't noticed they had drawn even with the now fading Wisconsin runner. They flew around the last turn and they both veered wide of the runner in red when Brett realized his legs were beginning to shut down. It was only a well-timed sharp elbow by the Kid that shook him from his doubt and he felt a fresh surge of adrenaline. You bastard! he screamed silently. He strode desperately down the homestretch and caught a side-long glimpse of the eyes he had held in such wonder, and for the first time noticed a brief flicker of uncertainty in them. "Strike!" he could hear his father say from somewhere far away. Their eyes met again and he felt his drawn lips curl into a cruel smile. He gathered the strength for one last drive and charged to the white line before the blackness had a chance to envelope him completely. The fibers in his tortured legs trembled as they approached their breaking point, and his heart hammered wildly. He refused to concede and he drove with all of his passion and fury as the line still seemed to be agonizingly far away. He sensed a tumble of arms to his left and it was all he could do to stay upright as he thrust his torso across the white line. He gasped hoarsely for air and looked back to see the Kid and the Badger runner crawling frantically toward the finish line in an attempt to grasp the final positions. Brett watched as the Kid clawed himself over the line a matter of inches before the plane was broken by the exhausted runner in red. With hands on his knees he continued to draw in the hot air as his body screamed for oxygen. He squinted at the stadium scoreboard where it boldly flashed his winning time of 13:22.8. The race behind him had taken on a surreal quality until he recognized the familiar grimace of another runner as he struggled past the finish line. He embraced his friend as they comforted each other in their sweat soaked weariness.

"Top ten," he whispered joyfully to Rip.

Rip was too drained to even mouth a response, but Brett saw the satisfaction buried deep in his friend's worn face. He released himself from the younger runner and staggered over to the Kid to help him in his unsteady walk down the track. Mutual respect had been earned by the two warriors and previous sins were quickly forgiven.

"Christ, that hurt," said Brett as they slowly continued on. "I was just trying to survive."

"That was one ugly run," said the Kid with a rueful smile. "And for all that I still get second. It's not my favorite place." He looked at Brett before he continued on with a measured response. "But you earned it. I knew you had some fast times in the past, and I thought you looked good in the prelims. And when you stared me down before the race I thought you might be trouble."

"Well, you pissed me off."

"That wouldn't be the first time I've heard that," he said as he licked at the salty sweat dripping from his lips. "But then again that was the whole idea. To get you off your game. I guess it didn't quite work out the way I had it planned." His dark eyes flashed before he spoke his parting words to that day's victor. "Congratulations...and I believe I'll be seeing you again soon."

Brett nodded after finally having been allowed inside the darkness that had once mystified him. With a drained satisfaction he gingerly walked to the infield to get out of his drenched singlet. As the final runners trickled in, he had to wait for their completion of the distance before he could begin his celebratory lap. When he neared his gear he heard the call of his zealous supporters and waved to them while he searched in vain for the one face he still hoped to see. But without its presence, the tens of thousands of eyes in the stands left him feeling terribly alone. He had finally been able to seize the Gift, but without Marie, the triumph of the race had an utterly hollow core. With downcast eyes he resigned himself to her absence and located his bagful of gear.

He sat down and stripped off his soaked top and dropped it in a heap. When he reached for his customary post-race t-shirt he was surprised to find a small package nestled inside of the faded garment. He noticed the numerous USA Track and Field committee blazers milling about, and he appreciated their first recognition of his accomplishment. He tore through the golden wrapping and curiously examined the small box it contained inside. He lifted the case up slowly and eased back the hinges before staring at its contents dumbfounded. He studied the hand written note enclosed and read aloud the four small words Marie had left unsaid at the track all those months ago.

He stood up once again and felt the warmth of the evening sun shine upon his face. And with the simple gift of a single broken track spike held firmly in his hand, he began the victory lap he had dreamed about for a lifetime.

Epilog

He could still feel the jet lag in his legs after the long flight home from Beijing. As he jogged through the campus he reminisced about the bittersweet memories of his Olympic experiences. Although he had not advanced past the qualifying rounds, he felt satisfaction that his new friend had returned with the first United States track and field distance medal in a generation. The Kid and he had promised to train together in the future.

He closed in on the old bike rack and heard his friends' chattering from a distance. The voices rose as he neared them, and he smiled at the expectation of the verbal wars that he would soon be part of. After slowing to a walk he breathed in the fresh air and tried to appreciate the simplicity of the moment. His future was with Marie and he knew he would have to grow up soon. But not yet.

1376315